SKI TRAILS IN THE CANADIAN ROCKIES

REVISED EDITION

A Guide to Banff, Jasper, Kootenay and Yoho Parks

Rick Kunelius

Dave Biederman

SUMMERTHOUGHT
Banff, Alberta

ISBN 0-919934-06-4

Revised edition 1981

SUMMERTHOUGHT LTD.
BOX 1420
BANFF, ALBERTA

Printed and bound in Canada

Forward

Ski Trails in the Canadian Rockies has always been a bit of misnomer to date since many important areas, namely in Jasper Park, were not included. The second edition is an attempt to rectify the situation with a major addition of selected ski routes in the Jasper area written by Dave Biederman.

There are no major changes in the original text. Typographical errors have been corrected, the Wheeler Loop at Sunshine has been deleted since it no longer exists, and alterations in the access at Bow Lake and Paradise Valley have been noted.

Each national park is developing its own network of recommended cross-country trails, but none of the systems seems to be confirmed or consistant to date. They have not been included because the information is available from the park offices and is subject to change.

Some readers may feel the equipment section is a bit outdated, but I did not feel that the new technology of the last four years was significant enough to warrant promotion or a major re-write. The principles are still the same.

Rick Kunelius
Banff

Acknowledgements

Many people both in Banff and Jasper have helped with encouragement, information and partnership on the ski trails. A special thanks to the following people for their extra help: Edward Cavell (photo curator), Jim Davies (pilot), Bruno Engler (photographer), Keith Everts (avalanche researcher), Linda Flygare (typist), Bruce Leeson (park preserver), Lynne Marriott (pharmacist), Brian Patton (editor), Willi Pfisterer (alpine specialist), Jan Sommer (phycologist and proofreader), Luxie Traschell (medical doctor), Joe Weiss (pioneer skier and photographer), Jon Whyte (editor) and the Parks Canada Warden Service.

Photo and Illustration Credits

Archives of the Canadian Rockies: vi, 5, 47, 173, 179
Tim Auger: Cover, 24, 37
Bruno Engler: 19, 31, 83, 87, 110, 114, 120, 122, 123, 124, 127
Joe Weiss: 131, 183
Author: 90, 106

Contents

Have you ever stood
above the wood
on the top of a mountain divide?
And you're full of gut rot
and your nerves half shot,
with an avalanche after your hide?

"A Birthday I Remember" from *Timberline Tales*
by Jim Deegan

Skiers on Deception Pass near Skoki, ca. 1932.

Introduction

Cross-country skiing as we know it today is a product of this decade, but its roots go back through the centuries. Skis may have appeared in the Canadian west prior to this century, but skiing did not develop to a sport level until the 1920's. The sport flourished for a time in areas such as Banff, Skoki, Assiniboine, and Jasper, but it did not become a popular form of recreation until the promotion of mechanical lifts. For two decades emphasis was placed on downhill skiing, until in the late 1960's when cross-country skiing began to catch on once again. Today it has developed into a promoter's dream.

In the 1920's my grandfather made his own skis, as did many other people. Skiers of that era wore work clothing and work boots with leather strap bindings. In the last fifty years the principles have not changed, only the technology has been modified. Techniques have also changed, but not always for the better. The beautifully carved Telemark turn executed with a full pack or the ultimate double-pole plant turn are rarely seen today.

The object of skiing for pleasure has outgrown the original purpose of skis as a tool to assist in winter work, and it is the principle of pleasure that motivated me to compile this book.

Though, I may never completely understand why I wrote this book. It is the type of book which can never be finished. Trails have sometimes been included or rejected on a personal bias, and sometimes because of popularity or lack of popularity. Some areas such as Skoki and Assiniboine deserve expansion, but due to incomplete notes, poor memory, or the inability to get back to them again, they did not receive a full treatment.

The summits of many mountains can be reached on skis, but the dangers involved seemed to warrant their exclusion. Castle Mountain was included as one example, allowing advanced skiers the option of doing other summits on their own.

One can never say enough about safety. Yet, it is impossible to describe on paper the nature of snow and the peculiarities of avalanches. Avalanches claimed the lives of over a dozen persons in the Canadian west during the winter of 1976-77, and every winter people succumb to hypothermia and frostbite. The art of winter travel and survival can only be learned through actual experience. Yet the simple pleasures of winter travel in a natural environment can be experienced through all levels of development. The opportunity to experience Canada's mountain parks during the winter season is unique and wonderful, but also potentially dangerous. Hopefully this book will encourage people to experience the natural environment during the winter months at a level which will always result in pleasure rather than pain.

Some of the material in this book must be credited to Parks Canada. For a period, I worked on a research project to inventory cross-country trails in the Lake Louise area. A transfer into the Warden Service and experience with avalanche control and more mountain rescues than I care to remember, forced me to attempt to put on paper some of the basic principles for safe winter travel in the mountains. For many skiers the initial text may seem overly long and unnecessary, for which I can only say that my experience as a ski guide indicates the majority of skiers will find something of value.

Winter skiing in the mountains should not be approached in the same manner as hiking in the summer when almost all trails are suitable for the majority of hikers. Begin your exploration of winter by underestimating your ability. Slowly work upwards to bigger trips as physical condition, experience, and ability improve.

Using the trail guide

The routes described in the last two-thirds of this book have been layed out along a progression of difficulty and are classified quite generally under the headings of novice, intermediate, and advanced. This should facilitate the choice of a trip appropriate to ability. Within these three classifications, the routes are arranged in a rough sequence of location from Banff East Gate westward. If you are approaching from the west, thumb through the appropriate section backwards.

Maps

The maps within the trails section are mere sketch maps and should not be used for travel. Ability to travel by map is necessary for many of the intermediate and most of the advanced trips. The descriptions have been written for use with the Canadian government 1:50,000 topographical maps. Indeed, the Katherine Lake—Helen Lake route was written as a practical map exercise which should be completed before attempting more advanced routes. Maps are available from the National Park information offices, the Banff Book and Art Den, the Institute of Sedimentary and Petroleum Geology (just north of the University of Calgary), and other official map dealers.

Weather

The ski season in the Canadian Rockies begins slowly in November. Conditions reach their peak in February and March. Skiing begins to disappear from the lower levels in early April, but at higher elevations the season may extend to the middle of May. Snowfall and weather conditions vary significantly each winter. Since 1956, the lowest snowfall in Banff was 162 centimetres in 1962-63; the highest, 455 centimetres, occured in 1971-72. The average winter snowfall for Banff townsite over the last twenty years is 250 centimetres, a figure which is exceeded at higher altitudes and westward near the Great Divide. Suffice it to say, there is absolutely no general trend or pattern for predicting long-range mountain weather.

Banff Snowfall and Temperature, 1941 - 1970:

	Nov.	Dec.	Jan.	Feb.	Mar.	Apr.	Annual
Mean snowfall, cm.	32	34	36	30	23	30	207
Max. snowfall 24 hrs, cm.	53	50	33	50	41	36	
Mean temperature, °c.	−3	−9	−11	−7	−4	+2	+2
Record max. temp, °c.	+15	+12	+12	+14	+17	+24	
Record min. temp, °c.	−40	−48	−50	−45	−40	−27	

Registration

The National Parks policy directive states that the Warden Service shall be responsible for the safety of the visiting public. Accordingly, a registration system to assist backcountry users was developed many years ago. With the dramatic increase in backcountry use beginning in the early 1970's, first with hikers and more recently with cross-country skiers, the registration system became cumbersome and somewhat unmanageable. The system is presently being revised and some problems have yet to be solved. Regardless of its actual structure, it is always operating and is for your protection.

Before beginning your trip, register out at a warden office in the appropriate park where you intend to ski. Besides assuring your safety, up-to-date information can be obtained from Warden Service weather forecasts (usually much more applicable to the mountains than the general synopsis from the radio) and avalanche condition reports. Occasionally you will be lucky enough to find a warden who can provide further details on your proposed trip.

And of utmost importance: **Return your registration immediately at the end of your trip.** If a registration is not returned, the wardens begin to mobilize a search and rescue operation to find the missing party. Unnecessary searches consume time and money and may tie up the rescue helicopter when it is needed for a real emergency.

Equipment

SELECTING SKIS

The most difficult decision in selecting skis is whether to purchase wood or fiberglass skis. Cross-country skis were traditionally made of wood. If you're seeking craftsmanship, fiberglass will never compare to a good wooden ski. To date, I have not encountered a fiberglass ski which can compare with the "life" available in wood.

Understanding the background development of various skis should make the choice self-evident. Cross-country skiing developed first in the Scandinavian countries, each country developing a ski particular to its own requirements.

Finland has gently rolling terrain, hundreds of thousands of lakes, and its snow is generally cold and dry. Finnish skis were primarily birch because of the availability of the wood and its suitability for moderate conditions.

Sweden's terrain is much rougher than Finland's although the southern quarter of the country is quite similar. The Swedes added hickory edges to their birch skis to withstand the additional stresses of rougher topography and somewhat harder snow conditions.

The lignostone edge was developed in Norway where the terrain is steeper and the snow is hard because of the cold, damp maritime climate. Norwegian skis use hickory for a base to withstand the abrasion from hard crusts and ice.

Plastic-coated wood and fiberglass skis were developed in the middle European countries to cope with a warm, damp climate. The non-porous plastics require little maintenance, even when skiing damp conditions, to ensure that moisture is sealed out of the ski. They stand up well in icy conditions, especially when a narrow metal edge is added.

The Canadian Rockies are most similar to the geographical and climatic conditions of Norway. Although the Rockies are not influenced by a damp maritime climate as such, regular chinook winds warm the snow to melting and are followed by severe cold periods which set a crusty surface to the snowpack. Strong winds also set a hard abrasive crust on the snow.

If you started when skis were inexpensive , or if you can afford it today, the ideal combination is a pair of wooden skis with hickory bases and lignostone edges for the cold winter, and a fiberglass pair with metal edges for easy maintenance during the spring klister season.

Waxless skis are a recent innovation of the television mentality. They can be compared to real skis as TV dinners to home cooked meals. Surely you have enough energy to wax your skis if you have enough energy to go cross-country skiing. Waxless skis are never as efficient as well waxed skis, and more energy is in fact expended using them.

Fish scale type bases will not work under all conditions and waxing them is the only way to make them work on certain days. Removing wax from all those little pockets is a painstaking process. On downhill runs strange whirring type noices murmur from the bases, which can be quite disconcerting.

Mohair strips, a modification of the old seal skins used on mountaineering skis, are a poor compromise indeed. Mohair is certainly smooth to the skin but can hardly be construed as a slippery surface for sliding. The greatest problem with these strips is that they ice up on wet, warm snow alternating with cold, frozen snow.

Whether a ski is wood or fiberglass, it should possess the following characteristics:

1. The tip should be high and encompass about 90° of arc to ensure that the skis track well when their tails are raised and to guide the skis up in loose snow.
2. The shovel should be flexible so that it moves easily over bumps in the track and allows the tip to ride up in loose snow.
3. The mid-section must be thick and stiff. The core should contain some hard woods to hold the binding screws.
4. The tail carries more weight than the shovel and is not required to perform extreme flexing. Thus it is stiffer than the shovel but not as stiff and the mid-section. On wooden skis the tails should be finished with metal protectors to prevent splitting and delamination when skis are stored with their tips up.

The "life" of a ski comes from a careful relationship of its various laminations. Place the skis base-to-base and squeeze them together at the mid-section. They should approach each other easily at first but with gradually increasing difficulty until, when the bases are nearly together, a dramatic increase of pressure is required to hold them flush. A good pair of skis will have a natural springy feeling between your hands and respond quickly to changes in pressure.

Matching serial numbers should guarantee matching camber. Check by laying the skis side by side base down on a flat board and make sure that the tops are level at the mid-section. Or, stand the skis upright base-to-base and visualize equal bow from an imaginary straight line between them.

Some stores have charts illustrating the tensile strengths of the various materials which are used in making skis. From these charts sales staff attempts to show which skis will be strongest. Tensile strength, however, has little to do with the functioning of skis. What is of importance is the divergence strength of the glue bond between the laminations. No charts illustrate divergence strength. The test is how far a salesperson will bend a ski before he's afraid of breaking it. Let the salesperson show you. If he breaks it in the store, you won't have to pay for it.

Finally, and of prime importance, see that the skis are not warped. Place the skis base-to-base and hold loosely. The shovels should be flush and the tails should be flush. Very often, especially in fiberglass skis, when the tails are flush, one side of the shovel will have a gap. A warp gap of one or two millimetres can be tolerated, but beyond that it will noticeably affect your skiing.

A warp in the wooden ski may be corrected during summer storage, but it's impossible to correct a fiberglass ski. A warped ski will not track flatly, and the wax throughout the warped section will not bind with the snow.

The Final Selection Process. Once you've decided on wood or fiberglass and the price range you can afford, you are faced with the dilemma of discovering which ski is right for you.

The whole principle of skiing is to travel over the surface of the snow, or at least as near the surface as possible to minimize effort and speed travel.

The old rule of thumb was to find a ski which reached to your wrist when you stood straight with your arm vertical above your head. Quite simple. But consider: I am 173 centimetres (5′8″) tall. With my arm up the formula says I should have a ski 205 centimetres long. My usual weight is 150 pounds. On a hard-packed trail I can comfortably ski anything between 185 centimetres and 215 centimetres. In fact, on a shorter ski I am much faster through the corners. I try to ski fresh snow whenever possible, especially good powder slopes. On short skis I sink too far into the powder and find it harder to break trail, but easier to turn on a good downhill. Extra long skis make it very easy to break trail because the extra surface area keeps me from sinking, but they are more difficult to turn because of their extra length.

As it turns out, 200-205 centimetres is my ideal ski length for a combination of snow conditions, and I stay high in the snow pack so it's easy to maneuver in the trees.

I almost always ski with a pack which weighs 15 to 20 pounds. With normal clothing, boots and so forth, my effective total weight is about 175 pounds. A light touring ski with a width of 50 millimetres is not sufficient to keep me up in loose snow, so I always choose a wider ski—55 millimetres with a corresponding increased surface area.

If I weighed 170 pounds to begin with and added the dead weight of clothing and a pack to a total of 200 pounds, I would probably have to use a wide ski 210-215 centimetres long and simply would have to learn to ski on it. Otherwise, I would have to put up with both breaking deeply through the snow and the extra work of trail-breaking and turning.

If I weighed 130 pounds I would probably choose a shorter ski because it would be more maneuverable while still fulfilling the basic functions of gliding on top of the snow.

If you ski packed snow only, it matters little what length or width you choose, but if you intend to ski loose snow, the longer and wider the better.

Consider that the old rule of thumb is for persons of average weight for their particular height. If you are overweight, compensate with a bigger ski. If you are lighter, either enjoy the extra freedom of travel or choose a slightly shorter ski for ease of handling.

For some people no cross-country ski available will be large enough to carry them on top of the snow. For these people the only solution is to try to avoid breaking trail and ski the loose snow as well as possible.

The next problem is to decide how stiff a ski to purchase. A soft ski under a heavy person will not have any life and the kick and glide process will be restricted. A ski which is too stiff will not contact the snow fully and there will be a tendancy to slip which can only be partially corrected with over-waxing.

Ideally, when you are gliding over the snow squarely on both skis, the underfoot section (where the kicker wax is) should barely touch the snow and the weight should be concentrated on the faster tip and tail sections. When it comes time to kick on stride, the majority of body weight comes onto one ski and the centre is depressed fully into the snow.

How to decide in a ski shop? Any good shop will either have a hard, smooth, flat floor or at least a narrow sheet of stiff, smooth plywood to accommodate a full pair of skis. Place the skis on the floor and stand squarely on top of them. The salesperson should be able to slip a sheet of paper between the skis and the floor under foot. If it won't go through, the skis are too soft; if a whole pile would go through, they are probably too stiff. (Take your normal pack with you and wear it, or pick up some appropriate weight in the shop to approximate your normal total skiing weight.)

Transfer your weight from one ski to the other and back and forth. You should feel the off-weighted ski springing up under your foot quite comfortably. When your weight is on one ski a piece of paper should no longer slip under the weighted ski. If it does it is too stiff. Try another pair.

If you are very, very lucky you will find a pair of skis which is the right length for you, is of sufficient width, and which responds correctly to the floor test. As is generally the case with mass production articles, quality control suffers. You may not be able to find a ski which will pass the floor test. But try it, you may be lucky. Many store clerks will claim the above test is useless or is no longer used, but it seems more likely they do not use the test because they do not have a ski which will pass it. Ask them how a good racer chooses his skis.

SELECTING SKI POLES

Ski poles, or ski sticks as they used to be called, seem to be the least important item on everyone's equipment list. It is impossible to ski without poles and totally frustrating to ski when one is broken or missing a basket.

The old long downhill ski poles with large baskets and metal shafts are still among the most appropriate poles available for cross-country skiing in the mountains. Look around your basement, ask a neighbor, or watch your local dump for a pair of these increasingly rare oldtimers. Heavier than the new poles, they take only a couple of trips to get used to.

If you're buying new poles, consider them carefully before accepting the first thing a salesman offers. In skis and everything else, cheap purchases are often cheap quality.

Bamboo (Tonkin) poles are the least expensive and the weakest. Many people use them for years with no problems. Many others have broken them in a fall and have limped lopsidedly back to their car. Every season I pick up at least a half-dozen broken pieces lying alongside various trails.

Fiberglass poles, which cover the mid-price range, are significantly stronger than bamboo. Fiberglass does become brittle at cold temperatures and may break in a good wreck. These poles, if you find them with large baskets, are an acceptable compromise.

Metal poles, usually alloy tubing, are the most expensive but are consistently the strongest. If bent, metal poles can be straightened and they will accept repeated bending before the metal fatigues. The major problem with metal poles is finding them with large baskets for loose snow. Thus the note on finding old ones. Metal poles are strongly recommended for use in the mountains.

Each brand of pole has its own particular type of handle. Cork handles are expensive but warm, though they do disintegrate in time. Leather handles are inexpensive, warm and durable, but they are very difficult to find. Plastic handles are somewhat colder, inexpensive, shed snow readily, and are often moulded to your hand for comfort. Any of the above handles is acceptable.

Rough-out leather (suede) handles are the most common and the most impractical. Handles become warm from your hands. If you fall or otherwise get snow into a suede handle, the snow melts and the moisture is absorbed into the suede. Wet handles transfer water back to your gloves, and wet gloves are cold gloves. If you can't avoid rough-out grips, a covering of plastic electrician's tape, paraffin, or hard green ski wax will shed snow.

Straps should be adjustable so that they may be enlarged on cold days when you need extra mitts. It's a minor point since most fixed straps are large enough for such occasions. Check your straps regularly, replacing them if they wear thin. If you break one on the trail, you will quickly discover how dependent you are on your straps.

Baskets provide resistance to keep the pole from punching too far into the snow. The new plastic half-baskets are only useful on well-packed trails or in shallow snow. Great for races, they're useless in the mountains. The old large baskets, ideal for loose snow, can be cumbersome and hard to find. Once you find the pole and handle you want, you probably won't have a choice of basket. Obtain at least a ten centimetre (4 inch) diameter basket and buy an extra one to keep in your pack. Wax the cross pieces if they are leather to shed snow.

Ideally, the shaft should be canted below the basket, but this is only significant in hard-packed snow. For the non-racing skier the bit of extra ease extricating the pole tip from the snow is inconsequential.

Cross-country ski poles should reach comfortably into your armpits when you are standing on a hard floor. Slightly shorter poles are handy if you intend to do a lot of downhill skiing on your cross-country trips.

A recent innovation in ski poles is a must for advanced cross-country skiing in the Rockies and ski mountaineering—the new "probe poles." They are especially designed for persons travelling potential avalanche terrain. The baskets and handles slip off and the shafts screw into each other providing an immediate, although short, avalanche probe.

SELECTING BOOTS

Do you hike in running shoes or do you hike in relatively sturdy hiking boots? Apply exactly the same logic to cross-country ski boots.

Above-the-ankle, hiking weight, cross-country ski boots are recommended for mountain skiing. The sturdier boots go with cable bindings on wide skis to attain maximum stability and ultimately realize the full potential of skiing in the mountains.

Fleece-lined boots have the major drawback of soaking up moisture and taking longer to dry out. You can change wet socks easily to maintain warm, dry feet. Thus simple leather or leather-lined boots are the best.

Avoid plastic boots at all costs. They will break in extreme cold and do not maintain the flexibility of leather when it is cold.

You get what you pay for and should expect to pay about $60.

SELECTING BINDINGS

Cable bindings are recommended for use in the mountains. They are strong, stable, and used with a strong, durable, supporting boot. If you intend to enjoy the full potential of cross-country skiing in the mountains, cable bindings are the only answer.

Pin bindings are lighter and designed for maximum flex of the foot to provide maximum thrust on the skis. Originally created for racing, they have been adapted for light touring and are associated with light touring shoes. They are sufficient, but limited for touring on mountain ski trails.

CLOTHING

If man had been meant to ski, he would have been born with fur and board feet with sealskin bottoms. Compensation for lack of the above may be accomplished in a multitude of various ways. What follows is my way of doing it. However you go about doing it, do it brightly, for the simple reason that it's easier to see you if you wear something red, orange or yellow, it's easier to keep track of your partners, and if you ever need to be found, it will help speed up the rescue process. Meanwhile, from the bottom up:

Socks. What makes you feel warm and helps you avoid blisters? For me it's light wool work socks under heavy wool knicker socks. Many people prefer silk or nylon socks under their heavy wools; others swear by thermal socks. Regardless of your system, there is no substitute for wool to keep you warm when the going gets damp.

Pants. Synonymous with knickers (but not the British type). Blue jeans or cotton trousers get wet and cold, the wind blows through them, and they usually restrict free movement of the legs. There are a multitude of brands of fancy, stretchy, colorful knickers on the market, and perhaps one brand will make you go faster than another. Wool is the warmest: tight weave wool to keep the wind out. If you can't afford good tightly woven wool knickers, buy a pair of army surplus wool trousers, cut them off below the knee and make your own.

Gaiters (Leggings). To keep the snow out of your boots and your legs dry now that you're wearing knickers. Canvas should be preferred. The most colorful gaiters are made of nylon, but it's a rare piece of nylon that breaths. For years I used bright red nylon gaiters and at the end of every day found their insides soaking wet, even with the zippers halfway undone. Finally I switched to ordinary, mundane, blue canvas gaiters and discovered warmer, drier legs. Zippers should be at the back of the leg so that snow doesn't tend to seep in as easily (unless you own the super-fancy ones with storm flaps over the front zippers).

Underwear for legs. Cotton, wool, thermal, duofold or fishnet. I've found if it's fairly warm, then no long underwear. If it is simply cold, then duofold or fishnet, preferably duofold since fishnet tends to lose its qualities when your knickers flap about. If it is really cold, then fishnet next to the skin covered by duofold. And if it is super-cold, fishnet covered by duofold, covered by knickers, covered by wind pants or warm-up pants.

Underwear for torsos. Cross-country skiing usually involves sweating somewhere along the trail, thus the advantage of fishnet undershirts next to the skin. No, they don't really have an influence on how much you sweat, but they help to create the illusion that you aren't really as wet as you should be. By getting that clammy, wet, absorbing layer of whatever away from your skin you stay warmer and actually have some chance of drying out. Whether your fishnet has net shoulders or cotton shoulders is not overly important, though the cotton shoulders leave less imprint from your pack straps. The wider the weave (the bigger the holes), the more efficient the fishnet feels.

Underwear for crotches. British Knickers, panties, jockey shorts, or briefs. Whatever keeps your long underwear cleaner and your knackers warmer by holding them closer to your body. (Women do not have the same need to keep special parts close to the body, with the exception noted immediately below.)

Underwear for boobs. If you are one of the unfortunate women who suffer from cold boobs while cross-country skiing, then try the following proven recipe. Buy a bra your size. Cut a liner from a rabbit skin or angora fur and stitch it (fur side to skin) inside the cups accordingly. Then, depending on your comfort factor, wear under or over a fishnet undershirt.

Shirt. Over your fishnet undershirt wear an ordinary cotton turtleneck or light wool turtleneck when it is very cold. On top of the turtleneck according to your needs, wear a cotton, flannel, or wool shirt. The main considerations are long sleeves and long tails. Nothing worse exists than a shirt that keeps coming out of your pants, allowing wind in around the midriff or creating uncomfortable rolls under your pack.

Sweater. One light sweater for most days, a second one for very cold days. Numerous light layers are easier to add to or discard from than singular heavy layers. I use one light sweater with a full zipper up the front on most occasions. Varying the zipper opening takes care of minor temperature fluctuations. Cheap cardigans, sufficient for skiing, are easily obtained at any second-hand clothing store.

Jacket. Jackets and tents possess the same inherent problem: keeping you dry from the outside elements without causing you to get wet from interior condensation. Fortunately rain in winter is rare and the only concern is to keep out wind and snow while allowing body moisture to evaporate. I still favor a tightly woven cotton (Grenfell) cloth, though the new 60/40 or 65/35 material is most common and works very well. The main features to look for are: ample size so you can still move with all your sweaters on, a built-in hood with drawstring, snug wrist and neck closures, large pockets, a drawstring around the waist to keep out wind and snow, and a style long enough to reach to the bottom of your buttocks. Full zipper fronts naturally allow some cold air to get in, but this can be minimized with a good storm flap, a feature found on most zippered anoraks. The ease of temperature control with a full front zipper outweighs the minor heat loss. The pullover style is somewhat warmer but inconvenient. And whatever you buy, obtain it in a bright color.

Stopping jacket. Anything will do—a down parka, another sweater, or usually just your anorak. It is easier to stay warm than to get warm. Whenever you stop for lunch or to fix something put on your extra jacket and preserve whatever built-in heat you have. If you started properly—cold, you can expect to be even colder when you stop unless precautions are taken to preserve your warmth. If it is windy get out of the wind or put something on top that is windproof. (Remember the wind chill factor.) I usually carry a down jacket stuffed near the bottom of my pack at all times; the weight is negligible and the down will compact smaller than any equivalent sweater.

Neck scarf. A woman's silk head scarf is absolutely ideal. It should be large enough so that the diagonal wraps twice around your neck with enough end left to tie securely. Minor temperature fluctuations can often be handled by pulling a scarf out of your pocket and tying it around your neck. Ordinary winter neck scarves are generally too bulky to be handy. The scarf also doubles very well as a bandage and is handy for cleaning sunglasses.

Headgear. Over fifty percent of the body heat can be lost above the shoulders (or something close to that). Wear a toque (toques will also work as a head-bandage when pulled down securely). Balaclavas are great but their ultimate design only works if you have a windproof hood or pullover over them. In the springtime baseball caps are ideal.

Hand-gear. On very cold days mitts are warmest, especially if they have a windproof outer shell. However, one usually creates enough heat while skiing that gloves are quite sufficient, and in fact, preferable for their extra freedom. The best gloves are leather with a woolen-elastic cuff to keep the snow out. The combination leather outer glove with wool inner glove is very handy in that either glove can be replaced when worn out, they come apart to dry quickly, extra dry liners can be carried, and they are less expensive than the usual ski gloves. If it is not very cold, I often use cotton work gloves of a sixty-nine cent or dollar-fifty variety. They dry quickly, are inexpensive, and very versatile. If you can see spending ten dollars or more on light gloves, the new cross-country gloves with leather palms and fishnet-type backs are excellent indeed, though it seems the sponge linings do not last as long as the ones with a simple flannel type lining.

Overboots. Unless you have double boots, you have boots that are often too light to be used in the mountains in winter. However, double boots are overly expensive, overly heavy, and an unnecessary duplication. An effective compromise can be obtained by simply pulling old worn-out wool socks over your boots. Immediately they will become caked with snow which will stay frozen on top to provide an additional insulation layer. For those who can afford it, specially tailored oversocks may be purchased from a local sports store. If your feet still remain cold, try putting on an extra sweater.

REPAIR KIT

Not everyone need carry a repair kit, but there should be at least one complete kit in every party. If you are depending on someone else now, can you depend on him to be with you always? Half of your repair kit is already lying about in various parts of your house—just put it together. It doesn't weigh much, and it takes little space. The following is a suggested list with reasons for including the various articles. (If you are ski-mountaineering, you should also include extra parts for your particular bindings.)

Spare basket. The slip-on rubber centre with a metal outside ring is simplest. Skiing with one basket broken or missing on your ski pole can make life more awkward than skiing with a broken tip. It may not seem you use your poles very much, but in actual fact you are heavily dependent upon them, and they do an incredible amount to maintain upper body balance. Vice-grips are the handiest tool to remove or replace baskets.

Swiss Army knife. Always in your pocket, of course! Everyone seems to have his own favorite model. Regardless of which model you select, make sure it has at least the following features: 1) cutting blade, 6 centimetres; 2) awl or leather punch; 3) can-opener with small screwdriver end; 4) bottle opener with large screwdriver end; 5) ring, so it can be tied on a string or thong to prevent loss.

The basic Swiss Army issue knife is described above. It has aluminum sides rather than plastic and will last a lifetime. The fancier knives with corkscrews (which often pull through the center of dry western Canadian corks), toothpicks, saws, scissors, files, spoons, forks, drills, shovels, tweezers, measuring tapes, sharpening stones, and so forth, probably all have their application at one time or another. However, all of these super-fancy knives have one thing in common with fat people—they bulge. They are excess weight and bulk. Ideally your pocket knife should ride in your pocket unnoticed. If you have a big thick one, you are always removing it and leaving it behind because it is not comfortable; then when you suddenly need it, it is not there. If such is the case, leave it in your repair kit, not in your pocket (unless, of course, you are trying to impress Mae West).

Vice-grips. Small, 13¼ centimetres (5½ inches) long. A luxury item worth its weight in gold. Vice-grips can be used for almost anything: straightening a bent binding, cutting wire, tightening nuts and holding them while undoing, tightening a jury-rigged wire cable, removing and applying ski pole baskets, holding hot pots, and clamping almost anything shut including a spurting artery.

Screws. Carry a small assortment of screws that match standard ski binding screws and some just one size larger. Remember, someone in your group may not have bothered to glue his screws in, or screws just might pull right out of a soft centered ski. When replacing screws cut a small bit of wood to fill part of the hole if the screw isn't big enough. If you have Phillips screws on your bindings, either replace them with a universal slot head or carry a Phillips screwdriver.

Nuts and bolts. A couple of bolts long enough to go through the thickest part of your ski. If a binding pops and everything else fails, you can always drill right through and bolt your binding back on. I know of someone who skied (floundered) all the way from Assiniboine to Sunshine (35 kilometres) with a binding bolted on!

String (cord). A few yards of cord take up no space at all and do anything from lashing together an emergency shelter, improvising boot laces, repairing torn garments, holding on bandages, and holding down gaiters, to cutting off the circulation in the end of your finger while you remember to put everything in your pack.

Wire. Any old farmer will tell you "hay wire holds the world together." I generally carry a coil of about 3 feet of hay wire, another of about 9 feet of stove pipe wire, and a small spool of hobby shop wire. Where cord is too thick and thread too weak, wire will usually fit the bill. Everything from jury-rigged bindings to reinforcing a broken ski pole, holding a pot over the fire, or repairing your car on the way home.

Spare strap. Usually this is the one that holds my skis together anyway. With it you can strap on a splint, rig a cable-type binding, or strap it around your ski to climb a hill when no wax will work. You can use it for a tourniquet or simply to hold your skis together when not skiing.

Sewing awl or speedy stitcher. These are available at any saddle or leather shop and are quite inexpensive. They are invaluable for mending boots, mountaineering seal skins, clothing, tents, pack sacks, and ski pole straps.

Fiberglass tape. Rather than depend entirely on the adhesive tape in your first aid kit, carry a small amount of fiberglass tape for emergency repairs.

Stuff bag. Sew yourself a small stuff bag with a drawstring top to contain your repair items so you won't lose the small ones and won't have to rummage all over your pack to find various pieces. If you are using cable bindings, this is a handy place to store your extra cable. Numerous other items will probably find their way into your kit: rivets, cotter pins, multi-head screwdrivers, spark plugs, wrenches, and so forth. But keep it light and simple or you'll find yourself leaving it behind.

In addition to your repair kit there are a few more items to stuff into your pack. A spare ski tip should be carried at all times, and a shovel is imperative for advanced trips. The shovel should be accompanied by a snow saw when you are winter camping.

Ski tip. Spare ski tips are available in both aluminum and plastic. The aluminum tip is cheaper and easier to remove if you are going to have your ski repaired. It also conforms better to the shape of your ski if your tip is only cracked and not broken. The main drawback of the aluminum tip is that it will bend in crusty snow or upon impact with another object or a sharp dip in the trail. it can easily be bent back into shape, but repeated bendings cause the metal to fatigue and ultimately break.

The plastic tip may cost twice as much, but it is pliable and will not fatigue. It is easier to pack since it is a one piece item without protruding wing screws. To hold the plastic tip on better if you have narrow skis, drill two holes just ahead of the grip plate and screw in two short screws which can be driven into the ski after the tip is slipped over the broken end.

Shovel. Aluminum snow shovels with removeable handles can be purchased at most mountaineering stores for $8.00 to $15.00. These are generally of scoop size 19 by 24 centimetres and fit conveniently into any pack. They are ideal for internal work on a snow cave and are generally sufficient for most digging jobs.

A less expensive and more useful shovel can be obtained from most hardware stores for $6.00 to $8.00. Obtain an ordinary aluminum snow shovel with a scoop size about 30 by 33 centimetres. Simply cut off the handle at a convenient length or shorten by the following method. Drill out the rivets holding the shaft to the scoop and drill the holes through to a clean one-quarter inch diameter. Obtain two one-quarter by two inch machine bolts with wing nuts to secure the shaft when needed (one is sufficient but two provides greater strength and covers the situation if one is lost). Cut off the handle to a convenient carrying length and coat it with varnish or plastic. The top of the handle can be left plain, fitted with a wrist loop, or a plastic handle may be refitted to the shaft.

With the larger shovel you can move a greater amount of snow much more easily than with the small backpack variety. In an avalanche accident this fact is critical. The ideal combination for digging snow caves is a large home-built and a small backpack shovel, and accordingly one person carries the large and the other the small one. To make the large scoop more convenient to carry drill a hole in each corner of the blade and tie it to the outside of your pack.

Snow shovels also double very well as frying pans.

Snow saw. Snow saws are essential for igloo construction and very handy for extra fancy snow caves. Again, they can be purchased from $8.00 to $12.00, or you can build your own for next to nothing. Regardless of bought or made, paint the handle (if wooden) with varathane or some sort of plastic sealer to preserve the wood and prevent wet snow build-up under your hand while working.

To build one, obtain a piece of aluminum (snow shovel weight) about 50 centimetres long. If the aluminum is slightly thicker then the blade does not have to be more than 5 centimetres wide. Cut to blade shape and drill out one edge with a three-eights inch drill leaving about three-eights of an inch between each hole.

Or build two by drawing out a double blade, edge-to-edge, and drill down the center line. Then cut through the center of the holes. Carve a wooden handle from a short piece of two-by-two, halve it, insert the blade and secure the halves with glue and screws, or glue and rivets. Cut a hole for a wrist loop, plasticize the handle and you're done.

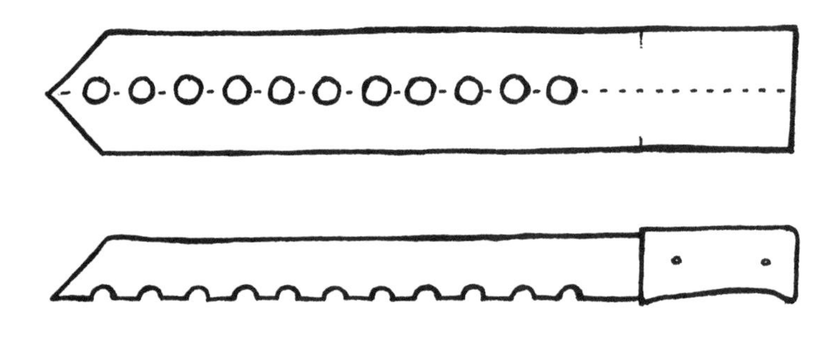

Survival

EMERGENCY SURVIVAL

Guide books succeed when they encourage people to new experiences, but they can lead to tragic results by involving people in trips beyond their ability. If an accident occurs with which the person cannot cope, the guide may be at fault. A short chapter on survival is at the heart of the whole reason for this book.

The stress on safety throughout this book may lead readers to feel numerous trails have been overrated in difficulty. After spending many hours analyzing accidents with the victims involved, and in carrying out rescues for the parks service, I realize that writing can never adequately cover the subject. Accidents befall even the most experienced mountaineers. Some of the world's greatest mountaineers, in fact, have died in ludicrously simple incidents.

The following chapter is a presentation of some ideas about staying alive if an accident occurs and you find yourself stranded. Success most frequently depends upon common sense and the resources available in your pack.

I assume you carry a complete day pack. If you ignore some items in order to travel less encumbered, your safety is solely your responsibility. Forewarned is forearmed. Enough said.

Something happened forcing you to stay out overnight. To remain alive you must stay warm. You should direct all of your efforts to conserving what bodily heat you have, and secondly, to creating whatever heat you can.

Keep active and add spare clothing from your pack as you need it. Move slowly and efficiently. Avoid working up a sweat as damp clothing draws warmth from your body like a wick. Save that down jacket or extra sweater for settling down when you will really need it.

Look around. If you are not in the trees, can you get down into them? Is there a natural shelter nearby? Is there enough snow for a snow cave? Is there wood for a fire?

And, once again, is there anything you can do to get out of the situation and avoid being stuck out overnight?

Lighting fires

It is astounding how many people fail at successful fire building in the summertime, not to mention the wintertime. So we belabour the point.

Stamp down a small sheltered area in the snow where your fire will be, so it will not disappear into the soft snow pack. Tear off a couple of green boughs as a base for your kindling and place them in the bottom of this pit.

Begin building with small dead, dry twigs, or lodgepole pines. The low dead, needleless branches of spruce trees provide the best kindling. The driest twigs will be on the lee side of the tree. If they do not break off with a clean snap they are not sufficiently dry. Gather at least two handfuls of these brittle twigs pencil size and smaller.

If twigs are not obtainable, use your pocket knife to slice up larger branches into feathered sticks or to remove the damp outer wood and get down to the dry center of a dead branch.

Stay calm and resist applying matches. To ensure success keep following the procedure.

Rummage through your pack for whatever available paper you may have: toilet paper, food wrappers, notebook, or this book. If it is this book, tear out the title pages or trips you have already done and crumple about three pages.

Lay your crumpled paper on top of the green boughs and cover with your twigs. Now grab a couple of handfuls of larger dead, dry twigs and pile one handful on top of the established kindling pile. Set the other handful nearby within easy reach.

Next, get an armload of dead branches and keep them within easy reach. Finally take an extra look for another handful of those tiny kindling twigs and select only the very driest. Keep them nearby but don't use them yet.

Then, light a match or put your butane lighter to the paper and start your fire. If everything catches and begins to burn well, add progressively larger bits of wood until you have a roaring blaze.

What? You say it started, blazed up, burned for a moment and then went out? Either the wood is too damp and you only had a few dry pieces or your twigs were too few. Start again with that extra handful of carefully selected tiny twigs. But before you light it this time, go and find some more of those twigs which you just observed are the kind that burn. Or cut out more dry shavings.

If it looks like you cannot obtain sufficiently dry twigs, dig out that short piece of candle from your repair kit, waxing kit, or first aid kit. Hold a bundle of the smallest twigs over the lit candle. The sustained heat from the candle will help dry them and get them started burning. Place the blazing twigs in the fire pit and add more of the small twigs before beginning your progression to larger wood.

Still having a hard time? Dig through your pack to see if you have a piece of fuel pellet or a can of sterno. Use that as the centre of your fire and build upon it.

There will still be some poeple who cannot get a fire going. God bless you. Before you simply give up and pray, try building a snow cave.

Building snow shelters (Ukrainian high rises)

There are essentially four types of snow shelters, or if you count igloos, five. However, igloos are usually premeditated and, besides requiring a snow knife, they require both practice and skill. Thus we disregard them as practical emergency shelter.

The Desperation Trench. This is for those who do not carry a shovel. Dig as best you can with your ski, spoon, cup, hands, whatever, a small trench large enough to sit in, deep enough for your head to be below the surface. In other words a hole, a pit in which to hide. (You might have to look for a snow drift in order to obtain sufficient depth.)

Line the bottom with spruce boughs or dead wood to provide insulation from the snow below. Place your skis and poles across the top of the hole and cover with a groundsheet or more boughs. Leave enough room to drop in. For added insulation cover the groundsheet or boughs with the excavated snow.

Perform your evening ablutions and crawl in. Do what you can to cover your entrance hole from the inside. It is unlikely that you need worry about suffocating as there will be air leaks everywhere.

Put on all of your extra clothing and loosen your boot laces. If you have extra socks or mitts, pull them on over your boots. If you do not need your pack to sit on, place your feet inside. Settle down as comfortably as possible and think about warmer places you have been. Do not assume the full lotus position as it will restrict blood flow to your feet.

The Powder and Prayer Dome. It is possible to build a snow cave in loose powder snow if you cannot find a snow drift or enough snow for a desperation trench. A shovel is almost mandatory, but with enough time and desperation the task can be accomplished by hand.

Unsettled, loose powder snow will settle after it has been disturbed. So disturb it. Throw together a pile of snow large enough to provide walls about 25 cm. (1 foot) thick once you have cleared out an inside to accommodate your needs. Roll your body over top and along the sides of the pile to help consolidate it. Powder snow is dry snow so there is no worry of getting wet. Allow things to settle for about 15 minutes while you have a coffee break.

Tunnel out the inside starting at the lowest possible point. Work from the bottom up so that what will be left for walls will have the maximum opportunity to consolidate. To assure the proper thickness of wall, insert branches of the appropriate length into the pile from all sides and when you expose the end of a branch you know it is time to stop.

Cover the entrance with a wind sheet or a pile of loose snow from the inside. Punch one or two small holes through for ventilation. In the morning you will be able to walk out of this shelter at any point you choose, and the entrance is of little consequence except as a cold air leak.

Until you have built one or two of these shelters you will not believe that they will stand throughout the night. Thus the name, Powder and Prayer. In fact, they become structurally stronger through the night, although the roof may sag a bit by morning.

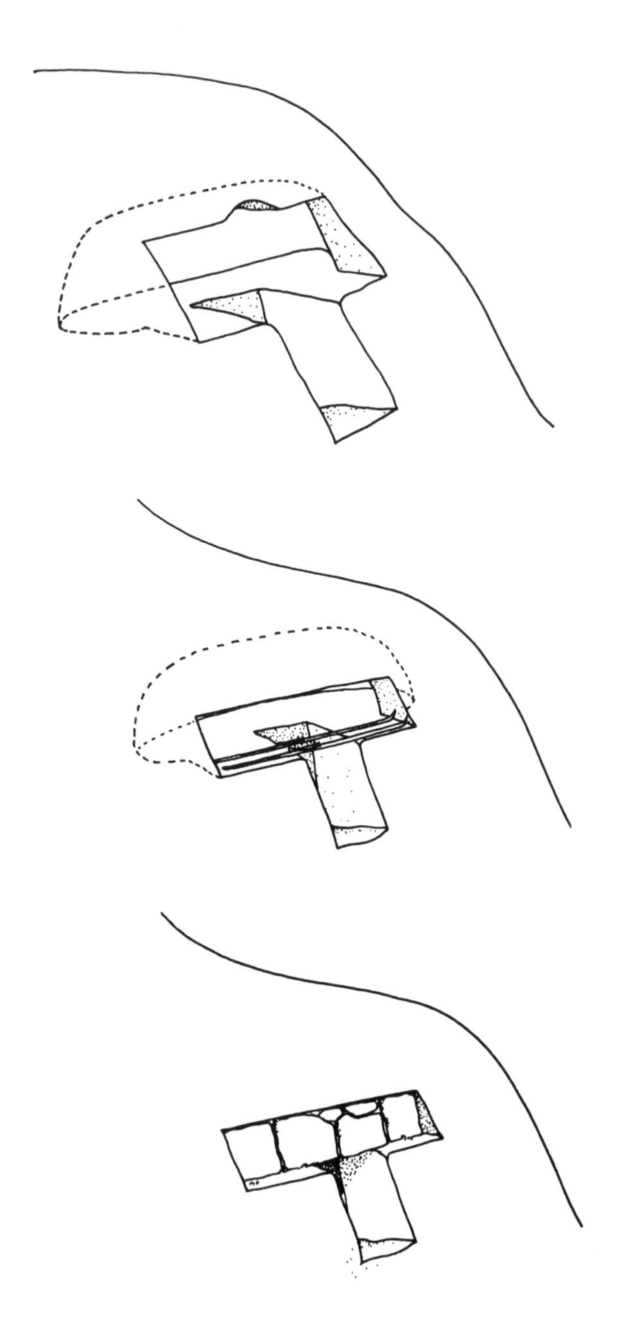

The Basic Split Level.

The Basic Split Level. There are three pre-requisites for a Basic Split Level: a snow drift, a shovel, and skis. The Basic Split Level is the simplest way to construct a proper snow dwelling to take advantage of the basic principle of living in snow. The basic principle is to create a pocket of warm air in which to live and trap the colder air below you. A proper snow cave or igloo will maintain a relatively constant temperature of 0°C. regardless of outside air temperature.

Face the snowdrift square on and mark out a cross as tall as you are and as wide as your skis are long. Clear away any loose snow on the surface. The arms of the cross should be about one half meter wide (2 feet). This will vary as you progress, but not to worry.

Carefully cut out the first layer in blocks as large as possible. Set them aside for use in the final stages.

Scoop out the vertical section of the cross until you are standing feely inside the drift with at least 25 centimetres (1 foot) of snow wall in addition. Now clear out the arms tc enable you to throw out the snow from inside easily while standing in your trench.

Do not trench any further. As you face into the drift, scoop out a domed area in front of and around you. You are developing a cavity with its bottom at waist level or just above the bottoms of the arms of your cross. Enlarge it to sufficient size to accommodate you comfortably.

Place your skis base down across the arms of your original cross to bridge the trench at the entrance. Now fill the arms and upper section of the cross with the snow blocks which you so carefully cut out earlier. Seal off with loose snow. Entrance and exit will be through the trench under your skis.

There is no need to seal the entrance, because as you warm the air inside the cold air will gravitate into the trench and remain there. Since you are on the lee side of a hill, and thus the snow drift, there will be no direct wind blowing in. Light your candle to maintain a temperature just above freezing. Pleasant dreams.

The Architectural Dream. The Architectural Dream is the ultimate in snow caves. There is only one rule, following the basic principle - keep the top of the entrance below the level of your living quarters. The design is limited by the scope of your imagination, the depth of the snow drift, and the amount of expendable time and energy to dig.

Usually the Architectural Dream is built only when you intend to live in it for at least a few days. In a survival situation, lacking a sleeping bag and ensolite to enjoy a good night's sleep, you might as well keep digging to keep warm if you cannot sleep in your Basic Split Level.

Once your Basic Split Level is complete, you can enlarge it by throwing snow out the bottom of the trench or by temporarily removing a wall. The Architectural Dream is nothing more than a Basic Split Level on a grander scale.

As a group project it is hard to beat. Many small chambers are preferable to a major cathedral, and sleeping chambers should be kept small. Multiple entrances facilitate snow removal. When the chambers are complete, punch crawlways through to connect them and seal off all but one entrance to minimize drafts.

Those who can sleep will sleep in peace, and the others can keep warm by digging. In the morning it will be an architectural prize and difficult to leave. Design is often a function of topography, and it is always interesting to see what can be developed.

Lean-to's

The least acceptable shelters are the standard Armed Forces or Boy Scout lean-to's. They are inefficient insulators, require a reflector fire to keep warm, are a waste of wood, and generally create an unacceptable mess. Their only true application is in northern Saskatchewan where there is ample wood to burn and insufficient snow to create snow shelters.

Lean-to's violate the basic principles of the National Parks. If you are intent on creating one for survival purposes, read through an Armed Forces or old Boy Scout manual. A proper waterproof lean-to made only of boughs is a work of art and a worthy structure, but the majority are embarrassing failures and should be limited to tarpaulins stretched over a rail.

KEEPING WARM

On those especially cold days when you cannot seem to keep warm but still want to ski, some simple remedies may help. (Check back through the clothing section for more hints.)

Cold feet are often the result of overall body cooling rather than a lack of foot insulation. If you neglect to correct the situation, you could be setting yourself up for a good dose of hypothermia or frostbite. A gram of prevention is worth a ton of cure, and all that.

Heat distribution varies from 37°C. in the body core down to 33°C. under the peripheral skin. For reasons of its own, the brain considers the interior vital organs much more important than fingers and toes. Accordingly, blood volume to the extremities is reduced when the body core cannot be kept warm enough. Thus the old axiom: "If your feet are cold, put on an extra sweater."

You can lose a hand or foot and still ski, but just try skiing without a brain. Always wear a good hat or toque when it is cold.

In addition to adding garments, look yourself over to see if you have any metallic ornaments which can be removed. Earrings are one of the best devices for freezing earlobes. If you are wearing earrings, necklaces, bracelets, rings or metallic watchbands, remove them and carry them in your pack or pocket.

If you are still cold, ski out as fast as your can and get into a long hot bath. Hypothermia can immobilize you if you keep on going, and frostbite can be unnoticeable once your toes are numb. A reputation for stoicism will never compensate lost limbs.

HYPOTHERMIA

Hypothermia is the accepted term for the old common concept of exposure, as in "he dies of exposure." Not to be confused with cameras, climbing or flashing. The recently popularized catch phrase for hypothermia is "killer of the unprepared," and yes, even Boy Scouts get it.

Hypothermia (hypo, "below", thermia, "temperature") is the lowering of the body's central core temperature which results in a diminishing ability of the vital organs (brain, heart, lungs, kidneys and liver) to function properly. The body's central core must remain close to its normal temperature of 37°C., regulated by the continual reactions of sweating, radiating, shivering and so forth. Lowering of the core temperature by even one degree brings on noticeable symptoms.

Blood vessels constrict in response to cold. Available blood volume and effective perfusion through such a part are thereby reduced, and the cells receive a restricted ration of their normal supplies of oxygen, nutrients and heat. You can have cold feet, even frozen feet, and a warm heart and continue to function—the frostbite situation.

If you reverse the situation and lose heat from your entire body rapidly, the central core temperature will drop. Your feet may, in fact, seem warm, but if your heart or brain are cold you cannot function normally.

In other words, cellular starvation in your feet is not critical to overall function, but cellular starvation of your brain or other vital organs definitely affects your overall body functioning. Your vital organs fail to function at optimal efficiency when they are not fed properly. Thus the immediate symptom of hypothermia is mental disfunctioning, similar to drunkeness but physiologically more complicated. Since hypothermia is initially a minor brain disfunction, it is difficult to recognize either in yourself or in others.

Overall body heat loss occurs most rapidly by immersion in cold water or by being wet or damp in windy conditions. Hypothermia can occur in seemingly moderate conditions. In fact, many incidences are recorded on cool days in mid-summer. A skier who has skied too far too fast, carried too heavy a pack, is hungry, tired, and/or demoralized is a prime candidate.

Adults are less likely to become victims of hypothermia than are children and adolescents for numerous reasons. Adults generally carry more fat (insulation) and have a lower body weight—surface area ratio than spindly teenagers. Adults usually have greater stamina, mental reserve, experience, and the training to travel at a more regulated pace. It is imperative when leading a group to travel at the pace of the slowest member and to observe the progress of any member who lacks physical or mental stamina.

Since it's impractical to ski around with your waxing thermometer in a rectal position, hypothermia must be recognized in its initial stages through its minor symptoms. Hypothermia is reversible if recognized early and treated rapidly. The initial symptoms are not obvious but require an analysis of actions. Watch carefully for erratic variations in walking, talking, co-ordination, and attitudes. As a person becomes progressively colder, symptoms are more easily recognized: shivering, slurring of speech, slowing of pace, stumbling, loss of orientation, amnesia, irrationality, and even hallucinations. Finally, physical manifestations become apparent: dilation of pupils, blueish tone of skin, slower breathing rate, and weak or irregular pulse. At this point the victim usually falls into a stupor and may experience an overwhelming sense of warmth before oblivion and death.

You might practice symptom recognition at home by getting drunk and keeping track of your gradually diminishing brilliance and grace. Learn to admit you no longer have it all together. If you are like me, however, you tend to believe you are being profound before you begin the downslide into drunken oblivion. It's often the same with hypothermia; the victim believes that everything is absolutely alright with himself.

Know your companion's normal personality since the initial symptoms could easily be excitement or swearing rather than lethargy and slurring. And, for your own sake, believe your partner when he or she says that you are not up to normal, even though you think you're still strutting along with grace and aplomb.

If you recognize the symptoms in anyone in your group, even if it is a nice day and hypothermia seems unlikely, stop immediately and initiate treatment. Act quickly and decisively!

Mild hypothermia

In an exposed windy area, ski quickly for the nearest shelter, a large boulder or a clump of trees. Ski back in your own tracks for speed rather than break fresh trail. If you are a long way out, it may be wise to send someone for help, since the victim may languish too far to ski out before dark or, through exhaustion, may slow the entire group down on the retreat. Do all you can and attempt to get out, since the rescue party may be held up for various reasons. There is nothing wrong in calling off a resuce if you have performed the rescue yourself. It is better to opt on the side of safety.

Back to the situation. Get the victim warmed! Find a sheltered area. Give the victim something to eat, especially high energy sweets; and, if possible, make something hot to drink. Insulate the resting victim as thoroughly as possible and cover him with any extra clothing. Remember the other members of your group who will be getting cold due to their inactivity. Keep everyone busy and helping. Discourage smoking because nicotine causes blood vessel constriction. "One puff of a fag can reduce the calibre of small and middle-sized arteries by half." (Peter Steele. p. 170-171).

Chances are your victim will resent what you are doing for him and may not appreciate being singled out as a victim. One simple way to avoid the problem is to declare a lunch break at a convenient sheltered spot. If it is nowhere near lunch time, declare that you yourself are getting tired and hungry and need a short break. See to it unobtrusively that the questionable member of the group puts on an extra jacket and gets rested and replenished. He will likely be happy to take advantage of the chance to restock his boilers while you receive the ridicule for being the weak member. If you can prevent hypothermia or treat it early you'll save time and prevent greater risks later.

Severe hypothermia

If someone has stumbled on and finally reached the advanced stages without being treated, stop immediately. By now the victim is probably beyond the shivering stage and can proceed no further. Dig in where you are if you fail to find immediate accessible shelter. In his rapidly weakening condition the victim must stop. Start re-warming without delay. The most efficient way to re-warm a person in the field situation is to strip him of his clothing, put him into a sleeping bag, and have someone crawl naked into the bag with him. Cuddle until warmth is restored. Naked bodies transfer heat much more efficiently than clothed ones, especially when the clothing is damp due to a day's exertion. It is a life or death situation. There is no time to waste with social protocol. Get in there and get the victim warmed up as quickly as possible.

Remember to insulate under the sleeping bag with ensolite, boughs, packs or whatever you can find. If you have a tent erect it immediately, or use your bivouac sack. Anything to keep the wind away from the victim and his companion. Think of all possible things which you can do to conserve and create heat, and do them.

Meanwhile, someone else should have the stove going and be preparing hot sweet drinks. Someone else should calculate the position accurately on a map, write down the required information on the emergency form (see first aid chapter), and be off on the way for help.

If the group is large enough and sufficiently equipped, dig a snow cave. It will be warmer than a tent while awaiting rescue. Remember, you won't be able to hear the rescue party coming if everybody is in a snow cave. so maintain an outside watch.

If you have no camping gear with you, get down into the trees whatever way you can, even if you have to lay the victim on his skis and drag him. Build a shelter and a large fire. Insulate the victim from below with boughs, skis, packs or anything else available. Skis make a good frame for a shelter from the wind. Change whatever wet clothing the victim may have for dry clothing, even if you have to exchange your own with his.

Once your victim is well looked after, see to it that the rest of the group is also in good shape, receiving that needed hot drink, and getting some of the extra food.

If the victim improves significantly, encourage him to begin skiing out toward the rescue party. Any exercise will help to warm a person. Do not leave your packs or extra equipment behind in hopes of travelling faster. Lighten the weaker members' loads if you can by sharing out some of their goods to stronger members.

To travel or not to travel, it's a tough decision to make. Your victim may be getting colder lying immobilized, but he may also collapse again on the way toward help, requiring that the whole process be begun again.

Do not depend on a helicopter coming to pluck you out of your situation. In stormy weather a helicopter cannot fly, and even on a good day there may be no helicopter available to rush to the scene.

Above all, keep the rewarming process going. Do not give up. Even "corpses" have been known to come alive!

If the hypothermia has been anything more than minimal, check into a hospital as soon as possible.

Proper trip-planning and decision-making can prevent all of the foregoing except in a catastrophic situation. Dress warmly and properly, pace yourself to the slowest member, carry survival equipment, make the vital decision and abort your trip if it looks as if the going may get too rough or if someone is weakening. The life you save may be your own.

For additional information, see the bibliography at the end of this book.

FROSTBITE

Frostbite is literally freezing of the body tissues. It varies significantly from hypothermia in that rapid cooling of a specific area, such as fingers or toes, can be extreme enough that those sites may actually begin to freeze without the central core temperature of the body being altered.

Mild frostbite may occur without any other associated problems in any healthy individual, but it is often associated with hypothermia and fatigue in a weaker person. Severe frostbite in a skiing situation is almost always complicated with hypothermia.

Frostbite is a constant hazard in cold weather, especially when the wind chill factor is high. Facial areas such as the cheeks and the tip of the nose may be partially frozen without the victim's realization. Watch the faces of other members of your party on extreme days.

If a person is immobilized through accident or hypothermia, the threat of frostbite is extreme. Bodily resources are already being conserved and immobility further reduces the ability of the blood to reach the extremities to maintain the required heat flow.

As explained under "Hypothermia," the body attempts to maintain a constant central core temperature for optimal functioning of the vital organs. If a person cannot maintain the required core temperature because of poor clothing, lack of energy or extreme conditions, then the blood vessels in the extremities automatically constrict to avoid losing heat to the extremities. You can live without a finger or foot but not without a satisfied heart. The tiny capillaries which keep your fingers warm and your skin alive shrink and the blood is shunted directly from arteriole to venule for the return trip to the heart.

The photos on the opposite page graphically display the grim progression of severe frostbite. Top, one day after the accident. Middle, seven weeks later as physicians are still waiting to assess the full extent of the damage. And finally, bottom, the post-operation—four months after the accident.

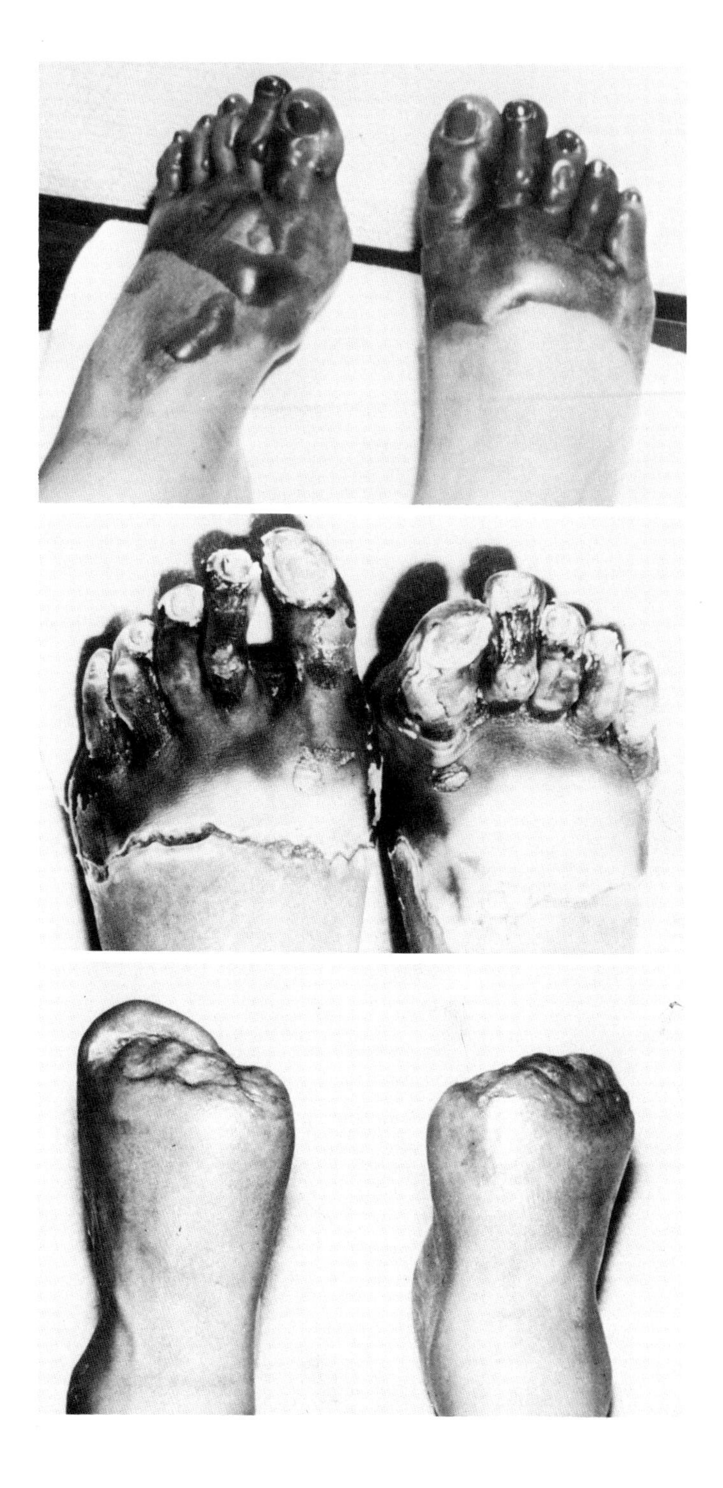

Once the situation is ripe for frostbite, two things happen which lead to actual death of the cells in question. Cells starve to death if the blood fails to get through to them with oxygen and nutrients. If the tissues in question lose heat to below minus one degree celsius, the fluid surrounding the cells freezes and ice crystals form. Freezing upsets the osmotic balance and draws water out of the cells, destroying their physical and chemical balance, injuring or killing the cells.

If the area can be thawed quickly before excessive damage, the water will move back into the cells and everything may be alright. If the fluid inside the cells freezes and the nucleus of the cell dies, it is too late and the cells are dead. Thawing will not revive them. Thus the importance of identifying the situation early and treating it immediately.

Treatment

A skier suffering from frostbite may also be suffering from hypothermia and fatigue. Peter Steele recommends that before treating the frostbite, make certain the victim is warm, comfortable, and free from pain and anxiety (see *Complete Accident Care).* However, do not waste too much time before beginning treatment.

Superficial frostbite

If the area is still soft and spongy, regardless of color (usually white by now), and if the victim still has some feeling (reacts to pain), warm the area quickly and head for home. Put extra clothing on the victim, keep him moving, and get out to somewhere warm. At this point damage is usually limited to the surface cells which are replaceable. Pain indicates things are still alive and a pain reaction (minor scream) can be a very reassuring sign.

Have the victim exercise: jump, clap, swing arms, twist, jive, anything to create heat. If exercise is not sufficient try the following variations. For facial areas, hold your hands over your face and warm with breath or warm skin. Do not rub. For hands, put them into your armpits or between your thighs. The closer you can get them to naked skin, the quicker they will warm. For feet, remove your boots and hold your feet in your hands. Or better yet, put them between someone else's thighs, into their armpits or onto their stomach. Anything to get the freezing flesh rewarmed. Other alternatives are to use your stove or build a fire, but work quickly before overall cooling begins to set in due to your immobilized situation.

Do not rub frozen areas or use snow. Rubbing may break the skin and introduce infection. Snow is cold and abrasive, and it can cut the skin, again allowing infection.

Deep frostbite

If the flesh in question is rock hard and elicits no pain response when provoked, the situation is severe. Do not attempt rewarming in the field or you will have a basket case on your hands. If rewarmed (thawed out), the victim will discover excruciating pain, likely to the point of immobility. If the area is thawed and becomes refrozen again, the cells are further damaged and more tissue is lost.

You can walk-out/ski-out on frozen limbs without further damage if you can contain general heat loss. Get out and get to a hospital. If possible, notify the hospital that you are coming and inform them what has happened and of the severity of the incident. Turn the heat in your car on high and do what you can to re-warm the victim on your way to the hospital. As in hypothermia, discourage smoking.

For field treatment in remote situations, dig your copy of Peter Steele's *Medical Care For Mountain Climbers* from the bottom of your pack.

Once again a gram of prevention is worth more than a ton of cure. Re-read the section on keeping warm, stay in good physical shape, avoid exhaustion, and cut a trip short if symptoms are arising.

EQUIPMENT ESSENTIAL FOR TRAVEL IN AVALANCHE TERRAIN

When travelling in potential avalanche terrain you should always carry the following list of extra essential equipment: a rescue transceiver, a probe, and a shovel.

Rescue transceiver. The avalanche rescue transceiver has replaced the old avalanche cord for everyone except those who feel their lives are not worth more than two dollars. Numerous brands are available, but the two most popular brands in the Canadian Rockies are "Pieps" and "Skadi." They work equally well and they are compatible systems. Another well known transceiver is the "Autophone." However, the Autophone will not work with a Pieps or Skadi. Until one frequency becomes standard, it is important to see that everyone in the group has the same brand of transceivers or that they are compatible.

Reading the instruction booklet which comes with a transceiver is insufficient. The principle of their use is so basic and simple it seems one must use the instrument perfectly on a first try. Experience with thousands of skiers has shown that this is not the case. It takes practice, lots of practice, repeated practice. Even if you had it down to a fine art last year, you should still practice this year.

When you practice, you should attempt to simulate a real situation. Bury three or five transceivers in the snow at once in various depths, organize your group, and work with military precision. Keep at it until everyone is equally proficient. Take turns being the leader. Remember, you may be the one lying buried in an avalanche hoping for the best help possible on top.

The group leader must always be certain everyone in the group has his transceiver turned to the transmit position when travelling in potential avalanche terrain. It is not enough just to ask, be certain by having each skier ski past you in turn. Ensure that the transceiver is not in a pack or an outside pocket where the turmoil of an avalanche could separate it from its owner. Carry it around your neck, hanging down the front inside of your shirt. (Batteries work best when they are warm.)

Avalanche probe. Prior to the advent of the rescue transceiver the probe was the only way to find a buried victim, unless his avalanche cord was on the surface. Except for the avalanche dog it is the only way to find a buried victim if electronic detection devices fail or are not used. Even with the transceiver the probe is important to discover exactly where to dig and how deeply to dig without fear of injuring the victim with your shovel.

Avalanche probes are available in many types. Some are narrow, long steel sections which screw together; others are hollow with a connecting wire similar to tent poles; in ski areas they may be as simple as ten or twelve feet of straight steel rod. Try to find probes which when fully extended are fairly rigid. If the probe whips like a fishing rod, chances are it will deflect easily in the snowpack and a consistent probe pattern will not be maintained.

Probe ski poles are now available and, except for a slight lack of length, they should be the answer for all serious skiers. Some brands telescope and adjust for downhill or cross-country skiing lengths as well as to maximum extension for probing. Their one drawback is they they are not as strong as a rigid pole. Regardless of type, the principle is the same. When needed for probing one basket is popped off and the handles are removed. The tops of the shafts screw together to provide a probe equal in length to the sum of the poles. Obviously, the longer the better, but even an ordinary ski pole is better than nothing. Be certain you can remove the baskets easily.

Shovel. Time is critical in all avalanche rescues. Hands or skis are insufficient tools to move the quantities of snow required to excavate a victim. Small shovels with removable handles designed to fit easily into a pack are available for from eight to fifteen dollars.

Everyone in the group should have his own shovel. If those carrying shovels are buried, the others will be left pawing away fruitlessly on the surface. (See the general equipment section for ideas on how to improvise less expensive avalanche shovels.)

In addition to the above essential equipment, the overall general equipment list includes items you might carry on a day trip. For example: a bivouac sack, stove, or ensolite. Share out equipment among your group, considering the extras you might need if you did have an avalanche accident in which someone was perhaps immobilized and you are forced to stay out overnight.

Travelling unavoidable avalanche slopes

The safest thing to do is to avoid potential avalanche slopes entirely. Since it is not always possible, certain precautions can minimize the hazard.

1. *Analyse the slope.* Try to find a way around the slope by getting above it. Take your skis off and travel the ridge. If avoidance is impossible, attempt a route across the slope as low as possible, well into its run-out zone. If there is still no way around it, think about it some more. If conditions are hazardous, why not turn around and go somewhere else? If you persist in your determination to cross, and a low route is impractical, select a route as high as is practicable and note possible protection points. Minimize the amount of snow which could engulf you.

2. *Pick an escape route.* Unlikely as it is, it is occasionally possible to ski out of an avalanche. Some persons actually track slightly uphill to the midpoint hoping to be able to perform an instantaneous helicopter turn should the slope fracture, skiing out to the side on a broken track. Great in theory, but the odds of successful execution are weighted heavily on the side of the avalanche. Anyway, if the slope fractures, try to remain upright and ski for one side. Burial depth will be less along the sides of an avalanche than in its main course.

3. *Check transceivers.* Take a moment to assure that your own and everybody else's transceiver is operating in the transmit position.

4. *Prepare to jettison.* Take your hands out of your ski pole wrist loops, undo ski safety straps, undo the waist loop on your pack, and slip off one shoulder strap from your pack. If you are engulfed, attached skis and poles contort the body excessively as well as beat upon you as you tumble; your pack will weigh you down, decreasing your chances of coming out on the surface.

5. *Seal up.* Do up any open zippers, close collars, and put on your toque. If you are buried, you will want to be as well insulated as possible.

6. *Attempt external initiation.* If a large flat rock or a dead tree stump is nearby, throw it out onto the slope to attempt a release before you have to step on the slope yourself. This is often successful in isothermal spring conditions but rarely releases a good slab.

7. *Pray.* If you are so inclined.

8. *Consider once again.* What happens if it does slide? If the path below goes over cliffs or channels into deep gullies, could you even survive?

9. *Cross one at a time.* The rest of the group must remain in a safe position from which it can view the entire route and as much of the slope below as possible. When the first skier is across, the next one may take his turn. You

can never assume a slope is stable because one, two, or ten persons have crossed it safely. Deep slabs often take their time releasing; many avalanche accidents have happened to the last man across. It is important to be able to see the slope below; in the event a slide occurs, you must be able to mark the victim's last seen point.

10. *On being a victim.* You have taken all of the previous precautions. Suddenly, part way across, the world begins to move underneath you. What to do? Go for it! Try to ski for the side.

When you realize you are not going to make it, ditch your ski poles and pack. You won't have time to undo your skis, you can only hope they will release.

Try to stay on top of the sliding snowpack by swimming, usually the backstroke. Try not to exhaust yourself in your frenzy. Swimming can be very successful in a small slide or in a slow slide; in a major slide you will probably be flying, tumbling, and rolling all at once.

Maintain calm and try to figure out which end is up. As you slow down (if you are aware of it) thrust one arm up to the sky, you might luckily punch through to daylight. The other arm should be in front of your chest and face attempting to clear some breathing space.

Try to relax in order to conserve oxygen, and if you feel you are blacking out, enjoy your dreams. An unconscious person consumes less oxygen than someone in a conscious panic and thus may survive longer.

Avalanche rescue procedure

In an avalanche accident or observing one while travelling in the backcountry, remain calm and think your way through the situation. The victim's chances of survival are minimal if he is not recovered within one hour, desperate if he cannot be found within two hours. In most backcountry situations, there is not time to go for help. By the time an organized rescue party can arrive, rescue has usually become a recovery situation.

Do not ski madly to the scene of the accident and begin frantic attempts to find the victim(s) unless you can see an actual body part sticking out of the snow. Maintain control of yourself and the rest of your group. If you are carrying this book in your pack, take the time to take it out and follow through with the proper procedure. **STOP** and **THINK!**

1. *Check for further danger.* Is there immediate danger from other avalanches? Can you make it to the accident site without getting caught?

2. *Quick visual search.* Scan the slope for arms, legs or skis sticking out of the debris.

3. *Mark the last seen point.* If the victim(s) was observed in the slide, there is no reason to search above that point. Mark the spot clearly with your ski or ski pole; begin searching down slope from that point.

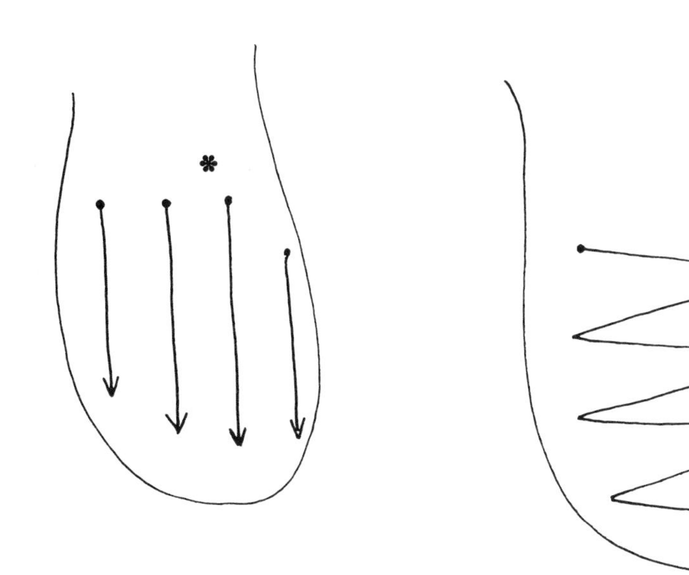

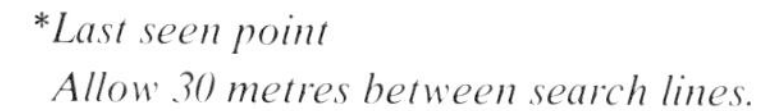

*Last seen point
Allow 30 metres between search lines.

4. *Use your transceiver.* Turn the switch to receive and stick the earphone in your ear.

5. *Make a hasty search.* Identify any gloves, toques, packs, ski poles which may have come to the surface. Scuff your boots through the snow as you cover the slide; you might encounter something or somebody just beneath the surface.

6. *Establish probable trajectory.* If various articles have surfaced and show a continuous pattern of travel, chances are the victim may be located in that same path. Use your transceiver while following these guidelines until you pick up a signal. Machines do not lie; if you get a signal, follow it through even if the location appears improbable.

7. *Stop, organize and execute.* Stop long enough to see that the others are carrying out the procedure systematically and thoroughly. Simple organization will save time and energy.

8. *Hasty search.* If transceivers are being used, comb the slide in one of the patterns illustrated above.

If transceivers are not being used, probe the probable burial sites. These include the probable trajectory, areas around trees, ledges or benches, and corners—the places where the victim may have become lodged by an obstacle or deposited by slower moving snow.

If the victim(s) still cannot be found, make some executive decisions. If you are the sole survivor, keep probing for at least two hours, unless you are certain a rescue party can reach the scene within one hour. It is your decision whether to keep looking or go for help.

If you are two survivors, keep working until you have exhausted all possibilities. Then send for help. One survivor should stay at the scene and keep probing.

If you are three survivors, send one for help and probe the slide with the other two.

If you are more than three survivors, you might consider sending two for help to ensure safety. Keep everyone else working.

Going for help

Your objective is to get your message to the Park Wardens. They have a trained avalanche search dog and the manpower and resources to carry out any required full-scale rescue.

Travel quickly but safely. The victim depends on your getting through without being caught in another slide, injuring yourself through reckless skiing, or becoming too exhausted to reach the objective.

Mark your route if it is snowing. The rescue party will want to know it is on the right track. You may have to guide the rescue party back yourself if the location is obscure.

Carry your pack. Jettison only the few non-essentials you might have or the essentials the victim may require if he is found while you are gone. You may need repair or survival items yourself in order to succeed in getting help.

Write down the details of the accident and accident site before you depart for help. The wardens need to know at least the following: the precise location, the time of the accident, the number of victims, the number of survivors, what equipment is already available at the accident site, and the nature of the terrain.

Meanwhile back at the accident site

Keep probing and scuffing through the snow. If you are a group of survivors, organize a course probe line and systematically probe through the likely areas. Stand in a line facing uphill almost shoulder to shoulder. In unison probe directly in front of you, take one short step forward maintaining the line and probe again. Continue systematically uphill. When you reach the top of your search area scuff your way down to the base of your next search area. Do not work a probe line downhill; your steps will be too long and it is difficult to maintain uniformity on a steep slope. Maintain orderliness.

Do not urinate on or in any way litter the slide area. Things of this nature will only serve to confuse the avalanche search dog when he arrives.

Keep at it! You may be getting tired and despondent, but think about the victim. Although sound cannot be transmitted out of the snowpack, very often the victim can hear the rescue party working above. Knowing that the rescuers are still trying may provide the victim the extra enthusiasm he needs to stay alive.

When the rescue party arrives, explain the situation clearly and point out what you have done. Turn over command of your group to the rescue party and work with them.

When the victim is found

1. Excavate head first. Check for breathing. Clear the airway, apply artificial respiration if necessary and loosen any restrictive clothing.

2. Do not move the victim until breathing is restored, unless it is absolutely essential.

3. Continue treatment according to standard first aid practice. Treat and move with care.

4. Improvise anything you can to help restore warmth to the victim.

If the victim is conscious and apparently unharmed, cancel your original plans, ski out and escort the victim to a hospital for a thorough examination. Internal injuries may not be immediately apparent.

If the victim is found unconscious, treat as outlined above, but remember that even though snow is a good insulator, you may be required to treat for hypothermia as well. Also, check and continue to watch for frostbite.

Above all, do not give up. Some apparent corpses do come back to life.

COMPLETE ACCIDENT CARE

Most first aid courses and books underrate or ignore the psychological trauma which an accident victim undergoes. These additional stresses are especially pronounced in winter accidents where basic survival against the elements is an ever present additional burden. It is not enough to treat a victim for only his physical injuries; and so I have summarized a paper by Cameron C. Bangs, M.D., which was delivered at the Mountain Medicine Symposium, Banff, 1976.

Most accidents involve an error somewhere, and the immediate reaction is to blame oneself for the mistake, leading to a loss of self-esteem or self-respect. It is embarassing to be a victim and often an initial overreaction leads to further embarrassment. The loss of independence which a victim experiences is especially important to adults. No one enjoys being a burden and ruining a trip for others.

Each victim will have many specific fears. The primary fear is, of course, the extent of the injury, followed quickly by the concern over the quality of care the rescuers can provide. Finally, there is the very real fear for the immediate future. When other persons are involved, the worries are correspondingly complicated over concern for the others.

Many factors will influence a victim's behavior, including pain, hypothermia, shock or head injuries. It is possible that a victim will only be concerned for himself and his own survival, which may lead to greater complications when there is more than one victim.

As a survivor and rescuer, try to put yourself in the place of the victim. Realize his fears and anxieties and talk to him. If you do not already know the victim, find out who he is, use his name as you talk, and treat him like a real person, someone you know. Introduce yourself and explain briefly that you are qualified to help to whatever extent.

Reassurance begins with overall orderliness and calm, deliberate actions. Establish someone as a leader and support him. Discuss questionable procedures intelligently in front of the victim rather than hiding away or arguing.

Warn the victim if you think some procedure may cause pain or if you are about to move him.

Be as honest as you possibly can. If the victim is badly hurt, it is better to admit it rather than have the victim discover it bit by bit himself.

Do not diagnose if you do not know. Honesty can be simple, it does not need great descriptive details to get the message across.

Work efficiently and completely. Often there will be spare time to repeat your complete examination and tidy up loose ends.

Comfort of the victim does not end with seeing that he is merely warm and comfortable. See to his hunger, thirst, and that he does not have to go to the bathroom as well.

It is difficult to maintain concern once you have succeeded in the basic treatment. Regardless, stay with the victim, let him help whenever he can in whatever limited way, and encourage him to talk about the accidet to get it off his mind. Avoid moralizing during the discussion; judgements and reprimands can wait for another time.

Finally, keep the victim informed as the rescue and evacuation proceeds. If it is going to take time explain why, what you have done, and what the victim can expect to happen.

If you can, visit the victim in the hospital the next day and let him know that you are still friends regardless of the incident.

FIRST AID KIT

Always be certain there is a good first aid kit with your group. Build your own kit and always keep it in the bottom of your pack. It should never leave your pack except when it's needed or being refurbished. No prepared kit available on the market is as versatile as the one you can build yourself for a reasonable price.

Contents will vary according to personal preferences and degree of experience in the medical and mountain situation. The most important thing, next to knowing how to administer first aid, is knowing exactly what is in your kit and how various parts may be adapted for multiple uses. A good kit can be small, versatile, inexpensive, almost sufficient, light (less than a pound), and unobtrusive, even in your day pack.

Just because you haven't had an accident on a ski trip is no reason not to be equipped to handle one. Things happen: someone falls and is punctured by a ski pole; someone loses control, runs into a tree where he is scraped, cut, or impaled; someone falls and dislocates a knee, sprains an ankle, even breaks a leg; a clumsy move around camp results in a severe burn; or someone is injured in an avalanche. Anything can happen, and it's much more pleasant to bring back an injured friend in relative comfort, or maybe even save a life.You might be lucky and never have to open your first aid kit in all your skiing, but won't you feel stupid if you find yourself unable to patch up your friend or yourself if something does happen.

Enough good books and courses are readily available everywhere so I will not go into actual first aid, except where I can't resist throwing in a comment. The list at the end of this chapter recommends books and courses. Remember: if you don't practice what you read, you will be fumbling when the time comes to do it.

A check list for a first aid kit I developed over a two year period serving on the Mountain Rescue Team in the Banff Warden Service follows. The first list contains what I consider to be the basic kit for everyone to carry; the second list contains several extra items which I carried to perform my job and which can be considered optional items for a basic kit.

Customize your kit to your own ability. You can never carry enough to handle all situations, so be prepared to improvise. For example, guaze is bulky, so once the initial layer of sterile gauze is applied, improvise further absorption, if required, with clothing, extra wool socks or mitts from the bottom of your pack.

If you are intent on having an ultimate first aid kit, ask your local doctor for his suggestions; or ask three doctors and come up with three different lists; or ask a public health nurse and get a different list again. The important factor is that it works for you, that as many parts as possible have multiple applications.

Some items might appear more logically in a repair kit (candle, matches, sewing kit, etc.), but since they do have first aid applications I keep them readily available for when I will need them in a hurry. It doesn't matter where you carry them so long as you have them in your pack. My basic kit lives at the bottom of my pack and rather than dig to the bottom for recurring minor items, I keep the starred (*) items in a small bag at the top of my pack or in an easily accessible side pocket.

Obtain a polyurethane fridge container, rough size 4 x 5 x 3 inches high, to protect your basic kit—keep bandaids dry, gauze sterile, pill containers from opening, and packages from wearing out. Fit the container with the leftovers (space blanket, etc.) into a tight nylon stuff bag with a drawstring.

First aid materials are expensive. Get together with some friends to purchase what you can in bulk.

Pills are most easily carried and identified if purchased in the more expensive blister packs rather than bulk bottles. Include as many blister sheets you feel may be required.

Unqualified persons cannot legally administer prescription drugs. You may assist a person to take such medications at that person's request. It's a fine line but important.

**Band-aids*. Lots of ordinary large ones (top pack, with extras in the main kit).

**Adhesive tape*. Two or three rolls of one inch wide (one roll top pack). Useful for taping down gauze pads, covering heels to prevent blisters, taping splints, repairing split skis, taping your boot to your ski if a binding breaks beyond repair, and temporarily patching torn down-filled garments.

Triangular bandages. Useful for everything from splints to slings to towels to improvised socks, mitts, or scarves. Obtainable in compressed form to save space. I carry only two because clothing, tape, gauze rolls, and other materials can be used for the same purpose.

Safety pins. Assorted sizes. Generally handy for triangular bandages or anything from diapers to bras to pinning two sleeping bags together (if the occasion warrants and the zippers don't match).

Kling bandage or panty hose. Kling bandages are similar to roller gauze except they're woven in such a manner that all parts stick to each other. There is then no necessity of fancy ties, knots, and aids in application to non-conforming body parts. If you can't find or afford these bandages, wash out an old pair of panty hose and stick it in your kit. Cut out whatever portion is needed when the need arises. Severe head wounds can be quickly and effectively treated by covering with gauze pads held in place with a section of the nylon stocking pulled over, but not so tight as to restrict circulation (a toque pulled down tightly would serve the same purpose).

Moleskin and/or molefoam. Sophisticated adhesive tape. Basically nothing more than a felt or foam pad with an adhesive surface. Cut to required shape with your folding scissors. If you expect to develop blisters, apply the moleskin to potential trouble spots before you leave home.

**Sun cream and lipsaver*. Top pack or pocket. Some of the good commercial names are Screen and Glacier Cream. Any cream heavy in zinc oxide is not only good to prevent sunburn but can also be used as a universal ointment (or to pack a cavity until you're back to a dentist). A good layer of greasy cream will also help to prevent windburn.

Tensor (Ace) bandage. Three inches wide. For sprained ankles, twisted knees, and general psychological support. Many doctors feel these bandages do no good at all, are only psychological, and in fact, impede circulation. Use your discretion.

Sanitary napkin (Kotex). As many as you have room for. Aside from their usual purpose, they outperform standard gauze pads, are thicker, and may be used for padding. Cut one to required size for any wound. Some brands come with their own tie strings. Unless you obtain them individually wrapped, keep them in a plastic bag to maintain relative sterility and dryness.

Alcohol towelettes. About four. If you do have to repair major cuts, why not clean your hands first to reduce the risk of infection? If someone has bled profusely, especially over facial areas, wipe off as much of the blood as possible to make the victim more acceptable to himself and the rest of the party for the remainder of the trip. (Be careful not to disturb clots when cleaning deeply cut areas.) Accidents are a psychological strain on everyone, and even visual appearance makes a noticeable difference. Finally, it's nice to clean off parts (if not all) of your body on extended camping trips.

Folding scissors. Folding, only because they're easier to pack. Your pocket knife will serve, but for the additional weight and size scissors are extremely handy for cutting gauze pads or Kotex to size, preparing doughnuts of moleskin for blisters, removing bandages, or cutting off pieces of clothing in extreme injuries. Obtainable from most sewing stores and some drug stores.

Tweezers. The kind with sharp points. Slivers don't often occur in the winter, but you never know. Handy to clean deep wounds.

**Matches.* In top pack and also various pockets. Butane lighters are inexpensive and sometimes more useful, but be careful when you pack them that nothing can trip the switch and cause all the gas to leak out. Some waterproof matches require a special scratch pad which sometimes disintigrates when wet, leaving you with great matches and no where to light them; test them before you take them.

**Short candle.* Top pack. Three or four inch ordinary white paraffin candle. Always handy to help start a fire, sterilize needles, work in the dark, or generally illuminate your emergency snow cave. Paraffin also works very well as a hard, fast, sliding wax on the base of your skis.

**Sewing kit.* Top pack. As simple as two needles and a small roll of strong thread stuffed into a 35 mm film container. Besides repairing torn clothing, tents, or sleeping bags, it may be necessary to perform a rough suture job on a wound which cannot be closed by other means.

Condoms. Not really a first aid item, but where else do you carry them? Men will find them invaluable for urinating into when inside tents, caves, or on a cramped bivouac when it is too much to get clothed and coordinated to step out into a storm. Exercise caution: do not store in living area when they've been used for this purpose and are full. The cheap, heavy-duty ones tend to out-perform the super sheer sense-it-alls in this situation.

Emergency space blanket. Shirt pocket size. Replace after each use since they're quite fragile and do not repack well. Indispensable for protecting or wrapping up an immobilized person while awaiting rescue or for covering yourself or for use as a groundsheet on a forced bivouac.

**Tylenol, Tempra, or Campain (Acetaminophen).* Rather than the acetylsalicylic acids such as Aspirin, Anacin, or Bufferin. Acetylsalicylic acid is a standard pain reliever and antipyretic (fever bringer-downer), but has certain disadvantages as an analgesic in emergency situations. It has a tendency to cause acid stomach upset in some people, and when they are already injured is not the time to cause another problem. In accidents that involve bleeding, either external or internal, aspirin has been found to delay clotting time by inhibiting formation of one of the clotting factors—in other words, more profuse, longer bleeding. Since internal bleeding may not be apparent even to skilled observers, it's best not to give aspirin to anyone who has had a severe fall or other accident. The alternative is acetaminophen (trade names Tylenol, Tempra, Campain) which is very good as a pain killer and antipyretic and does not cause stomach upset or influence clotting. (For severe pain neither Aspirin nor acetaminophen will be effective; go to your doctor and ask for a prescription for a dozen Codeine phosphate ½ gr. or 30 mg. tablets).

Chlor-tripolon (Chlorpheniramine). A simple non-prescription antihistamine which helps to slow down dripping noses and relieve occasional itches or allergies. Note: any antihistamine tends to make one drowsy, but Chlor-tripolon less than the others; second choice would be Actifed.

Gravol (Diphenhydrinate). Ordinary non-prescription Gravol which many people take to prevent travel sickness. Tends to help persons suffering the first effects of minor altitude sickness which may hit some people as low as 8,000 feet.

**Salt Tablets.* Top pack, especially for spring skiing. Sweating may not be so easily noticed when perspiration evaporates rapidly in dry mountain air. If it looks like a long hot day coming up, pop one or two in the morning; they can't hurt you and may make a world of difference.

Luggage label and soft lead pencil. If you are involved with a serious accident where the victim is to be evacuated by a rescue group and you are not accompanying the victim to the hospital, it is extremely important that the receiving end know exactly who they are treating, the age of victim, what happened, when it happened, the environment where it happened, and what treatment has already been performed, especially drugs and amounts administered. It is not enough to tell a member of the rescue group the above information: write it down! A luggage label (old large kind) is durable and has a string so that it can be attached to the victim, and a soft lead pencil works even in slightly damp conditions.

Optional Extras

These don't add much more bulk; it's more a matter of cost, imagination and ability.

Elastoplast. At least a 12 inch strip. It's simply an oversized band-aid with a gauze strip down the middle and elasticized adhesive sides. Cut to required length.

Steri-strip (butterfly) skin closures. You should carry about ⅛ in. x 3 in. and ¼ in. x 3 in. sizes. Difficult to obtain in individual packages of three or five (a box may be shared by a club or friends). They are essentially a cosmetic-type dressing and replace the need for sutures where situations are not overly extreme. Very useful on facial cuts.

Airway. Cheapest and smallest is a Guedel airway. It's a small item which you may never need to use. but if the situation ever occurs where you need to move an unconscious victim, it provides the easiest way of keeping an airway open. Refer to a first aid manual.

Pneumatic splint. A good air splint for a leg is bloody expensive—upwards of fifty dollars. The possibility of frostbite may also be increased when these splints are fully inflated. If you can afford one, they are convenient to pack and provide additional comfort in transporting a person with a broken leg. The can also be unlaced, spred out, and used as an air mattress. Usually a splint can be improvised from ski equipment, pack frames, or trees.

Folding metal splint. Compact, inexpensive, and obtainable from most safety supply stores. Not effective for anything larger than an arm, and then just barely. Its great advantage is that it can be folded into any position, even down to finger-splinting size.

Antiseptic ointment or powder. Polysporin is a readily available broad spectrum ointment. However, ointments tend to jam up under freezing conditions. A powder (BFI Powder) is more appropriate for winter use, though powders available over the counter aren't as effective as Polysporin. Luckily, under arctic-type conditions there are relatively few free-floating infectious organisms. Polysporin in the small opthalmic size can also be used for pinkeye and other common eye infections.

Antacids. Usually only required for extended trips. You should know if you are likely to require them. Enquire of others in your group before setting off. Diovol tablets seem to handle most uncomplicated situations.

Opthalmic ointment. Sunburn-to-the-eyeball ointment. As always, prevention is better than cure; keep one pair of good sunglasses in your pack at all times. Polysporin in a small tube with opthalmic application tip is the handiest medication. If possible, cover the eyes and keep in darkness. Minor burns should heal in twenty-four hours.

Analgesics, antibiotics, and sedatives. These all require prescriptions and specific knowledge for administration. If you feel you would like to carry them, contact your local doctor for prescriptions and instructions. Once he understands why you need them, he will probably be glad to help.

For a complete overview of medical supplies, see the pharmacopoeia list in chapter 19 of *Medical Care For Mountain Climbers* by Peter Steele. Also see appendix *First aid reading.*

Banff, Kootenay and Yoho Trails

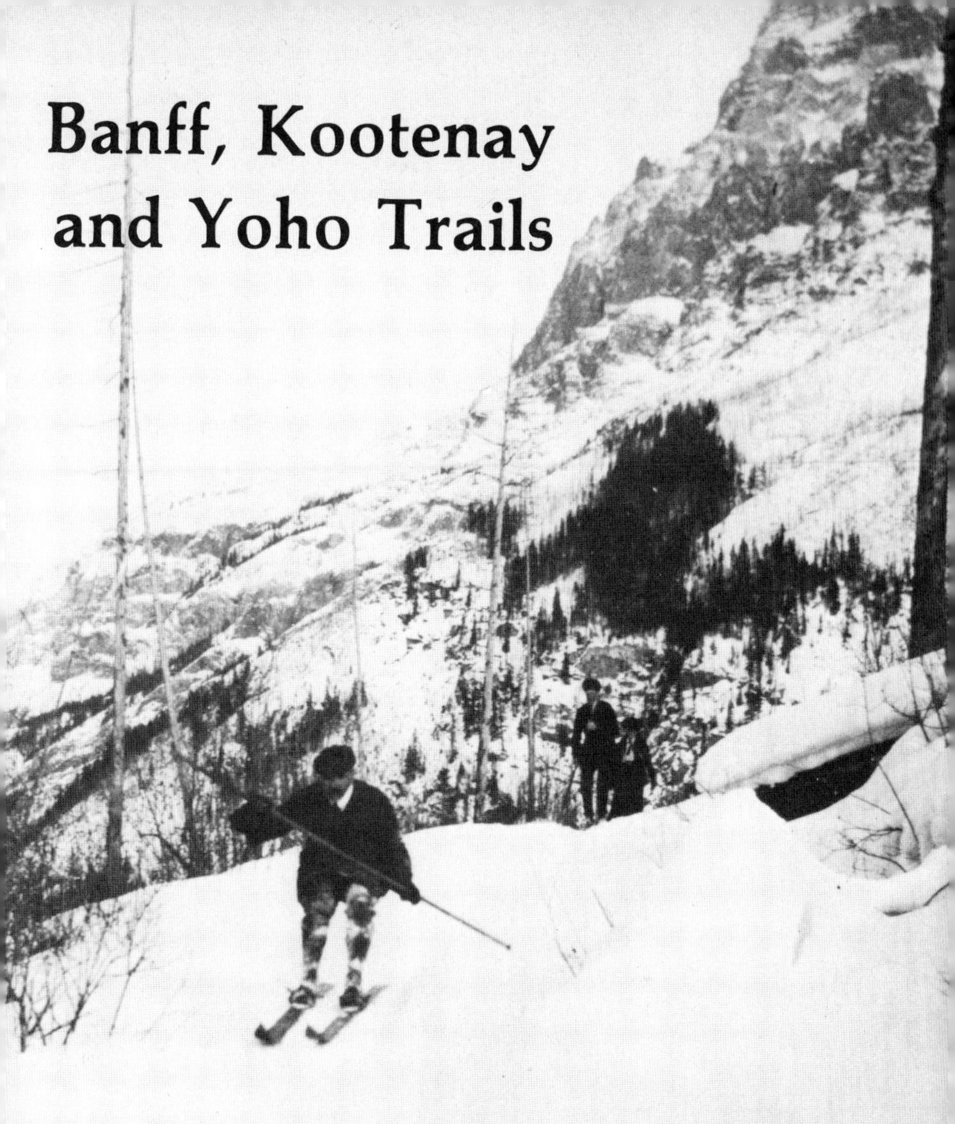

Manager of Mount Stephen House at Field, B.C. tries out an early pair of skis in the Canadian Rockies, ca. 1894.

CLASSIFICATIONS

Classification of ski trails is next to impossible except in very general terms. A trail normally accepted as *novice* could become temporarily *intermediate* after a large fresh snowfall where one is required to break trail and perhaps even do some route finding. Or conversely, after a long dry spell the track may become hard-packed with holes and icy stretches rendering it treacherous to a novice skier. The system also works the other way; an intermediate trail under ideal conditions, in some instances, might be felt to be nothing more than a novice run.

Conditions in the mountains are very rarely "ideal" and everyone's "ideal" is different—powder or packed, warm or cold; the possibilities are near endless. Areas throughout the mountains also vary in conditions with the time of year. Generally the higher one goes, the better the snow, but also as sometimes occurs, the more critical the avalanche hazard. The lower Bow Valley is generally best in January and February, until a chinook comes along and temporarily ruins everything. Often by the end of March the lower Bow is almost ruined and skiers will have to go to Lake Louise and north to find acceptable snow conditions. Your best update on general ski conditions can be obtained by listening to the morning radio ski reports, calling the Banff Warden Service trail condition recording phone (762-3600), or stopping in at the Banff, Lake Louise or Yoho Warden Offices.

I have attempted to come up with a precise classification system from which a logical progression of increasingly more difficult trails could be followed as a skier gains expertise. However, as each winter has passed with its differing climatic conditions and patterns, all precision has blown away with the westerly winds and has become so much wind itself. The system which follows is very general, very opinionated, and subject to climatic variations. However, it will provide you with a rough indication of the kind of trails to either avoid or seek out according to your own personal ability. When travelling with a group choose the trail according to the ability of the "least able member of your party." The basic philosophy behind this whole book is enjoyment, not endurance or suffering.

The National Parks, each in their own way, are gradually developing a cross-country ski trail program and information hand-out. The main emphasis is on safety and simplicity and so they concentrate mainly on novice type trails. Thus many of the simpler trails have been left out of this book and can be found in the park brochures. These can be obtained at park information bureaus and warden offices.

Very little information has been provided on Kootenay Park for two simple reasons: first, the park brochures will cover the west end, and second, much of Kootenay Park is too dangerous to ski without experienced leadership.

Novice Trails

Once bored with the Park Nordic Trails and, ideally, having completed a couple of cross-country lessons and gained an understanding of how wax works, you can enjoy the novice trails. Essentially they are wide trails varying from 7 - 13 kilometres (4 - 8 miles) in length and involve both flat running and gentle hills. They provide a good opportunity to perfect striding, gliding, climbing, and downhill sliding.

Novice 1: straightforward, follow the road or the trail markers and enjoy yourself.

Novice 2: almost straightforward, but beginners may encounter minor route finding difficulties or ankle wobble on the downhill sections.

Novice 3: slightly steeper with some sharp corners, but still short. When these are perfected and enjoyed, it's time to move on to the longer and correspondingly harder intermediate trails.

And remember, always ski with your full day pack even if it seems ludicrous.

Intermediate Trails

Intermediate is a catch-all classification which encompasses the majority of the established trails in the Park system. Properly these routes should be termed "intermediate mountain cross-country" since numerous problems will be encountered which one would not face on a classic foothills course. There is a greater chance of accidents on these trails and your "complete day pack" should always be carried.

Intermediate 1: half day, steep sections, some difficulties, minor route finding problems, and requires good skiing ability.

Intermediate 2: full day and all of the above.

Intermediate 3: overnight or a very, very long day and all of the above.

Advanced Trails

Advanced means decision-making, expertise, and experience. An advanced trail may only be of upper intermediate difficulty, but if there is an avalanche slope which must be evaluated before it can be crossed, then the trail automatically falls in the advanced category. A section which may be safe one week may have to be re-routed the next, or perhaps a whole trip may have to be aborted if it is not judged safe. Attendance at one avalanche school does not qualify you to lead an advanced trip; knowledge of avalanches can only be acquired slowly through experience. Travel with someone who knows and can explain to you the ingredients of his decision-making. Advanced also includes those trips which require expert skiing ability to enjoy them and those which would require endurance beyond the intermediate level. Any trip which entails crossing a glacier is also considered in this category.

Trail Courtesy

Some of our cross-country ski trails are becoming very crowded, and the time has come for that little extra bit of courtesy which provides a more enjoyable day for everyone.

When someone skis up behind you and calls out "track," it means that you should step out of the track and let the faster skier by. If you are training for a race, remember that you are in the minority and most people are out to find peace and quiet. Use your extra ability to go around occasionally instead of yelling.

Downhill traffic has the right-of-way over uphill traffic for two very simple reasons: 1) the downhill skier usually has less control than the person slowly working uphill who can easily step aside, and 2) a good downhill swoop is often the highlight of a ski trip for a good skier.

Don't litter and when you can, flick fallen branches and other natural debris off the trail. Help keep the track clean and fast.

Fires should only be lit in park fire circles, except in an emergency situation. With your co-operation and encouragement, the park might provide expanded fire facilities in the future.

Drain your internal systems well off the trail and behind a tree.

Keep your dog under control, preferably on a leash, and clean up after it if it decides to drain its internal systems.

If you stop for repairs or re-waxing, step well off to the side so that you do not block the trail or ruin the track stomping around with your skis off.

In other words, remain mindful of others. It is an easy way to keep a simple sport enjoyable, and as always, the responsibility rests with each individual.

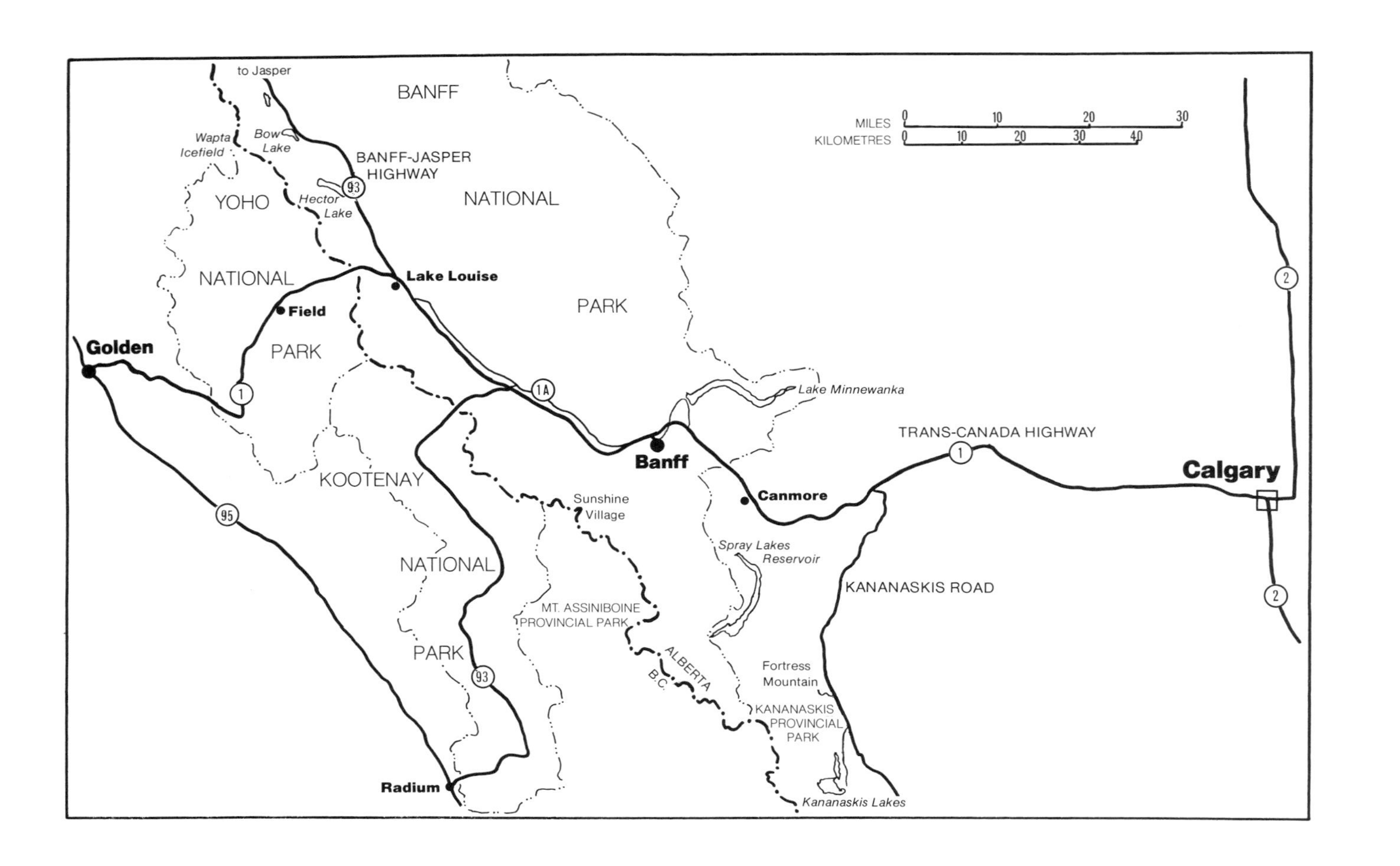
to Jasper
BANFF
NATIONAL
PARK
MILES
KILOMETRES
Wapta Icefield
Bow Lake
BANFF-JASPER HIGHWAY
93
Hector Lake
YOHO
NATIONAL
PARK
Lake Louise
Field
Golden
1
1A
Lake Minnewanka
TRANS-CANADA HIGHWAY
Banff
Calgary
2
Canmore
KOOTENAY
NATIONAL
PARK
Sunshine Village
95
Spray Lakes Reservoir
KANANASKIS ROAD
MT. ASSINIBOINE PROVINCIAL PARK
ALBERTA
B.C.
Fortress Mountain
KANANASKIS PROVINCIAL PARK
Radium
Kananaskis Lakes

Novice

CASCADE FIRE ROAD TO FOUR MILE BRIDGE

Novice 1
Trail and road tour
13 kilometres (8 miles) return
Maps: Banff 82 0/4
Castle Mountain 82 0/5

An ideal, very popular, and sometimes overcrowded trail.

Until the park service decides to build an official parking area, begin from the C-level Cirque Parking Lot at upper Bankhead. Ski across the open meadow to the northeast corner where an obvious trail through the trees will be seen. Following along, the trail brings one quickly past the Bankhead warden residence (please appreciate that it's a private residence and not a public washroom). Continuing behind the yard and up a small rise followed by a short downhill, the route brings one onto the Cascade Fire Road.

The road may remain a restricted road for a few years yet or it may revert to a wide trail. Regardless of what happens to the road, the general geography won't change. When you have passed the old gravel pit on your right you reach the first of two large hills—the first real test of your waxing skills. They are rather long hills, so if your wax isn't working properly stop and rewax before you wear yourself out.

The road is very straightforward and wide, as roads are, and once up the two hills you continue along a gentle grade past the Stenton Pond, all through relatively open country. The last quarter-mile to the bridge provides a continuous downhill glide to the Cascade River.

The return is precisely the same as the approach.

Time in: 1 - 2 hours
Time out: 30 minutes - 1½ hours

SPRAY RIVER PICNIC SITE LOOP

Novice 1
Trail and road tour
10 kilometres (6.5 miles) return
Map: Banff 82 0/4

An ideal trail for novice skiers and for those seeking a dash more adventure than the standard novice trail provides.

Park at Bow Falls viewpoint below the Banff Springs Hotel. Cross the bridge and bear slightly right across the first fairway. An obvious opening will appear in the trees up which the trail begins. Immediately one begins a long climb up a wide trail which is steep until just beyond the golf course boundary fence. From the fence the grade lessens, but the climb continues on past a sign on the left which indicates the summer hiking trail to the summit of Mount Rundle. Soon the high point is reached, and the grade remains relatively level until the gradual descent begins to the Spray River bridge and picnic site.

Tables, firewood, and a fire circle are all provided at the picnic site. If all the tables are covered in snow when you arrive, take the time to clear them off and lift them onto the top of the snowpack so they'll remain usable throughout the winter. Confine all fires to the one fire circle provided to help alleviate further damage to an already heavily-used site. It may be wise to carry some form of fire starter along with you since most of the small wood will be used up. Do not throw snow over your dwindling fire when you leave as there will probably be another group arriving twenty minutes after you have left.

Return the same way or choose one of the below:

Spray River Fire Road. A very simple, direct return may be made along the Spray River Fire Road from the picnic site. Returning this way, you end up at the Banff Springs Hotel where you can either walk back to your car or search for a ski trail below the hotel and back to the parking site. This road is part of the oversnow vehicle course from Canmore to Banff and is often very hard-packed and somewhat rough from snow machine traffic; if one abhors roaring snow machines, this may not be an enjoyable option.

Spray River. By far the most interesting and enjoyable return route is along the Spray River bank itself. Leaving the picnic site, cross the bridge and drop down to the river bank as soon as it is convenient. The route will vary slightly depending on the time of season. Generally the upper section is most conveniently skied on the east bank, a short section near the Spray River Hostel on the west bank, and the lower half again on the east bank. At no time should one have to climb high above the river bank. If you are not already on the east bank in the lower section when you encounter a foot bridge, then cross over. From here out to the golf course one is again on an obvious trail. This route will bring you out below the hotel and directly back to the starting bridge. (Do not attempt the Spray River return in early winter or spring as river crossings may not exist.)

Time in: 1 - 2 hours
Time out: 1 - 2 hours

OLD HEALY CREEK ROAD

Novice 2
Road tour
13 kilometres (8 miles) return
Map: Banff 82 0/4

Though there may be some conflict with oversnow vehicle traffic, this is one of the classic cross-country tours in the immediate Banff area. (Snow machine use in the park is dwindling, so chances are you won't encounter any.)

Park at the Cave and Basin swimming pool and ski down the closed road toward Sundance Canyon. Impressive beaver lodges occur along the south side of the road. Just beyond two kilometres the Sulphur Mountain Cosmic Ray Station road comes in from the south while immediately beyond, the old Healy Creek road branches off to the right (the topographical map is inaccurate at this junction). Take the right fork, also known as the Brewster Creek Fire Road. From here on the track is wide and gently rolling in the tradition of the finest cross-country ski terrain.

The Sundance cross-country race course intersects with the road and follows along below for short sections. Just three kilometres beyond the Sundance Canyon fork the Brewster Creek Fire Road branches off to the south. (See the notes on *Brewster Creek* for this trail.)

Continue along the Healy Creek Road for another two kilometres to the Healy Creek crossing. At time of writing there is no longer a bridge over the creek but it will likely be reconstructed. Across the creek is the road to Bourgeau Parking Lot and the Sunshine Ski Area.

On the north side of the road, 100 metres back from the Healy Creek crossing, is an ideal picnic area lunch stop.

Return the same way or ask at the Warden Office before you go if the bridge has been replaced and perhaps an alternate loop added.

Time in: 1 - 2 hours
Time out: 1 - 2 hours

ROCK ISLE LAKE LOOP—SUNSHINE

Novice 1
Cross-country trail tour
5 kilometres (3 miles)
Map: Banff 82 0/4

On a bright sunny day, the high alpine meadows above Sunshine provide one of the finest, easily accessible, cross-country ski areas in the Canadian Rockies.

The trail begins near the base of the Strawberry triple chairlift. Climb to the left up the side of Rock Isle ski run onto the Rock Isle Flats. The top of the chairlift will appear above to your right. Locate the cross-country sign and follow the orange poles to Rock Isle Lake.

The trail turns southeast from the lake and makes a large loop through the open meadows. Follow the orange poles around and back to the Rock Isle Lake run, and down the ski hill to the lodge.

The trail should be avoided during bad weather since visibility can be reduced to zero on the open meadows. On a nice day the loop can be extended as far as you wish. From the lake follow the trail southeast to the next corner and then simply continue out onto the meadows toward Citadel Pass. Below Quartz Ridge stay sufficiently away from the potential slide slopes, but do not drop too low into the trees and the Howard Douglas Creek drainage. Back over your left shoulder, the Great Divide Chairlift on Lookout Mountain provides a good return reference point.

The development and expansion of the Sunshine Ski Area has caused changes in the available cross-country ski trails in the immediate vicinity. Check with the Warden Service at the Snow Research Office for up-to-date information and handouts. They are located in a log building above and to the left of the base of the Strawberry chairlift.

Time: 1 - 2 hours

WOLVERINE LOOP—SUNSHINE

Novice 3
Cross-country trail tour
7 kilometres (4 miles)
Map: Banff 82 0/4

The Wolverine Loop is the most difficult of the marked Sunshine circuits but also the most interesting since it provides an overview of the entire area. (When there is a danger of white-out conditions above timberline, the circuit should be avoided.)

The trail begins below the Wah Wah T-Bar lift and follows up the Meadow Park ski run—the third run to the right of the lift. The run makes a large, extended, open-hairpin loop to the top of the T-Bar. (Stay single file and to one side of the ski run to avoid collisions with the downhill skiers.)

At the top of the ski lift a cross-country sign marks the starting point of the marked trail. Follow the orange poles toward Twin Cairns Col then along a gentle contour below Twin Cairns and behind Standish. Once behind Standish a marvelous view opens over Grizzly and Larix Lakes and down into the steep Simpson River valley.

Continuing behind Standish the trail drops down to Rock Isle Lake and joins the Rock Isle Lake Loop. At this point one can short-cut back to Sunshine on the near side of Rock Isle Loop. However, in the interests of track maintenance and traffic flow, it is best to continue on around the Rock Isle Loop and then back to the lodge.

On a clear day, if you have extra time and energy, you can continue out onto the Sunshine meadows as described in the Rock Isle Loop report.

Time: 1½ - 3 hours

REDEARTH CREEK—FIVE MILE CAMPSITE

Novice 2
Road tour
15 kilometres (9 miles) return
Map: Banff 82 0/4

This is another one of Banff's unaccountably popular cross-country ski trails. The destination is merely a campsite below a bridge, the views are not overly exciting, and the area is short of sunlight for the first half of the winter. However, being a fire road, the track is wide and the grade is quite acceptable for cross-country skiing. Some fairly long hills on the return provide a more than ample opportunity for a novice skier to practice snowplowing (and to judge by the number of craters along the trail, it must be considered quite challenging to more than a few skiers).

Parking is in the cleared parking lot short of the highway, 20 kilometres west of Banff. A summer short-cut trail at the southeast corner of the parking lot cuts off almost one kilometre on the way up, but it is too narrow and steep to ski on the return.

Leaving from the northeast corner of the lot, the trail briefly parallels the highway until reaching the Redearth Fire Road. On the fire road the trail is straightforward. Simply ski up the road.

Remember, on the hills downcoming traffic has the right-of-way and is often out of control. Stay single file on the hills and be prepared to step out of the way to avoid collisions.

Return the same way.

Time in: 1½ - 3 hours
Time out: 30 minutes - 1½ hours

BOOM LAKE

Novice 3
Trail tour
8 kilometres (5 miles) return
Map: Lake Louise 82 N/8

In the past several years, Boom Lake has become one of the most popular novice trails in the mountain parks. Its high altitude (5700 - 6200 feet) provides sufficient snow early in the season when snow is lacking at lower levels, it is more accessible than the Lake Louise area, and at the end of the season the snow is generally in much better condition than in the Bow Valley.

On the Banff-Windermere Highway 6 kilometres south of Castle Junction, a plowed parking area and trail sign appear on the right. The trail begins at the far end of the parking lot and immediately crosses a footbridge. Just ahead the trail switchbacks twice and makes a short but rapid altitude gain. Beyond this initial hill the grade lessens, and the trail continues as a long, gentle rise through heavily-timbered old forest.

Before it reaches the final descent to the lake, the trail crosses the base of three distinct major avalanche paths. These areas provide the new skier with an appreciation for the awesome power of avalanches which keeps vegetation cleared and leaves an ample supply of broken mature timber.

At the lake one can continue easily along the north shore for further exercise and a closer view of Consolation Pass. Before skiing onto the lake surface itself, it is wise to scrape away the top snow layer to ensure that a layer of slush is not quietly waiting to freeze to the bottom of your skis and ruin the carefully-waxed base.

The trail as marked on the topographical map is, unfortunately, on the wrong side of the creek and should be ignored.

Return along the same trail. The trip out should be without incident so long as extra caution is taken near the start where the steeper sections and switchbacks occur.

Time in: 1 - 2 hours
Time out: 30 minutes - 1½ hours

STANLEY GLACIER VALLEY

Novice 3
Trail tour
6 kilometres (4 miles) return
Map: Mount Goodsir 82 N/1

The Stanley Glacier trail is the only real trail through the Vermilion Pass fire of 1968. Through the next decade at least it will remain primarily dead barren trees and fire-blackened snags. On a sunny day after a fresh snow it is one of the prettiest trails with its contrast of white, black, and blue. Once over the first 2.5 kilometres travel becomes very gentle along the creek bank, and one is treated to views of phenomenal frozen waterfalls hanging from the northeast face of Mount Stanley. Across the valley numerous avalanche paths dominate the slope, and at the end of the valley the impressive ice of the retreating glacier stands out against rock, snow, and sky.

Travel south on the Banff-Windermere Highway from Castle Junction and watch for the trail sign on the south side of the road about five kilometres beyond Vermilion Pass (the boundary of Banff and Kootenay Parks).

Across the footbridge at the trail head, bear left and gradually ascend the first bank. If the trail is not immediately apparent it can be picked up again by following obvious clearings to the right of the main drainage, roughly as shown on the map.

One of the great advantages of skiing through a recent burn of this magnitude is that a trail isn't really needed since the forest is so open it permits easy, obvious travel if the snow is deep enough. One can always see the obvious "U" shape of the Stanley Glacier cirque above.

Once over the major valley bench the terrain becomes quite gentle, and one should cross the creek to the north side at the first opportunity. Continue through the last of the burn and into the remaining old forest along the north bank. Within a short distance the forest opens dramatically into an impressive, barren hanging valley.

From the end of the forest one is free to wander along the bottom of this magnificent open area which in summer is an ankle-jarring boulder field. At the further end some gentle downhill runs can be attempted on the open slopes, but stay away from the side slopes which are avalanche areas.

The return trip is the same for the top portion until one is back into the burn and coming down the valley bench. From this point either follow your original trail or attempt some fancy skiing and minor route-finding in a more direct line down through the open forest.

Time in: 1½ - 3 hours
Time out: 20 minutes - 1 hour

MORAINE LAKE ROAD

Novice 1 to 3
Road tour
12 kilometres (7 miles) one way
Map: Lake Louise 82 N/8

The Moraine Lake Road is not plowed in the winter thereby providing an ideal course for all classes of skiers. And the road is paved so there is no fear of hitting rocks in early winter.

The road begins about half-way between Lake Louise townsite and the Chateau Lake Louise. The start of the road is plowed for parking, and road signs are obvious.

Novice skiers should keep close track of the time allowing enough daylight for their return. (The full trip of 24 kilometres requires proficiency and stamina beyond a novice level.)

The road is so straightforward it warrants little description. There are no major hills, and the total elevation gain over 12 kilometres is a mere 700 feet. The open slide paths along Mount Temple should be traversed as quickly as possible, however.

Return the same way.

Time in: 2 - 5 hours
Time out: 1 - 3 hours

PARADISE VALLEY—GIANT STEPS

Novice 3
Road and trail tour
20 kilometres (12.5 miles) return
Map: Lake Louise 82 N/8

The complete Paradise Valley return trip is almost too long to be classed *Novice,* but because of the ease of terrain, and the trust that skiers will keep track of the time to know when to turn around, it was rated *Novice 3.*

Begin at the Moraine Lake Road junction as for the Moraine Lake trip. About 2.5 kilometres up, the road crosses Paradise Creek. About 600 metres before the creek a trail sign indicates the turn-off to the right. A new trail start has been established along short-cut lines and narrow meadow openings to avoid the very steep and narrow rise alongside the creek.

At the top of the first section, the trail meets the old Moraine Lake trail and follows it along to the north (right) away from Paradise Creek. It feels like the wrong direction, but bear with it for five minutes to the next junction.

Watch for signs which indicate a sharp left turn back into Paradise Valley and the Giant Steps. The trail gains altitude coming around the corner of Saddle Mountain and then drops down to cross Paradise Creek. It is straightforward and obvious through to the first bridge.

Across the bridge the trail may be difficult to locate on the south side, and the creek may be used for a half-kilometre to the next bridge, where the trail crosses and remains on the north bank. Pick up the trail on the north (right) side and follow it to the Lake Annette junction. This section of trail crosses the run-out zones of two major slide paths where tracks may be obliterated. Gain a slight bit of altitude as you cross these run-outs to assure finding where the trail re-enters the trees.

The side-trip to Lake Annette is not recommended for skiing as the trail is very steep, narrow, and dark. The destination is not worth the effort in the winter. Moreover, avalànches off Mount Temple occasionally sweep right across the lake and pile debris through the outlet and across the trail.

From the Lake Annette junction to the base of the Giant Steps it is generally easier to ski the creek than follow the trail. Turn south (left) at the junction and follow the Lake Annette trail down to the creek, then turn up the creek and ski variously on and along it. (Keep watch of the time to ensure that you will have ample daylight for your return.)

The creek area opens up and provides magnificent views of the Horseshoe Glacier and surrounding mountains. Follow up the creek for two kilometres and take the right fork for the Giant Steps which will be visible from the fork. The Steps are huge bedrock and boulder fractures which in winter combine frozen waterfalls and snow caps to create an entirely unique phenomena.

Return the same way. Do not attempt to complete the high summer loop through Lake Annette as the trail is difficult to locate and traverses dangerous avalanche paths.

Time in: 3 - 5 hours
Time out: 1½ - 3 hours

HECTOR LAKE

Novice 2
Trail and exploration tour
4 kilometres (2.5 miles) return
Map: Hector Lake 82 N/9

A short fool-around tour for a half-day in the Lake Louise area. The old cabins on the lakeshore which were a historical destination have been destroyed, and the tour is so short that it's hardly worth the bother.

Park alongside the road at the summer hiking sign, 18 kilometres up the Icefields Parkway. The first half-kilometre is a bit steep and through heavy timber, but the trail quickly levels out to provide acceptable terrain. Most of the route is in heavy timber except when crossing the Bow River. If

you lose the trail blazes trying to find a place to cross the river, drop downstream for 100 metres and then head toward the lake. Either you will encounter the trail blazes or, with enough bushwacking, you will reach the lake.

Return the same way.

Time in: 30 minutes - 1 hour
Time out: 40 minutes - 1 hour

NO-SEE-UM CREEK

Novice 3
Exploration tour
4 kilometres (2.5 miles) return
Map: Hector Lake 82 N/9

No-see-um Creek has no summer trail, so it rates as an exploration tour. The route is not difficult but it doesn't go anywhere, so there is not much to explore. And to push beyond two kilometres puts one on steep and exceedingly dangerous avalanche slopes. However, if you have a couple of hours to kill and are in the area, it's an enjoyable tour into an impressive cirque.

Drive north up the Icefields Parkway and park at the No-see-um Creek bridge, about 23 kilometres from the Trans-Canada junction. To put it simply, ski up the creek. The trees are thin, the drainage is very open. After a fresh snowfall the upper boulder fields assume a personality of their own and are great fun to ski around and over. Once into the lower section of the basin, avoid the avalanche slope on your left (about 100 metres wide) and stop at the final treed area.

The head of the valley is very impressive with its steep scree slopes and numerous avalanche gullies dumping in. To go beyond the last trees without a very experienced person who can evaluate snow conditions, would indeed be courting danger. Be satisfied with an eyefull rather than a lungfull.

The return route is precisely reversed.

Time in: 30 minutes - 1 hour
Time out: 15 - 30 minutes

LAKE O'HARA FIRE ROAD

Novice 3
Road tour
24 kilometres (15 miles) return
Map: Lake Louise 82 N/8

The Lake O'Hara region, infamously popular in the summer, should be first explored on foot in order to appreciate the difficulties the trails present to the cross-country skier. Many of the short classic hikes do not translate into good ski trails due to their short, steep pitches and the great avalanche potential throughout the entire area. However, the access road provides a classic cross-country ski trail for the novice skier.

Begin at the 1A Highway junction two kilometres east of Wapta Lodge. (The map is incorrect for the first section of trail since the road was changed.) Ski across the railroad tracks and turn down the fire road to the right. Turn left up the access road and around the gate just above the O'Hara parking area. From here onward simply follow the road to Lake O'Hara.

The road is quite steep for the first kilometre but soon levels out and continues as marked on the map from the Narao Lakes onward.

About nine kilometres up, the road crosses Cataract Brook and begins to climb more steeply through the next kilometre before levelling out again for the final two kilometres to Lake O'Hara.

Return the same way.

Lake O'Hara Lodge is open at Christmas and again on weekends from mid-February through the end of April. One can drop in for afternoon tea in front of a blazing fire, if the lodge is not too crowded. If you wish lunch, phone ahead for reservations (604-343-6418). If you have a group of at least eight and not more than fifteen skiers and wish to stay in the area for a few days, arrangements can be made to open the lodge during the week. For information about Lake O'Hara Lodge write to Box 1677, Banff, Alberta, T0L 0C0.

The Alpine Club of Canada has a large cabin (the Elizabeth Parker Hut) in the Alpine Meadows, one kilometre southwest of the warden cabin. Use of Alpine Club cabins requires that at least one person in the group be a member of the club in order to obtain a key. Information on joining the Alpine Club and use of their cabins can be obtained by writing to The Alpine Club of Canada, Box 1026, Banff, Alberta, T0L 0C0, or phoning (403) 762-3664 during office hours.

Time in: 2½ - 4 hours
Time out: 1 - 2 hours

YOHO VALLEY ROAD

Novice 3
Road tour
13 kilometres (8 miles) one way
Maps: Lake Louise 82 N/8

The Yoho Valley Road, 13 kilometres west of the Kicking Horse Pass, is not plowed in the wintertime and provides excellent cross-country skiing. It is much more demanding than the Emerald Lake and Moraine Lake Roads and is also subject to avalanche danger during critical periods. (Check with the Yoho wardens for snow stability when registering out for this trip.)

Follow the highway signs for Takakkaw Falls and Kicking Horse Campground. Park in the plowed parking area off the Trans-Canada Highway before the campground.

Simply ski up the Takakkaw Falls Road for as far as you wish to go, or to the end of the road at the Takakkaw Falls viewpoint. Once above the switchbacks at Kilometre 5 the major avalanche paths from Wapta Mountain are seen above to the left; the road crosses through the run-out zones. Move across these run-outs quickly and efficiently.

The area around the Whiskey Jack Hostel near the end of the road shows ample evidence of the destructive power of the avalanches, with great piles of dead trees and other debris spread throughout the site. Indeed, some of the original outlying buildings are no longer in existance as a result of the avalanches.

Beyond the hostel and through a parking lot the road continues to Takakkaw Falls viewpoint where one of the greatest waterfalls in the Rockies hangs almost dormant in frozen splendor. The road continues beyond the viewpoint and gradually diminishes to trail width up the Yoho Valley. However, the highlight is the falls, and few skiers travel beyond unless headed up to the Little Yoho Valley.

Return the same way.

Time in: 3 - 5 hours
Time out: 2 - 3 hours

EMERALD LAKE ROAD

Novice 1
Road tour
6 kilometres (4 miles) one way
Map: Golden 82 N/7

The paved road to Emerald Lake, about three kilometres west of Field, is not plowed in the wintertime and provides an ideal novice cross-country ski

run similar to the Moraine Lake Road. Drive west from Field and watch for the road sign to Emerald Lake and the Natural Bridge. Park off the highway and simply start skiing up the road.

The topographical map is somewhat confusing in the area of the highway and the Natural Bridge, but a map is hardly necessary, as the road is obvious and the attractions are well-signed.

The Natural Bridge provides an interesting sidelight well worth the short diversion off the Emerald Lake Road. There are no hazards along the road and the grade is perfect for beginning skiers.

More advanced skiers or even strong beginners can take advantage of the pony trail around Emerald Lake, the hiking trail closer to the lakeshore, or even simply meander over the frozen lake surface. All in all, this is one of the most ideal areas for cross-country skiing in Yoho Park.

Return the same way.

Time in: 1½ - 2½ hours
Time out: 1 - 2 hours

OTTERTAIL FIRE ROAD

Novice 1 to 3
Road tour
14 kilometres (8.7 miles) one way
Maps: Lake Louise 82 N/8
Golden 82 N/7

The Ottertail Fire Road begins on the south side of the Trans-Canada Highway, eight kilometres west of Field. Originally this was the site of the Ottertail District Warden Headquarters, but now it is nothing more than an abandoned clearing.

The road is straightforward, climbing quickly in the first three kilometres to avoid a small canyon, then levelling out to continue at a gentle grade up the Ottertail Valley. Just over two kilometres from the start a very steep open bank drops abruptly to the river. Small hoodoos can be seen half-way down. This is a popular mineral lick for goats in the summer, but wildlife is rarely encountered in the Ottertail Valley during the winter.

Float Creek, the third creek up the road at Kilometre 6, makes a handy spot for most novice skiers to turn around. (A primitive campsite below the road is marked by the usual park camping sign.)

One-half kilometre beyond Float Creek the road climbs through a short series of switchbacks before levelling out again. An old burn opens the area for one kilometre in the area of Kilometre 10 before the mature forest closes in once again over the final stretch to McArthur Creek.

Looking west from the McArthur Creek Warden Cabin, the Goodsir

Towers provide one of the most spectacular views in Yoho Park, making the trip worthwhile for intermediate and advanced skiers who can complete the round-trip in one day.

Return the same way.

Time in to Float Creek: 2 - 4 hours
to McArthur Creek: 3 - 5 hours
Time out from Float Creek: 1 - 3 hours
from McArthur Creek: 2 - 4 hours

ICE RIVER FIRE ROAD

Novice 2 or 3
Road tour
0 - 32 kilometres (0 - 20 miles) return
Maps: McMurdo 82 N/2
Mount Goodsir 82 N/1

Skiing the full length of the Ice River Fire Road would definitely be an intermediate overnight trip, but since most people are likely to turn back at Steep Creek or Tallon Creek, the trail is listed as *Novice 2* or *3*.

Start either at the Leanchoil Bridge over the Kicking Horse River or at Hoodoo Creek Campground. From the bridge ski down the east bank to the fire road at the old Leanchoil Warden Station. From the campground ski past the entrance (which will be on your left) and continue down the road; within one kilometre you will reach the old warden station.

The fire road is very straightforward, easy skiing, with no major hills. The way is in heavy timber, but the swamps in the lower end provide an opportunity to sight moose or elk.

Eight kilometres up the road Tallon Creek is easily identified by a steep, hairpin approach and a small, old log warden cabin beside the road. The road continues another eight kilometres to its terminus at the Lower Ice River Warden Cabin. Unless you are camping out and planning to go up the Ice River, there is not much point going beyond Tallon Creek. There are no great viewpoints, and the road stays in heavy timber.

Return the same way.

Time to Tallon Creek: 1½ - 3 hours
Time out from Tallon Creek: 1 - 2½ hours

WAPTA FALLS

Novice 2
Trail and road tour
8 kilometres (5 miles) return
Map: McMurdo 82 N/2

A very short trip, quite out of the way, the Wapta Falls trail head is 25 kilometres west of the town of Field. But if you're in the area on a bright sunny day, it is definitely worth the extra effort to get there, for of all the frozen waterfalls in the mountain parks, Wapta Falls is among the most impressive and beautiful.

The trail head sign is hidden behind the snow banks on the south side of the Trans-Canada Highway between the Leanchoil Bridge over the Kicking Horse River and the Yoho west gate. The trail leaves the highway at a right angle, following a 50 yard-wide road slash for 2.5 kilometres. This section is ordinary, mundane, and straight. At the end of the slash a normal hiking trail takes off from the east side of the clearing (southeast corner). It is an easy grade with short up-and-down sections for 1.5 kilometres to the viewpoint at the top of the falls.

The falls are the width of the river and drop nearly 30 vertical metres over a sharp plate lip. On the north bank, massive 10 metre-high boulders are encrusted with spectacular layered formations of ice, snow, and frozen mist. To get to the bottom of the falls it is easiest to leave your skis at the viewpoint and walk down the short .5 kilometre trail. Take your ski poles along for balance. (If you must ski, make a long loop into the trees to the right and approximate a curve to the base of the falls.)

Return the same way.

Time in: 1 - 1½ hours
Time out: 40 minutes - 1 hour

Intermediate

CANMORE—GOAT CREEK—BANFF SPRINGS HOTEL

Intermediate 1
Trail and road tour
19 kilometres (11.5 miles)
Elevations: Trail head 5400 feet
Goat Creek junction 5000 feet
Banff Springs Hotel 4600 feet
Maps: Banff 82 0/4
Canmore 82 0/3

An ideal run if you can arrange transportation to Canmore for a drop-off. This is one of the rare trails in the Rockies which is downhill most of the way. Under good conditions the entire trail can be run in less than 3 hours.

Drive to and through Canmore, then follow the signs for the Spray Lakes. Proceed to the top of Whiteman Pass and to just beyond the first small lake (about 8 kilometres from the bridge in town). Below to the right are some old buildings and a conduit leading down to a small pumphouse. A short downhill run ends in a clearing where, proceeding uphill and slightly right, one is greeted by a decrepit fence and a boundary slash marking the entrance to Banff National Park. From the boundary to the Banff Springs Hotel the trail is almost entirely downhill. (The trail is also used by oversnow vehicles, so don't be offended if you chance to meet any.)

The trail through the Goat Creek valley is an old logging road—wonderfully wide and gently graded—and runs along the northeast side of the creek as indicated on the map. The southwest side of the valley was burned during the 1930's.

Do not attempt the cut-off trail marked on the map at 060611 as it does not hook up to anything (at least not according to my explorations). Continue down to the Goat Creek bridge and on to the Spray Fire Road via the Spray River bridge. (Some caution should be used between the two bridges where the descent to the Spray can be excessively fast when hardpacked.)

Junction with the Spray Fire Road is about one kilometre below the 8-Mile Warden Cabin. (Do not bother dropping in on the warden for coffee or repair items since no one lives there in the winter.)

Continue north along the Spray River Road for 6.5 kilometres to the Spray picnic site. The section is generally uneventful but does contain some rather long downhill glides as well as the occasional rise away from the river. The road is as marked on the map. From the picnic site one can avoid the road by crossing the bridge then carrying on along the river bank or along the novice trail back to the golf course. See *Spray River Picnic Site Loop* for details of this section.

Time: 3 - 5 hours

SPRAY RIVER—BEYOND 4 MILE

Intermediate 2
Road tour
Up to 48 kilometres (29.5 miles)
Maps: Banff 82 0/4
Canmore 82 0/3
Spray Lakes Reservoir 82 J/14

There is no trail along the east side of the Spray River beyond the 4-Mile Bridge picnic site. Follow the fire road as marked on the map. The road remains a fairly simple grade with occasional up and downhill stretches contouring the hillside. Straight ahead and up-valley you are looking into the Goat Creek valley, not the Spray. The Spray continues off to the right. (Goat Creek Valley can also be identified by the old burn on the northeast slope of the Goat Range.)

At present, and I don't foresee any policy changes, the Spray River Road to Goat Creek and Goat Creek to above Canmore, will remain as part of the park oversnow vehicle trail system. Thus you may encounter snow machines and a somewhat rough though generally well-packed trail. (For Goat Creek continuation see *Spray River—Goat Creek Trail.*)

One kilometre beyond the Goat Creek junction and downhill off the road is the old 8-Mile Warden Cabin (it is not for public use nor is it manned or stocked during the winter). Another 1.5 kilometres along is the junction of the rarely used and poorly maintained Sundance Creek connection. If the trail appears unused between Goat Creek and here, it is likely to appear the same or even less used beyond this point. Ski traffic beyond this point has been almost nil except for the occasional warden patrol, generally by oversnow vehicle.

There seems little point is saying more about this road in winter except that it continues roughly as marked on the map at the same basic grade, except for a section between the 16-Mile Warden Cabin and Fortune Flats where it rises about 300 feet above the river along the east bank. Following the road beyond Fortune and back again on the west bank brings one out at the upper end of the Spray Lakes, providing access to Bryant Creek and Assiniboine Park.

Except for Goat Creek and Sundance Pass (see appropriate reports), there are no side trips to be made out of the Spray River Valley until one reaches the reservoir at the far end.

Distances down the Spray measured from the gate at the Banff Springs Hotel:

Four-Mile Picnic Site	6.0 kilometres (3.7 miles)
Goat Creek confluence	11.0 kilometres (7.0 miles)
Goat Creek Junction	12.0 kilometres (7.5 miles)
Eight-Mile Warden Cabin	13.0 kilometres (8.0 miles)
Sundance Junction	13.5 kilometres (8.5 miles)

Sixteen-Mile Warden Cabin	24.0 kilometres (15.0 miles)
Fortune Flats	35.0 kilometres (22.0 miles)
Fortune Warden Cabin	37.0 kilometres (23.0 miles)
Park Boundary	38.5 kilometres (24.0 miles)
Spray Lakes Reservoir	40.0 kilometres (25.0 miles)
Spray Reservoir (south end)	48.0 kilometres (29.5 miles)

SUNDANCE PASS—SPRAY RIVER

Intermediate 2
Trail and road tour
27 kilometres (17 miles)
Elevations: Cave and Basin Parking Lot 4600 feet
Sundance Pass 5750 feet
Banff Springs Golf Course 4500 feet
Map: Banff 82 0/4

Sundance Pass is one of the least exciting skiable passes in Banff Park. There is no such thing as a view from the pass, and the broad flatness of the summit makes it second only in dullness to Spray Pass above Leman Lake. However, the circuit does provide an enjoyable day-ski accessible from Banff townsite.

Proceed down the Sundance Canyon Road west from the Cave and Basin. Watch for a sign on the left side of the road between the junction of the Cosmic Ray Station Road and the end of the Sundance Road which marks the start of the canyon bypass trail. The summer trail up the canyon is too steep and confined for skis.

The first kilometre is quite steep, but the trail follows a relatively constant grade and merely requires a good wax job. Once above the canyon area the trail continues along the lower slopes of Sulphur Mountain above the east bank of Sundance Creek. The rest of the trip through the pass and down to the Spray Fire Road is straightforward through trees and occasional small meadows. Stay on the east (left) side of the meadows in order to relocate the trail when it goes back into the trees.

From the pass down to the fire road there is a bit of enjoyable skiing through the somewhat open timber of an old logging area. Again, stay above and east of the creek.

The Spray Fire Road is rarely skied beyond the Goat Creek junction, so the two kilometres back to the junction may be a bit slow requiring trail-breaking through fresh snow. From the junction back to the Banff Springs Hotel is almost always a well-packed, fast track, and the usual variations may be followed back from the 4-Mile Picnic Site.

Total time: 5 - 8 hours

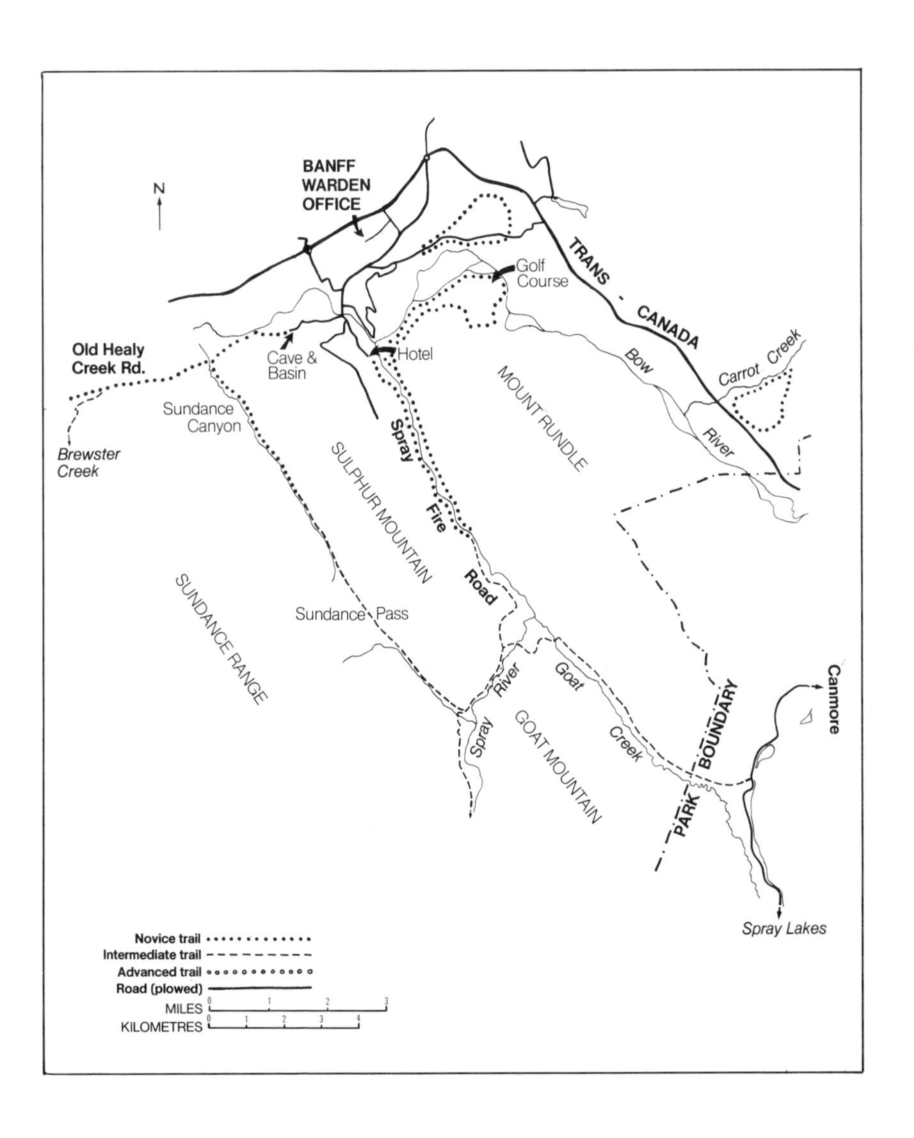
N
BANFF
WARDEN
OFFICE
TRANS - CANADA
Golf
Course
Old Healy
Creek Rd.
Cave &
Basin
Hotel
Bow
River
Carrot Creek
MOUNT RUNDLE
Sundance
Canyon
Brewster
Creek
Spray
Fire
Road
SULPHUR MOUNTAIN
SUNDANCE RANGE
Sundance Pass
River
Goat
Creek
Spray
GOAT MOUNTAIN
PARK BOUNDARY
Canmore
Spray Lakes
Novice trail
Intermediate trail
Advanced trail
Road (plowed)
MILES
KILOMETRES

TUNNEL MOUNTAIN LOOKOUT

Intermediate 1
Trail tour
5 kilometres (3 miles) return
Elevations: Banff trail head 4600 feet
Tunnel Mountain Lookout 5550 feet
Map: Banff 82 0/4

Handy, but not really an ideal ski trail. The trail gets hiked so often during the winter that is is often hardpacked and full of footholes. As on most steep, switchbacked trails, it is best skied after a fresh snowfall.

There are two places to start. If you don't have a car handy, walk up Saint Julien Road toward the Banff Centre and begin at the left side of the kids' toboggan gully, next to Aileen Harmon's log house. Between here and Tunnel Mountain Drive trail head there is nothing worth skiing. Best to walk. If you have a car, drive to the trail head on Tunnel Mountain Drive, just below the road's highest point (the main viewpoint for the Bow Valley).

The trail has sharp switchback corners, but the grade is quite gentle throughout and easy to follow. The only problems to be encountered occur on reaching the ridge where the trail swings back left to the fire lookout. Here the wind piles sharp four to five foot high snowdrifts. Once beyond these drifts follow the ridge through the trees to the lookout.

The summit is about 1000 feet above the town and it provides one of the best views of the Bow Valley east and west. From the top and along the way you can pick out numerous other hiking and skiing trails and obtain a full geographical feel of the Banff area. The trail is also the best place for observing huge, old Douglas fir trees, a species which is becoming rarer each year.

The return trip is along the same route as the approach and it should present no major problems if you slow down going into the corners. (The return can be treacherous if the snow is hard-packed then it may be wise to walk down some sections.) Use extra caution on the top ridge section; if you lose control here and slide out past the trees, it's almost 1000 feet clear to the bottom.

Time in: 30 minutes - 1 hour
Time out: 15 - 30 minutes

STEWART CANYON—CASCADE LOOP

Intermediate 2
Road, trail and exploration tour
15 kilometres (9 miles) return
Elevations: C-level Cirque parking 4800 feet
Cascade bridge 5050 feet
Maps: Banff 82 0/4
Canmore 82 0/3
Castle Mountain 82 0/5
Lake Minnewanka 82 0/6

The Stewart Canyon trail can sometimes be a dream; at other times it's a nightmare. Basically, this trip follows an unofficial summer trail perpetuated by enthusiastic fishermen. At the upper end the trail is literally non-existant. Steep rock bluffs force one down to the edge of the river, and minor rock scrambling is required to negotiate short sections. If the winter has been sufficiently cold to form continuous river ice, if the snow is deep enough, and if there are not too many windfalls, a most enjoyable loop can be made. (When I skied it there was insufficient snow, windfalls everywhere, and I found myself knee-deep in the Cascade River.)

Start either at C-Level Cirque or Lake Minnewanka. If you start at C-Level proceed as for the start of the Cascade Fire Road. Upon reaching the fire road follow it a short distance until just past the large gravel pit on your right. Leave the road and skirt the gravel pit. Beyond the gravel pit you will be forced to ski along the edge of the road to Minnewanka. An alternative is merely to ski along the road bank from the C-Level parking lot to Minnewanka, if you don't mind traffic.

At Minnewanka ski past the picnic shelters to the end of the road. At the top of the road loop the Stewart Canyon trail begins.

Do not attempt to ski up the river and through the canyon; open water and ice falls (the lake drains during the winter) make progress very treacherous.

The trail is straightforward to the bridge with the exception of a rocky corner which often lacks snow. Across the bridge turn left and proceed slightly uphill along the obvious trail. Do not continue too far up the most obvious trail since this ultimately switches back to become the Minnewanka north shore trail.

It is impossible to describe the right trail to branch left on since there is a profusion of small trails heading back toward the Cascade River. Pick one and hope. You should be off the north shore trail within a half-kilometre of the bridge. If you proceed upstream staying about 60 metres back from the top of the steep bank, you will ultimately find yourself on course and following tree blazes. Though the route is not obvious, a bit of careful looking will connect the blazes. In just under two kilometres a tributary creek comes in on your right, and the trail drops closer to the river level.

From this point on you can either continue along the trail or, if conditions are good, ski along the river bank where you will occasionally be required to cross back and forth over the river. Progress through this section to the big bend presents no problems. If you are continuing on the trail you will be forced onto the river about 033825 by steep rock shoulders which fall into the river. Travelling along the southwest bank is your best bet through this short section until you can resume the trail for the final kilometre to the Cascade Bridge.

Return down the Cascade Fire Road to C-Level parking lot or Minnewanka.

Time from Minnewanka to Cascade Bridge: 1 - 3 hours
Time out: 30 minutes - 1½ hours

C-LEVEL CIRQUE

Not Recommended

C-Level Cirque is a fine summer hiking trail but it has little to offer as a ski run. It is steep, at times very narrow, short on viewpoints, and heavy snow could hide dangerous mine shafts near the trail. If that's not enough to turn you off, the trail ends abruptly at a shallow but very high cirque which frequently funnels powder avalanches down onto the trail-end.

ELK LAKE SUMMIT

Intermediate 2
Trail tour
11 kilometres (7 miles) one way
Elevations: Mount Norquay Parking Lot 5550 feet
Elk Lake Summit 6850 feet
Maps: Banff 82 0/4
Castle Mountain 82 0/5

The Elk Lake trail is a very popular summer and winter route, but the lake itself, set within a very cold, dark, inhospitable pocket, is hardly worth visiting during the winter. Plus the final two kilometres to the lake can be hazardous. The summit before the lake provides a very worthwhile destination, however.

Begin at the Mount Norquay Ski Area, Parking Lot 3. Ski northeast along the base of the ski area to the Wishbone ski lift. The trail proper begins just beyond the last run which returns to the base of the lift.

Initially the trail is a wide cat track, and although there may be a confusion of tracks at the start, the main trail is well-signed. At Kilometre 1 the trail forks left to Forty Mile Creek and down to the right for Cascade

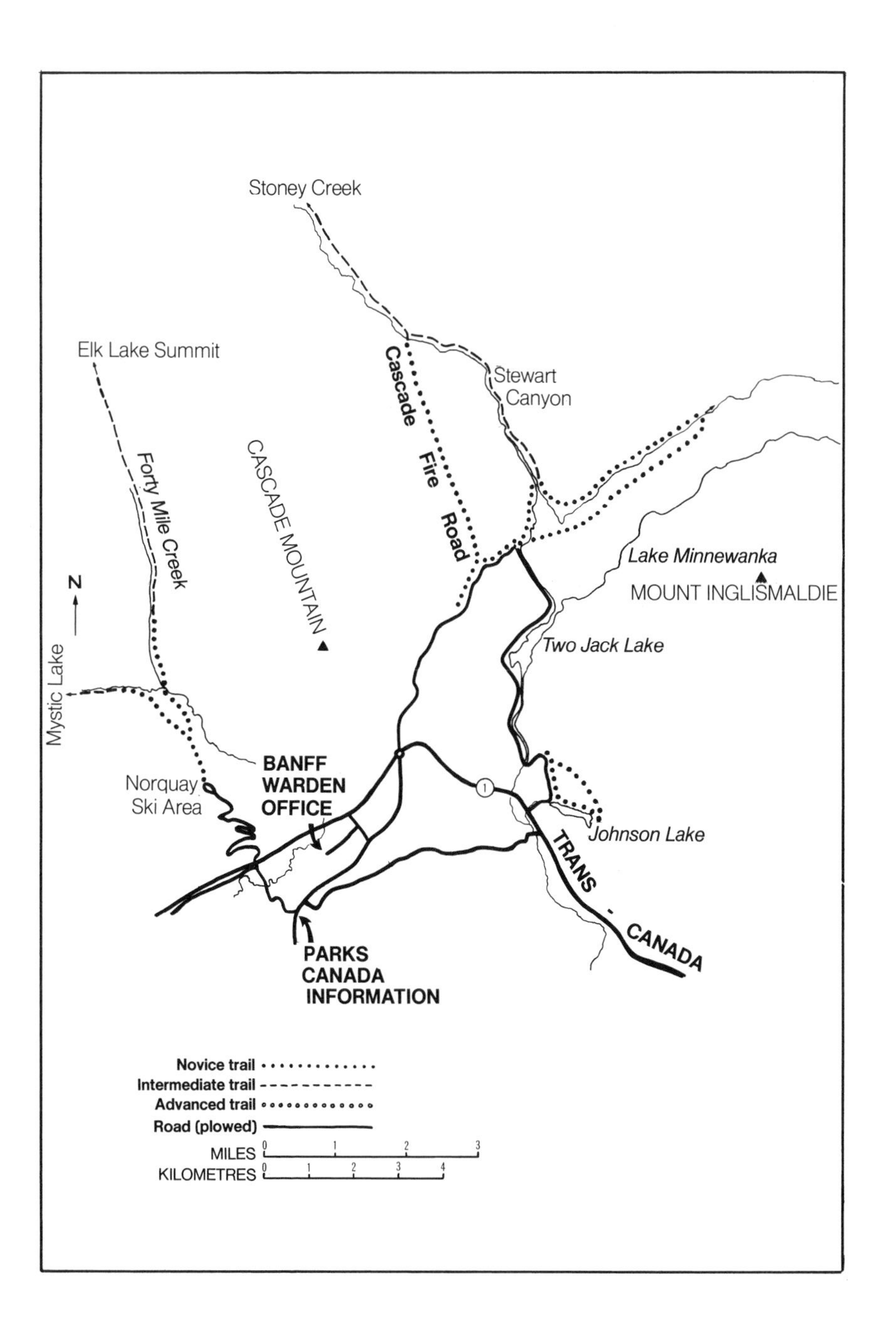
Stoney Creek
Elk Lake Summit
Cascade Fire Road
Stewart Canyon
Forty Mile Creek
CASCADE MOUNTAIN
Lake Minnewanka
MOUNT INGLISMALDIE
N
Two Jack Lake
Mystic Lake
Norquay Ski Area
BANFF WARDEN OFFICE
1
Johnson Lake
TRANS - CANADA
PARKS CANADA INFORMATION
Novice trail
Intermediate trail
Advanced trail
Road (plowed)
MILES
KILOMETRES

Amphitheatre and Elk Lake. The trail remains wide and descends gradually to Forty Mile Creek just beyond Kilometre 3.

Across the Forty Mile Creek bridge the trail is reduced to normal width and stays on the east side of the creek for the rest of the way to the summit. Between the bridge and the Amphitheatre junction at Kilometre 4, magnificent views of Mount Louis appear directly west looking up Forty Mile Creek proper.

Continue up the trail beyond the Amphitheatre junction (the Amphitheatre is not a recommended cross-country side trip due to its steep, tight, switchbacking corners). Easy travel through the timber with occasional clearings brings you to beautiful, open sub-alpine meadows at Kilometre 7. For the next 4 kilometres the trail can be followed, or you can ski anywhere along the creek or through the open meadows. The summit provides an ideal lunch stop. (For details on continuing to the lake or over the summit, see *Elk Lake and Stoney Creek* connection.)

Return the same way.

Time to Elk Lake Summit: 3 - 5 hours
Time out: 2 - 3 hours

ELK LAKE AND STONEY CREEK CONNECTION

Intermediate 3
Trail, exploration and road tour
36 kilometres (22 miles)
Elevations: Mount Norquay Parking Lot 5550 feet
Elk Lake Summit 6850 feet
High point of trail 7100 feet
Stoney Creek Warden 5300 feet
Cascade Road trail head 4850 feet
Maps: Banff 82 0/4
Castle Mountain 82 0/5

This ambitious loop should only be attempted in late winter or spring when a maximum of daylight is available. A pre-dawn start is recommended as may parties have been caught out overnight or have skied the Cascade Fire Road in complete darkness. (Bivouac equipment and/or headlamps would be well advised.)

For the initial section, Norquay to Elk Lake Summit, see the route description for *Elk Lake Summit.*

The lake can be approached from the summit by either of two routes. The simpler but longer route is over the summit and down along the summit drainage to the forks with the Elk Lake drainage. From the forks ski up the creek over easy rolling terrain to the lake.

The other approach to the lake, via the summer horse trail, leaves the west side of the summit meadow at approximate grid reference 952823. The trail climbs up a steep gully for 100 feet and contours along a ridge of heavy timber (access through this bench of timber without the trail is almost impossible). Near the point of the ridge the trail turns back sharply toward the lake. Just before the lake the trail descends very rapidly, a run which requires some extra caution.

The lake is always cold, dark, and inhospitable during the winter when the sun's rays are not high enough to reach over Mount Brewster and onto its frozen surface.

From the lake to the Cascade Road it is very difficult to pick out the barely-existant summer trail. Ski along the drainage from the lake through numerous small meadows filled with willow and alder. The bottom of Elk Valley opens onto wide meadows as indicated on the map. Stay with the creek to avoid being trapped on the upper benches as it turns east to join the Cascade River.

The narrow gap leading to the Cascade has very steep slopes on both sides, the open north side providing a favorite winter range for elk. Travelling through the gap, stay on the creek and numerous small shelves primarily along the north bank. Beyond the gap continue east and locate an ice bridge or wade the Cascade River. From the river bushwack due east to the Cascade Road.

At the fire road travel is straightforward for 13 kilometres back to the Minnewanka Road and C-Level Cirque parking lot.

Total time: 1 full day and possibly overnight

STONEY SQUAW, NORQUAY TO TOP

Intermediate but not recommended

Stoney Squaw summit provides one of the best readily accessible viewpoints in the Bow Valley. There is no difficulty in getting to the top if you can locate the trail, but the hazards on the return are almost too numerous to describe. To find the trail after a fresh snowfall is an art in itself, and the descent is barely feasible when there is sufficient loose snow to provide resistance to your speeding skis.

MYSTIC LAKE

Intermediate 2
Trail tour
20 kilometres (12 miles) one way
Elevations: Mount Norquay Parking Lot 5550 feet
Mystic Junction 6000 feet
Mystic Lake 6600 feet
Maps: Banff 82 0/4
Castle Mountain 82 0/5

The most enjoyable section of the Mystic Lake trail is the first quarter (5 or 6 kilometres) to the base of Mount Louis. The trail is a wide cat track, and behind Mount Norquay the timber opens up, to provide marvelous views in all directions. The trail is well-travelled, usually very fast, and the first section provides a worthwhile half-day outing.

Begin at the Mount Norquay Ski Area, Parking Lot 3. Ski northeast along the bottom of the ski area to the Wishbone ski lift. The trail proper begins beyond the last run which returns to the ski lift.

Although there may be a confusion of tracks at the start, the main trail is well signed. One kilometre from the parking lot the trail forks to the left for Forty Mile Creek and Mystic Lake and to the right for Cascade Amphitheatre and Elk Lake. Continue on the left fork, climbing fairly steeply in short sections for the next kilometre.

Use extra caution as the trail descends to Forty Mile Creek. The descent can be very fast, and although the corners are ample, they do not provide much warning of upcoming traffic.

Once down to the creek the cat track crosses to the north bank and continues along at an easy gradient through a semi-open valley bottom. At Kilometre 5 a summer trail forks south to Edith Pass—hardly a recommended ski trail (see separate write-up).

Continue up Forty Mile Creek. The cat track narrows to a normal horse trail which continues high along the northeast side of the creek for the next 12 kilometres to Mystic Forks. In this section the trail crosses many narrow avalanche gullies in their run-out zones, so be extremely cautious during periods of high avalanche hazard.

The trail does not cross the creek below Mystic Forks as marked on the map. At the forks ski left down to the old Mystic Warden Cabin. The summer trail leaves northwest from the cabin and climbs steeply onto a bench, gaining about 200 feet, then traverses along the hillside crossing the bases of two major avalanche slopes. At the end of the second slope the trail drops down to the creek. Ski down to the creek's triple forks and follow the middle fork to Mystic Lake rather than attempting the summer trail.,

Return the same way.

Time in to Mystic Lake: 4 - 6 hours.
Time out: 2½ - 4½ hours

EDITH PASS

Not recommended

Although a marvelous hiking area, Edith Pass is not recommended for cross-country skiing. From Mount Norquay along Forty Mile Creek the skiing is excellent and enjoyable. From Forty Mile Creek to Edith Pass the route has minor route-finding difficulties and the lower half is very steep. From Edith Pass to the highway the trail drops 1700 feet in three kilometres (it is outrageously steep, very fast, the corners are dangerously tight, and the timber is so thick that nothing can be seen.)

Reversing the directions of the trip makes it more plausible but less logical. The first third is an outrageously long, steep climb through heavy timber with little possibility of enjoyment. The remainder of the trip is enjoyable but for the fact that you end up at the Mount Norquay parking lot, 900 feet higher than when you started.

MYSTIC LAKE—JOHNSTON CREEK

Intermediate 2 or 3
Trail tour
37 kilometres (23 miles)
Elevations: Mount Norquay Parking Lot 5550 feet
Mystic Pass 7450 feet
Ink Pots 5550 feet
1A Highway 4650 feet
Maps: Banff 82 0/4
Castle Mountain 82 0/5

Another of the classic "hope to do it in one day but might get stuck out overnight" ski trips. Reserve this jaunt for late in the winter to obtain maximum daylight. A pre-dawn start is recommended, and it is futile to attempt the trip unless travelling conditions are hard and fast.

Follow the *Mystic Lake* route description to the three forks below Mystic Lake. From the three forks forget the summer horse trail for the next two kilometres. Ski up the north fork for a kilometre to where the stream branches. Follow the south fork of this second split for 0.5 kilometres then turn north onto the small ridge bordering this minor drainage. Ski over this ridge and contour into the main drainage from Mystic Summit.

At timberline simply pick the best line up the centre of the drainage to the summit (the right side is generally the best). Both sides of the summit are prone to severe avalanche activity.

Over the summit the first kilometre is rather steep, but the trees are sufficiently open to provide exciting free-skiing. The summer trail is almost as marked on the map and can also be followed to Johnston Creek. The bottom of the drainage provides easy skiing and either route is acceptable.

At Johnston Creek pick up the trail at the primitive campsite. Follow down valley above the east bank or ski along the creek and through the open meadows to the Ink Pots. From the Ink Pots climb up the west bank onto the well-used Ink Pot trail and follow it down to the highway. (Details for the last portion are found in the *Johnston Canyon—Ink Pots* description.)

Total time: 1 full day and possibly overnight

JOHNSTON'S CANYON—INK POTS

Intermediate 1
Road and trail tour
10 kilometres (6 miles) return
Elevations: Johnston's Canyon trail head 4700 feet
Ink Pots 5300 feet
Maps: Banff 82 0/4
Castle Mountain 82 0/5

A very popular and somewhat exciting summer horse trail cum ski trail. The descent down the short fire road can be very fast under packed conditions, and intermediate ability is advised for enjoyment of the run.

The trail is not at all as marked on the map. Begin behind (west side) the Johnston's Canyon bungalows and continue up the old fire road. Wax well, the first 3.5 kilometres are relatively steep. Beyond the outfitter's holding corral the road narrows to trail width and levels out. The trail at this point is well above the creek, and due to its narrowness some good technique is required for the descent to the Ink Pots. Since you are likely to encounter returning skiers, keep a watchful eye on the trail ahead.

The Ink Pot meadows are an ideal spot for lunch on a sunny day (don't forget your Thermos full of hot whatever). The Ink Pots are artesian pools which flow at a year round constant temperature of 1°C and whose bottoms bubble slowly like large pots of gooey oatmeal. Their intense, clear blue colour is all the more striking when bordered by white snow.

Return the same way, and since this is a very busy trail, ski slowly and carefully on the hills.

The top section of the fire road can also be joined from the 17-Mile Flats by following the trail as marked on the map, but it is simpler to go up from the bungalow camp.

Time in: 1½ - 3 hours.
Time out: 40 minutes - 1½ hours

JOHNSTON CREEK—LUELLEN LAKE

Intermediate 2
Trail tour.
17 kilometres (11 miles) one way
Elevations: Johnston Canyon trail head 4650 feet
Ink Pots 5550 feet
Luellen Lake 6450 feet
Map: Castle Mountain 82 0/5

Luellen Lake is not really a ski destination, but enough people ski up Johnston Creek beyond the Ink Pots that the route warrants a description.

Begin as for *Johnston Canyon—Ink Pots.* From the Ink Pots the summer trail crosses to the east bank of Johnston Creek rather than the west as marked on the map. For the next two kilometres travel either the trail, the open meadows, or the creek itself.

Two kilometres beyond the Ink Pots travel along the creek becomes more difficult. The horse trail can be located by skiing up the creek which comes in from Mystic Summit to the east. Just up the creek the main trail crossing can be identified by a primitive campsite sign.

The trail is very straightforward through heavy timber except for a few very steep pitches climbing to benches above the creek. If you seem to lose the trail, look up the hillside for an opening before skiing down to the creek. The creek is generally passable but not as efficient.

As you approach the Luellen Lake area the trail stays on the east bank rather than crossing the creek as marked on the map. The spur trail to the lake drops down steeply to Johnston Creek where another primitive campsite identifies the crossing point.

Cross Johnston Creek at the campsite and follow the steep summer trail or the side of the drainage to the lake. The lake is in a cold, shaded pocket and hardly worth visiting.

Return the same way.

Time in: 4 - 6 hours
Time out: 2 - 4 hours

BOURGEAU LAKE

Not Recommended

Although the lower five kilometres of this trail are almost acceptable, the upper section becomes very awkward indeed, especially through the rock bands above the creek crossing at Kilometre 5.5. When packed the return trip can only be described as treacherous, as numerous accidents in the past testify. The trail is best left to the summer hikers.

QUARTZ RIDGE LOW PEAK—SUNSHINE

Intermediate 2
Exploration tour
13 kilometres (8 miles) return
Elevations: Sunshine Lodge 7200 feet
Quartz Ridge Low Peak 8300+ feet
Map: Banff 82 0/4

From the Sunshine Ski Area head left of the Strawberry Chairlift and ascend the Rock Isle Run onto the Sunshine meadows (left from the top of the chairlift). Follow the marked trail to Rock Isle Lake.

Quartz Ridge runs right down to Rock Isle Lake and it can be picked up from the lake, but this adds unnecessary gain and loss of altitude. Proceed left below the lower section of the ridge as if headed for Citadel Pass. At about 806563 bear right, up and onto the ridge. Stay along the ridge, crossing back and forth over the spine as snow conditions warrant. As you gain altitude, do not ski too far to the left since minor cornices develop which may be impossible to see before it is too late.

While you are switchbacking up the ridge, remember where the best snow conditions are for the return run. The wind is a major influence on this ridge, and snow conditions alter markedly within short distances. Near the summit of the low peak the snow may be too wind-crusted to be worth skiing. If you wish to make the summit, remove your skis and walk up the wind-bared rocks.

The area is very susceptible to white-out conditions and should not be attempted if the weather is threatening.

Travel over the low peak and onto the main peak (8464′) is not recommended for cross-country skiers. The steepness of the main peak requires both ski mountaineering equipment and a thorough knowledge of avalanche conditions.

Return by the same route.

Time up: 2 - 3½ hours
Time down: 30 minutes - 1 hour

Two trails are shown on the opposite page—the Quartz Ridge route terminating on the lower peak and the Citadel Pass track crossing the east spur of Quartz Hill and descending to Howard Douglas Lake. Note the snow slides (slabs) on the steeper slopes just below the Citadel Pass trail.

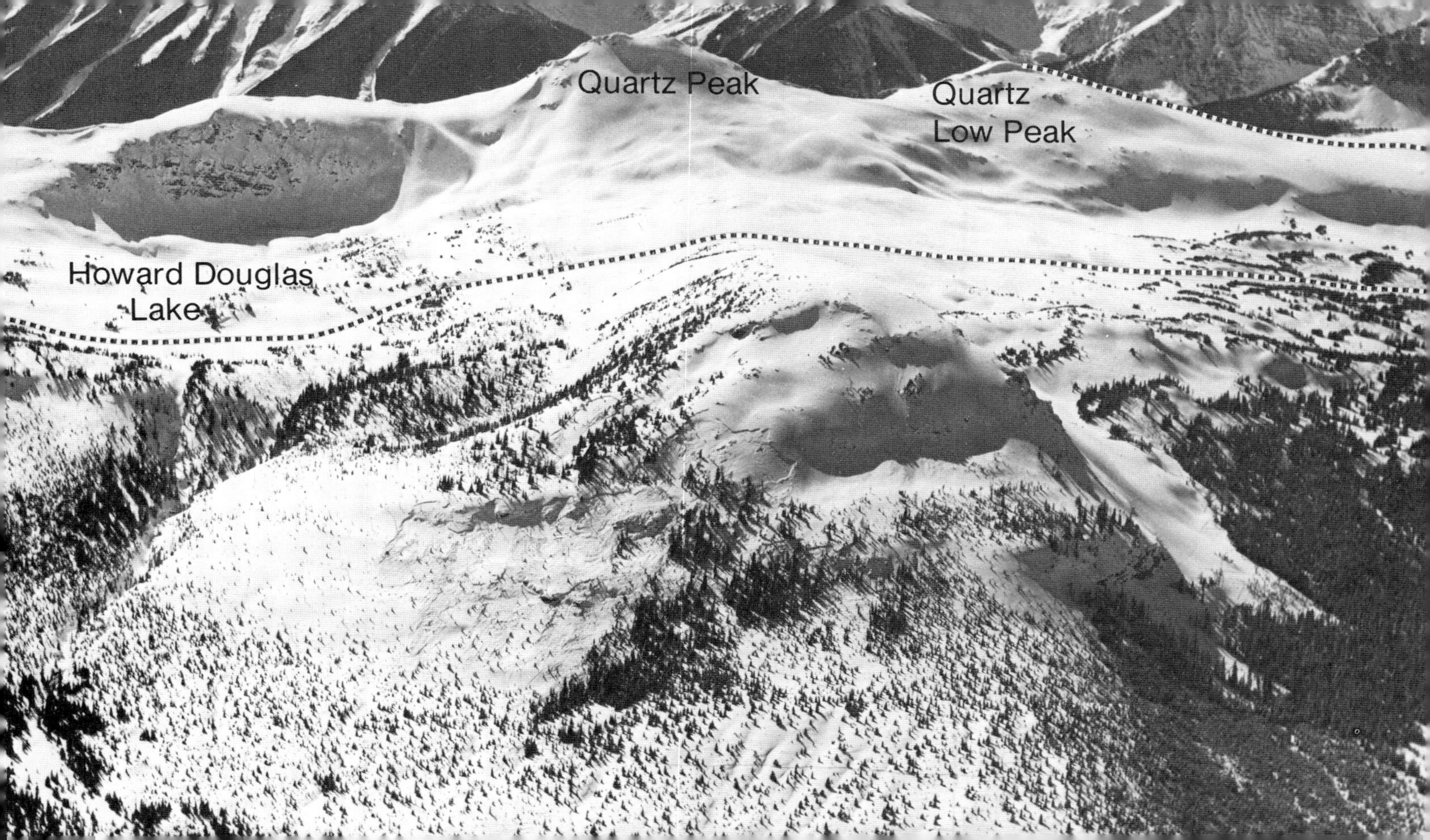
Quartz Peak
Quartz
Low Peak
Howard Douglas
Lake

CITADEL PASS

Intermediate 2
Exploration tour
10 kilometres (6 miles) one way
Elevations: Sunshine 7200 feet
Quartz Hill east spur 7750 feet
Howard Douglas Lake 7500 feet
Citadel Pass 7650 feet
Maps: Banff 82 0/4

Citadel Pass is an ideal return day tour from the Sunshine Ski Area, as well as being the first section of the standard ski route to Assiniboine.

Begin at Sunshine on the Rock Isle Lake novice route, skiing up the draw to the east (left) of the Strawberry triple chairlift. Once opposite the top of the lift and at the beginning of the Rock Isle Loop, ski across the meadows toward the peak of Quartz Hill. The last portion of the return of the Rock Isle Loop may be used for the beginning of the meadows, but it is better to keep just east (left) of it.

Once up the hill from the ski area the meadows are almost completely open and above timberline, providing direct travel, marvelous open scenery, and potential white-out conditions. If the weather is at all stormy calculate your bearings ahead of time and use your compass.

On a clear day the route is straightforward and obvious. Climb up to the saddle of the Quartz Hill east spur as marked on the map. Do not attempt to contour around the north end of it, as the north slopes are rather steep, avalanche prone, and confined with thick timber. It is also important to stay well above the Howard Douglas Creek drainage. In other words, do not lose any altitude except when skiing the section from the saddle down to Howard Douglas Lake.

Once across Howard Douglas Lake and up a short slope Citadel Peak stands out obvious and alone above the west side of Citadel Pass. Contour along the flats above the drainage and below the continuation of Quartz Ridge until near Citadel Lake. From the lake another easy, long slope leads around the northeast corner of Citadel Peak to the pass.

Return the same way or see Assiniboine continuations.

Time in: 2½ - 5 hours
Time out: 1½ - 3 hours

SUNSHINE—SIMPSON PASS—HEALY PASS—HEALY CREEK

Intermediate 3
Exploration trail tour
12 kilometres (8.5 miles)
Elevations: Sunshine 7200 feet
Twin Cairns Col 7750 feet
Simpson Pass 7050 feet
Bourgeau Parking Lot 5600 feet
Map: Banff 82 0/4

A classic day-run from Sunshine Ski Area back to the Bourgeau Parking Lot which also covers the initial three-fifths of the route from Sunshine to Egypt Lake.

Healy Pass has a reputation for being one of the few passes that will white-out while everything else is clear. More often than not the trail up over Healy Pass will be blown-in and require route-finding and trail breaking. To enjoy this route one must be a good intermediate skier—otherwise it's an agony of cold and wetness by the time one is back to the parking lot.

Take the bus up to Sunshine from Bourgeau Parking Lot. Sign out at the Snow Research Office (if you haven't already done so in Banff). From the bottom of the Wah Wah T-bar proceed to the right up the Meadow Park run to the top of the T-bar. (Watch out for downhill skiers.)

Once at the top of the lift pick-up the marked cross-country trail and follow to the notch between Twin Cairns and Carlyle Ridge. The marked cross-country trail heads south below Twin Cairns, but the route to Simpson Pass goes directly through the notch. Maintain a bearing left-of- centre through the notch while staying on top of the gully which drains Twin Cairns on your left. When the ridge begins to drop away, ski to the left and cross the gully. (Some year soon this route will be flagged, so watch for flagging.)

Lose altitude gradually, the aim being to drop into Simpson Pass about one kilometre south of the summit. A major boulder gully will lead you right into position—if you can find it. If the track isn't in the right place the way can be very difficult and is, under some conditions, an advanced trail.

Once you've skied, fallen, walked, or side-slipped your way down the cliff band, find the center of the Simpson drainage and ski up through the narrow meadow to Simpson Pass proper. Once on the pass, stop precisely on the summit. The monument will be buried, but you might be lucky enough to see the summer horse trail sign.

If the usual storms are moving in and you can't use a map and compass proficiently, ski north down the Simpson drainage to Healy Creek. It may be rough but at least it's in the trees, and after crossing the Healy Creek drainage and working a short way uphill you will run into the Healy Creek track.

If conditions are reasonable (or you are good with your map and compass), head from the summit of Simpson Pass directly west up a rather steep horse trail to gain the drainage of the lower Healy Lake on the Alberta side of the boundary. Follow this drainage to the lake, cross the lake, and attempt an easy contour bearing slightly left toward Healy Pass. (Keep well back from the Monarch Ramparts.) An almost level contour will bring you to the trail junction for Healy Creek—Healy Pass and Sunshine. If you intend to go to Egypt Lake, then contour gradually higher in the direction of Healy Pass (see the report on Healy Pass).

For the first two kilometres down Healy Creek from the junction sign the trail is insanely tight and requires proficient intermediate ability to be negotiated without wiping-out repeatedly. The trail follows the summer horse trail almost exactly as indicated on the map. Move through the avalanche paths quickly and do not linger in the open. Hopefully, your snowplow technique is perfected by now; if you can't snowplow, stem turn and make rapid parallel stops (keep the faith—you'll learn before this trip is over).

Once reaching the bridge which crosses to the south bank of Healy Creek it's only two more kilometres—although the last kilometre is down the super-slick, well-packed Sunshine ski-out. Once on the ski-out beware of downhill skiers—they tend to be most inconsiderate of cross country skiers and whistle by with no warning. Pick a side, stick to it, and don't spread yourself across the ski-out. The run is a bit dangerous but it's fun and fast down to the Bourgeau Parking Lot.

Don't bother doing this trip the other way around—it doesn't make sense.

Time from Sunshine to Bourgeau Parking Lot: 4 - 7 hours

EGYPT LAKE VIA HEALY PASS

Intermediate 3 overnight
Trail and exploration tour
13 kilometres (8.2 miles)
Elevations: Bourgeau Parking Lot 5600 feet
Healy Pass 7650 feet
Egypt Lake Shelter 6550 feet
Map: Banff 82 0/4

Healy Pass is notorious for white-out conditions even when the rest of the mountains look clear. Before beginning this trip phone the Warden Snow Research Office at Sunshine (762-2693) to obtain a local weather forecast. (Someone is usually in the office from 8:00 - 9:00 a.m., and you'll want to leave Banff by at least 9:00 a.m.) If the weather is unfavorable, use the Redearth Creek route.

Start from the Bourgeau Parking Lot, 18 kilometres west of Banff on the way to Sunshine. The trail begins up the ski-out at the upper end of the

The long ridge of the Monarch Ramparts leads northeast to the slight depression of Healy Pass. The summits of the Ball Mountain Group rise beyond.

parking lot. You shouldn't encounter downhill skiers early in the morning, but maintain single file on the ski-out just in case. Almost a kilometre up the trail branches off to the right. Continue on up the Healy Creek summer horse trail pretty much as marked on the map.

Across the bridge and on the northwest bank of Healy Creek, the trail crosses the lower sections of some fairly impressive avalanche slopes. Do not linger in these meadows. They are great rest stops for summer hikers but potential death traps in the winter.

The trail continues at a relatively constant grade to about Kilometre 6. For the next two kilometres it is quite steep, the corners are sharp, and visibility ahead is limited. Exercise great caution through here on the return.

Once beyond the steep section the forest opens up and the larches begin to appear below the expansive Healy Lakes meadows. A trail junction immediately ahead turns left to Simpson Pass and Sunshine, but continue straight ahead to Healy Pass. If the weather has closed-in obscuring the pass, turn back. Landmarks dwindle from this point onward.

Continue on as marked on the map or follow the uppermost drainage to immediately below Healy Pass. (This side of Healy Pass is prone to avalanche, and I trust you checked the avalanche forecast along with the weather before leaving.) Switchback your way up to the pass on the open southeast-facing slope.

From the top of the pass, Pharoah Peak stands out black and impressive in front of you. Egypt Lake lies at the southwest corner of this mountain. If you lose the track in the trees on the way down keep looking up to Pharoah Peak and work downwards toward its southwest corner. If the trail is not obvious then overcompensate by skiing gradually to the left all the way down. This way you will come out above the cabin and find it on your way downstream; were you to ski to the right you would either come out below the cabin and have to ski back upstream or possibly would not be certain which way to ski.

Details on shelter location and how to reserve space there are in the *Egypt Lake via Redearth Creek* report.

Return the same way or down Redearth Creek.

Time in: 4 - 7 hours
Time out over Healy Pass: 3 - 5 hours

EGYPT LAKE VIA REDEARTH CREEK

Intermediate 2 overnight
Road and trail tour
21 kilometres (13 miles) one way
Elevations: Trail head 4600 feet
Pharoah Creek junction 5700 feet
Egypt Lake Shelter 6550 feet
Map: Banff 82 0/4

A Parks Canada shelter at Egypt Lake provides free overnight accommodation, making this trip possible for intermediate skiers. The shelter is on a reservation system and must be reserved through the warden office in Banff. You should write ahead to the Park Superintendent, Box 900, Banff, Alberta, or phone (403) 762-3324, at least one week in advance of your proposed trip.

The shelter is rather large and barren. Sixteen people can fit on the plywood bunks in two sleeping rooms. The only other furnishings are two large tables and a small wood cook stove. Bring everything with you, especially foamies, pots, gas stove, and candles. Assume there isn't anything there, because there isn't. If you have a small collapsible saw, it would be wise to include it. Firewood is not pre-cut, and often the local axe and saw are broken. The woodpile is usually covered in snow, but there is a sign indicating where to look.

As for *Redearth Creek—Five Mile Campsite,* begin from the Redearth Parking Lot. Continue beyond the campsite along the fire road to the Pharoah Creek junction where the road ends. This last section of road is a bit easier than the lower section but uneventful. (Length of road: 11 kilometres.)

Cross the bridge to the Redearth Warden Cabin (even though it doesn't look like much of a cabin). A smaller bridge immediately crosses Pharoah Creek and puts one on the summer horse trail to Egypt Lake. Except for the first 1.5 kilometres, the trail is roughly as marked on the map. There is a high canyon by-pass in the summer but it is not recommended for winter travel.

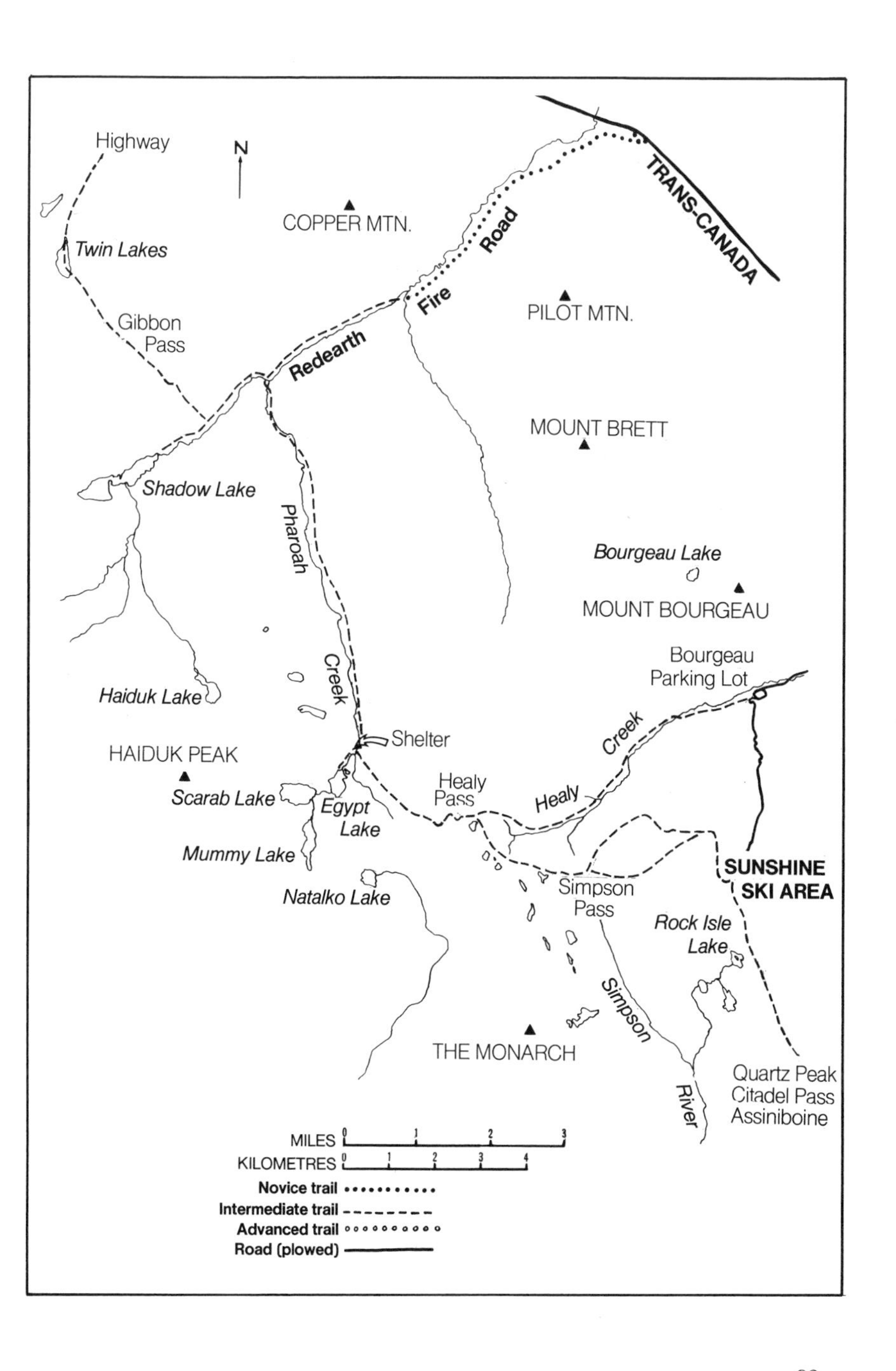
Highway
N
COPPER MTN.
Twin Lakes
Road
TRANS-CANADA
Fire
PILOT MTN.
Gibbon
Pass
Redearth
MOUNT BRETT
Shadow Lake
Pharoah
Bourgeau Lake
MOUNT BOURGEAU
Bourgeau
Parking Lot
Creek
Haiduk Lake
Creek
Shelter
HAIDUK PEAK
Healy
Pass
Healy
Scarab Lake
Egypt
Lake
Mummy Lake
SUNSHINE
SKI AREA
Natalko Lake
Simpson
Pass
Rock Isle
Lake
Simpson
THE MONARCH
Quartz Peak
Citadel Pass
Assiniboine
River
MILES
0
1
2
3
KILOMETRES
0
1
2
3
4
Novice trail
Intermediate trail
Advanced trail
Road (plowed)

Egypt Lake Shelter

The old trail has been washed out between bridges two and three above the Warden Cabin. Travel here for half-a-kilometre through the trees along and above the west bank (a short, steep, narrow hill may require removal of skis on the return trip). One-and-a-half kilometres up from the junction the trail eases out onto the old road grade established by the National Talc Mining Company. The "road" was originally constructed for hauling talc down from Natalko Lake in the wintertime, so it maintains a reasonably constant grade.

The first half of the trail is a touch boring due to the restricted view, but higher up the Pharoah Peaks come into view ahead on the right. They are a great landmark, and the shelter lies ahead just around those peaks.

Once through the old drift fence the track can go on either side of the creek, along or through the open meadows. Near the end of the meadow there should be the top rail of a bridge sticking through the snow. Above and slightly behind on the east bank is the Egypt Lake Warden Cabin. Ahead and to the right (west bank) up a short, steep, open slope is the Egypt Lake Shelter—home for the night.

The continued existence and success of the shelter depends on everyone doing his bit while he is there. Report cabin condition to the wardens when you turn in your registration. Some of the things you can do while at the cabin include cleaning it up, keeping it clean, shovelling some of the snow off the roof, shovelling out the windows, cutting extra firewood and bringing it in to dry, leaving kindling for the next group, and packing out everything packed in.

Return the same way or via Healy Pass.

Time in: 5 - 8 hours
Time out: 4 - 6 hours

SHADOW LAKE

Intermediate 2
Road and trail tour
15 kilometres (9 miles) one way
Elevations: Trail head 4600 feet
Pharoah Creek junction 5700 feet
Shadow Lake 6100 feet
Map: Banff 82 0/4

Shadow Lake has been a popular overnight ski destination in the past because of the availability of the Brewster Cabin at the Gibbon Pass trail junction, 1.5 kilometres below Shadow Lake. At the time of this writing, however, the future of the cabin is unknown. If you wish to use the cabin overnight, check with the Banff Warden Office (403-762-3324 or Box 900, Banff, Alberta, T0L 0C0) to find out who is operating the cabin, or indeed, if it is still there. Inquire well in advance of your proposed trip.

For the first section of this route see the description for *Redearth Creek—Five Mile Campsite*. Continue beyond the campsite along the fire road to within 100 metres of the Pharoah Creek junction, where the road ends. This last section of the road is uneventful and a bit easier than the section below the campsite. Watch for a sign near the end of the road indicating the start of the Shadow Lake trail.

The trail is a wide cut and very easy to follow. The initial section up from the road is quite steep but soon levels out to a comfortable grade. Follow the trail to the Gibbon forks and the Brewster Cabin meadow.

From the meadow to Shadow Lake either the creek or the trail can be followed.

Return the same way.

Time in: 3 - 5 hours
Time out: 2 - 4 hours

EGYPT LAKE—WHISTLING PASS—SHADOW LAKE

Not recommended.

This route provides a fine summer loop and possible alternative winter exit from Egypt Lake but for the initial kilometre between Egypt and Scarab Lakes. Short pitches over bedrock are so steep that one would reluctantly lead a horse over them in the summertime. In winter it is a case of removing skis then floundering and furrowing your way upward. A ski descent of this section is best described as "crash and burn."

TWIN LAKES—GIBBON PASS—REDEARTH CREEK

Intermediate 3 or Advanced 1
Trail and road tour
25 kilometres (16 miles)
Elevations: Trail head 4750 feet
Twin Lakes 6800 feet
Gibbon Pass 7450 feet
Shadow Lake 6000 feet
Redearth parking lot 4600 feet
Map: Banff 82 0/4

The Twin Lakes—Gibbon Pass loop is a rather uninspiring trip which, for some obscure reason, is becoming more travelled by the ardent skiers. The only rewarding portion on this trail is the short section running from Twin Lakes through Gibbon Pass, travelling as it does through open stands of larch with the impressive walls of Storm Mountain towering above. And if snow conditions are light and powdery, the run down from the pass through the trees can be very enjoyable. The rest is mundane.

If you insist on doing it, begin the tour at the Altrude Creek Picnic Site at the southeast corner of Castle Junction. Follow the access road straight along the east side of the creek and into a quarry, through the quarry, and across a small creek.

The trail climbs up a steep ridge to the west above the Twin Lakes drainage then continues along an uninspiring up-and-down, moving through switchbacks and finally to the open meadows about two kilometres below the lower lake. The trail is approximately as marked on the map. Follow the creek through the meadows to the lake.

Two alternative routes exist between Lower Twin Lake and Gibbon Pass. If you can locate the summer horse trail just below the outlet of the lake, a well-contoured route leads up to the pass, roughly as marked on the map. The lower two-thirds are easy to follow and well-protected in heavy timber. Open meadows and small sections of slide paths may present some confusion in the upper third, but this area is relatively open larch forest and one can ski almost anywhere through it to reach the pass.

If conditions are stable—especially if it has not snowed in the past few days, a route along the base of Storm Mountain's south spur is possible. Ski to the south end of the Lower Twin Lake then proceed along the base of the open scree slopes and through marginal meadows up to the pass. The steep slopes above are capable of discharging vast amounts of snow and loose rock, especially during or immediately after a storm. Consider the area dangerous.

Cross the open meadow of Gibbon Pass bearing left, or toward the east corner and main drainage. The drainage is a bit obscure near the top but quickly develops into a proper gully. Follow down either the drainage or the summer horse trail, or vary between the two. The trail, though a bit confining, is always just to the right of the creek as you proceed down.

In the lower sections it is best to attempt to stay on the trail even though steep skiing and tight corners are common. The lower section is again through very thick timber. The trail comes out at the Brewster Cabin meadow below Shadow Lake and joins the trail down Shadow Creek to the Redearth Creek Fire Road.

From the Brewster Cabin it is easiest to follow the trail to the fire road, but the creek can also be used. Thence, down the well-packed Redearth Road as always.

Total time: 7 - 10 hours

TWIN LAKES

Not Recommended

Twin Lakes as a simple day trip is not recommended as a winter ski route. Similar to other confined routes on the south side of the Bow Valley, it is mundane, cold, dark, uninspiring, and quite steep. In the summertime it is most enjoyable. Save it as a place to hike.

TOWER LAKE AND ROCKBOUND LAKE

Intermediate 2
Trail and road tour
16 - 18 kilometres (10 - 11 miles) return
Elevations: Trail head 4700+ feet
Tower Lake 6950+ feet
Rockbound Lake 7250 feet
Map: Castle Mountain 82 0/5

The trip to Tower Lake is only recommended for well-conditioned skiers (on the return you are required to hold an almost-continuous snowplow for 4 kilometres). In December or January it's wise to start by 8:00 or 9:00 a.m., since the sun is so low the upper half of the trail is shaded by the mountain by noon.

Park in the cleared lot at the Castle Warden Cabin, just east of Castle Mountain Bungalows on the 1-A Highway. Begin behind the warden house (please don't bother the warden for bathrooms or repair items) and continue along a wide track which climbs and switchbacks for the next five kilometres. Scenic views are rare along this section, but a good view of Copper Mountain appears higher up.

A proper wax job will save numerous headaches on this steep trail.

And try to remember the location of any fallen trees you might encounter on the way up, in case you're going at a good speed on your return.

As you turn around to the hind side of Castle Mountain the road track runs out and the trail becomes somewhat obscure. With luck someone will have been there before you laying in the approximate track. (The trail marked on the topographical map matches reality in only some sections.) Once into the trees on the narrow trail, do not drop down to the creek. Stay left above the creek and thread your way through the trees. An occasional blaze or passable opening will appear. In actuality, you never cross the creek but continue close to the base of the east buttress, crossing the very base of one or two small avalanche paths. The trees thin out into scenic small meadows while the rock towering above to the left provides striking contrasts of black and yellow. Continue left above the creek through easy terrain of alternating trees and clearings to Tower Lake.

If it takes you longer than 4 hours to Tower Lake you really shouldn't be here; it might be wise to take your skis off and walk down the steep sections on your return.

Rockbound Lake. The trail marked on the map is wrong. Find the north corner of the lake (752845) and cross where the creek empties the lake. Downstream on the right bank a sign "Rockbound Lake ½ Mile" will get you started in the right direction. It's almost straight up, bearing left, switchbacking and coming out to the right just below the upper rock band. It's really not as horrendous as it looks and it is definitely worth it.

Having gained 100 metres, you will probably be greeted by a cold, strong wind which seems always to blow through here. The area surrounding Rockbound Lake is open, and the wind creates exceptionally interesting snow sculptures on the boulders on the south slope above the lake. When the wind dies down, the lake circuit is easily toured.

Return on the same trail. If you are returning before 2:00 p.m., keep an extra careful eye for upcoming traffic. To repeat the warning: it's an almost steady snowplow for five kilometres; if you are not in shape, your thighs will be screaming.

Time into Tower Lake: 2½ - 4 hours
Time out from Tower Lake: 40 minutes - 1½ hours

CASTLE MOUNTAIN FIRE LOOKOUT

Not Recommended

For the first three kilometres the trail is a wide swath through the trees with little of interest and no significant viewpoints. The final kilometre, which provides magnificent views, traverses major avalanche slopes. Immediately below the lookout it is necessary to remove your skis to scramble through the final rock band. In brief, advanced skiers will find the trail too short to be worthwhile, intermediate skiers the potential danger too great.

WHYMPER VALLEY

Intermediate 1
Exploration tour
10 kilometres (6 miles) return
Map: Mount Goodsir 82 N/1

The Whymper Valley (also known as Chickadee Valley) is not marked on the topographical maps. It is the next valley south from Boom Lake and provides an excellent alternative trip when the Boom Lake trail is too crowded. However, it is a stage more difficult than the Boom trail.

Park at the Great Divide parking lot on the Banff-Radium Highway (Highway 93), four kilometres west of the Boom Lake parking lot. Walk across the road and start just east of the Kootenay National Park highway sign. There is no summer trail into the valley although there are a few old blazes in the lower section, but it doesn't matter if you can't find these markings since the creek is easy to follow. (This trip should not be attempted until late December when the creek is well-frozen.)

From the highway sign head straight into the valley bearing just right of centre. Within 100 metres the burned forest cover is replaced by live mature growth. You should be on top of the creek, and if not, work your way left until encountering it. From here onwards the creek and its banks provide the simplest means of skiing through the forest.

The initial section onto the river terrace is somewhat steep but soon levels out to provide ideal cross-country ski terrain. Numerous short sections require bushwacking and meandering route-finding. (This is a great valley for the practice of route selection if the usual ski tracks are obliterated or non-existant.)

The avalanche slopes on the north side of the valley should be detoured except where the avalanche fans reach across the valley and are unavoidable. Stay in the bottom of the valley when crossing these fans and do not linger out in the open. This valley should be completely avoided just after a major storm whenever the avalanche forecast is extreme, and on hot spring days when isothermal conditions can release natural slides to the valley bottom.

The tour is generally considered about five kilometres to where the forest cover is removed across the entire valley by a large avalanche slope. From this point magnificent views of hanging glaciers and broken ice falls on Mount Whymper dominate the cirque landscape.

Travel beyond this avalanche meadow becomes steep and more difficult through heavy timber and requires very skillful ski technique. Once through the upper timber one is confronted by massive rock walls towering above extensive scree slopes—a great place to be in the summer but entirely foreboding in the winter.

Return by the same track.

Time in: 2 - 3 hours
Time out: 1 - 1½ hours

TOKUMM CREEK (PROSPECTOR'S VALLEY)

Intermediate 2
Trail and exploration tour
21 kilometres (13 miles) one way
Elevations: Trail head 4850 feet
Kaufmann Lake Junction 5950 feet
Eagle's Eyrie 7400 feet
Maps: Mount Goodsir 82 N/1
Lake Louise 82 N/8

Prospector's Valley provides ideal, gently-graded, valley-bottom travel for the novice skier in the lower sections, but the upper half requires intermediate ability due to the length and minor route-finding difficulties.

The trail begins as a wide road-cut on the east side of Tokumm Creek, seven kilometres west of the Alberta-British Columbia Boundary on the Kootenay Parkway. (Avoid the Marble Canyon Nature Trail on the west side of Tokumm Creek.) At Kilometre 1.5 the road narrows to normal trail width and enters thick forest.

The trail through to Kaufmann Lake has been recently rebuilt with good blazes and new bridges (some of the bridges with long narrow spans skiers should best avoid). No difficulties should be encountered following the summer horse trail.

About three kilometres up, the trail leaves the trees and continues along the northeast bank of the creek. Travel is fast and easy if continued along the same bank, although the creek itself can often be used.

The trail continues upward along the creek, occasionally through trees, and often over snow bridges and avalanche debris. (The upper valley should be avoided during extreme avalanche conditions since numerous slides run down and across the creek.)

At Kilometre 14 the summer trail veers right, up to Kaufmann Lake. This trail is very steep, full of tight switchbacks, and hardly conducive to cross-country skiing. In other words, not recommended. The junction is the turn-around area for the majority of skiers enjoying the valley.

Return on the same track.

Time to Kaufmann junction: 2½ - 4 hours
Time out: 1½ - 3 hours

Travel beyond the Kaufmann junction continues along the creek and provides very interesting terrain for stronger skiers. Again, remain aware of the avalanche danger lurking on the slopes above.

The upper end of the valley is dominated by high peaks with the sheer, frozen walls of Curtis Peak effectively blocking out the afternoon sun. The Eagle's Eyrie looms ahead, a cold, barren, surrealistic landscape.

For advanced skiers, well-equipped and knowledgeable of avalanche slopes, access can be gained to Lake O'Hara over Opabin Pass or to Moraine Lake over Wenkchemna Pass. However, these are rather backward ways of approaching either area.

Return the same way, except as noted above.

Time to Eagle's Eyrie: 4 - 6 hours
Time out: 3 - 5 hours

BAKER CREEK TO MEADOWS

Intermediate 1
Trail tour
12 kilometres (7.5 miles) return
Elevations: Trail head 4950 feet
Baker Creek Meadows 5550 feet
Map: Lake Louise 82 N/8

Baker Creek is one of the more acceptable Bow Valley side trails since it does not include any major, prolonged descent runs on the return. The trail is generally narrow and requires some talent in cornering quickly.

Park at the Baker Creek Picnic Site, 15 kilometres west of Castle Junction on the 1-A Highway. The trail begins at the north end of the picnic site and immediately cuts upward to the left under the power lines to gain the top of the first river terrace. From here to the 4-Mile Meadows it is, with the exception of the occasional viewpoint, almost all solid timber.

The trail continues roughly as indicated on the map, always staying to the west side of the creek. Through Kilometres 2 and 3 there are some tight corners which should be remembered and respected on the return trip.

The old warden cabin two kilometres up the trail (shown on map) is no longer a warden cabin. The cabin belongs to the Banff boy scouts and is not open to the public. Because of past "scouting" activity in the area, there are numerous confusing blazes and markings throughout the woods. They are of no use to the skier, and one should look for the main trail.

About three kilometres up the first viewpoint occurs just as you come out of a steep left-hand curve. Step off the trail toward the creek (not too far, it's steep!). This is one of your best views. From here the trail levels out and continues close to the creek.

There is no official end to this tour, and one could carry on up to Baker Lake, through Boulder Pass, and down to Lake Louise—a trip of two or more days. Most people stop and turn around at the meadows which open up at Kilometre 5—a good lunch area with ample open space to burn off any extra energy before the return.

The return is precisely the same as the approach. If the trail is well packed on the way in, prepare to exercise extra caution below the first viewpoint where the trail leaves the creek. The thick timber does not provide clear visibility for any distance ahead; sharp corners appear rather abruptly. Watch for telltale signs of warning: trees stripped of their bottom branches, or numerous large holes in the snow.

Time in: 2 - 3 hours
Time out: 1 - 2 hours

SKOKI

Intermediate 3 overnight
Trail tour
11 kilometres (6.5 miles) one way
Elevations: Temple Ski Lodge 6500 feet
Boulder Pass 7600 feet
Deception Pass 8200 feet
Skoki Lodge 7200 feet
Maps: Lake Louise 82 N/8
Hector Lake 82 N/9

The Skoki Lodge was originally a major backcountry ski centre during the formative years of skiing in the Canadian Rockies. It was built by Clifford White and Cyril Paris in 1930 as the second ski hut in the Rockies, Mount Norquay being the first. There is more history, legend, and romance connected with Skoki than any other area.

Many skiers prefer to make simple day trips out from Lake Louise into the Ptarmigan and Baker Lakes areas, and strong skiers can make the Skoki return trip in a day. For overnight stays accommodation can be arranged through Lake Louise Ski Area, Lake Louise, Alberta (phone 403-522-3555).

Trail head access is a touch complicated but can be achieved in numerous ways: catch the bus from the Whiskey Jack Lodge at Whitehorn to Temple (the easiest start); ski up the ski-out 8 kilometres to Temple; or ride up the Whitehorn ski lifts and ski down the Pika run to Temple.

From the Temple ski lodge watch for the trail head sign and ski up the easy-to-follow trail through mature spruce-fir forest. Within two kilometres the trail breaks out of the trees, and travel continues free and easy through the open alpine valley toward Boulder Pass. A small hut (marked Ptarmigan Hut on the map) stands on a small protected bench in the meadow and is the original Half-way Hut between Lake Louise train station and Skoki.

Continue along the valley and follow a gentle ravine up through the boulders below the pass. Just below the pass a short steep section of 100 metres may provide minor difficulties as it leads up over the pass toward the east (right) side.

Over the pass a gentle downhill run leads to Ptarmigan Lake and a

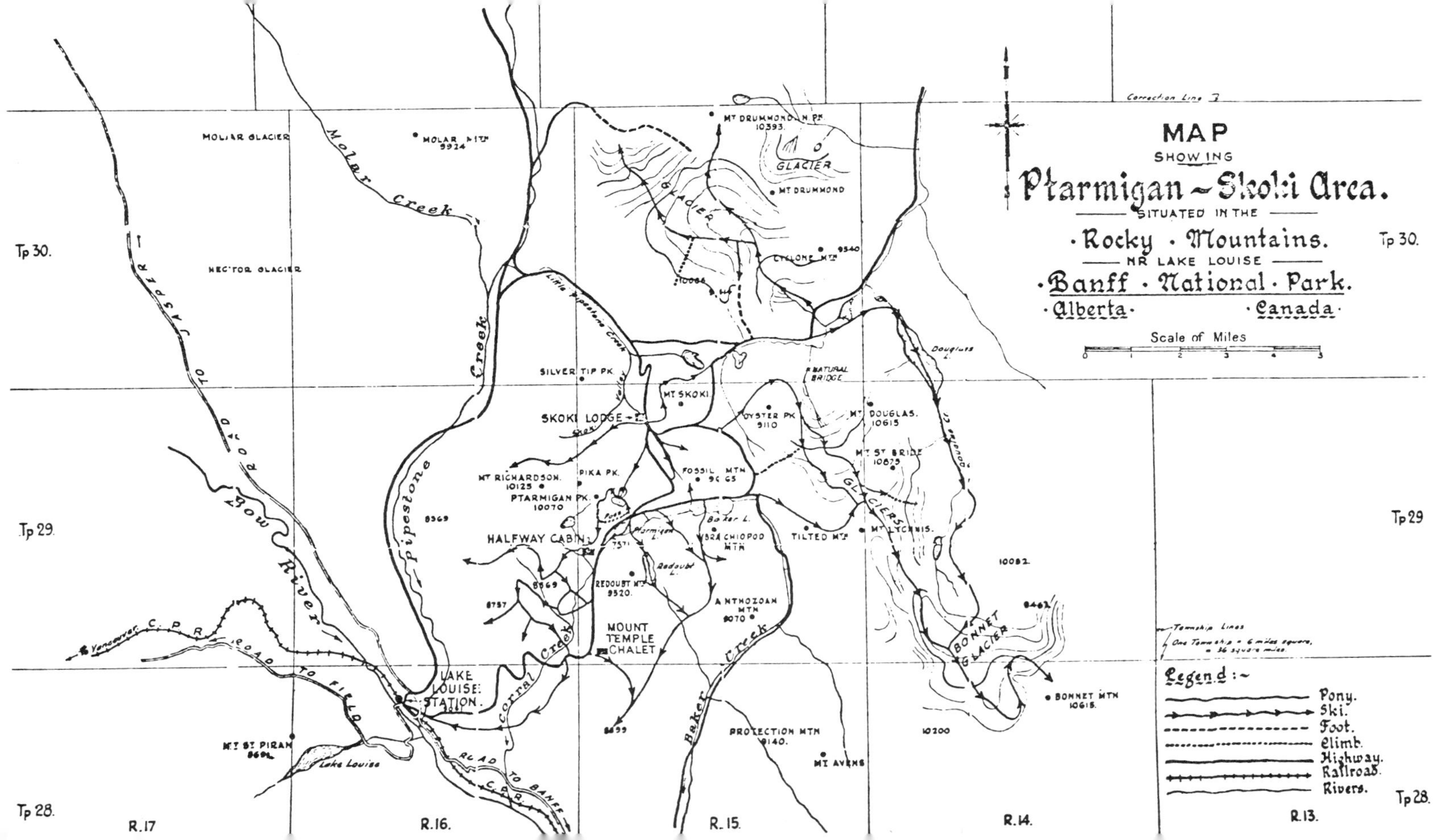

MAP
SHOWING
Ptarmigan ~ Skoki Area.
SITUATED IN THE
· Rocky · Mountains.
NR LAKE LOUISE
· Banff · National · Park.
· Alberta ·
· Canada ·
Scale of Miles
Correction Line 3
Township Lines
One Township = 6 miles square, = 36 square miles.
Legend :~
Pony.
Ski.
Foot.
Climb.
Highway.
Railroad.
Rivers.
Tp 30.
Tp 29
Tp 28.
R.17
R.16.
R.15.
R.14.
R.13.
MOLAR GLACIER
HECTOR GLACIER
MOLAR MTN 9924
Molar Creek
MT DRUMMOND N. PK. 10393.
GLACIER
MT DRUMMOND
CYCLONE MTN 9540
10086
SILVER TIP PK.
Little Pipestone Creek
MT SKOKI
SKOKI LODGE
MT RICHARDSON. 10125
PIKA PK.
PTARMIGAN PK. 10070
HALFWAY CABIN
FOSSIL MTN
OYSTER PK 9110
NATURAL BRIDGE
MT DOUGLAS. 10615
MT ST BRIDE 10875
Douglas L.
GLACIERS
TILTED MTN
MT LYCHNIS.
Baker L.
BRACHIOPOD MTN
Ptarmigan L.
Redoubt L.
REDOUBT MTN 9520.
ANTHOZOAN MTN 9070
MOUNT TEMPLE CHALET
BONNET GLACIER
BONNET MTN 10615.
10082
10200
PROTECTION MTN 9140.
MT AVENS
Baker Creek
Corral Creek
Pipestone Creek
8369
8969
8757
LAKE LOUISE STATION.
Bow River
ROAD TO JASPER
ROAD TO FIELD
ROAD TO BANFF
C.P.R.
Vancouver C. P. R.
MT ST PIRAN
Lake Louise

series of poles which mark the route across the lake during white-out conditions. Ahead to the north two passes lie between Ptarmigan Peak and Fossil Mountain. Deception Pass—the route to Skoki—is the more easterly (to the right).

Climb upward across the open slopes to the east (right) side of Deception Pass. Contour a short distance along the top of the pass before descending the open, gently rolling hills into Skoki Valley. Once to the valley bottom pick up the summer trail or simply continue down along the creek to Skoki Lodge.

Return the same way.

Time in: 3 - 5 hours
Time out: 3 - 4 hours

There are numerous ideal day trips in the Skoki area which the lodge proprietors will happily point out. For even more ideas see Sir Norman Watson's historical map of the Skoki area.

BATH CREEK

Intermediate 1
Exploration tour
8 kilometres (5 miles) one way
Elevations: Trail head 5280 feet
Bath Creek treeline 6200 feet
Maps: Lake Louise 82 N/8
Hector Lake 82 N/9

Bath Creek does not have a summer trail along it nor does it have any noticeable destination point. Once the creek is well-frozen, however, the area is quite accessible on skis.

Park along the Trans-Canada Highway just west of the Bath Creek bridge, about 10 kilometres west of Lake Louise. From the highway ski north to the railway tracks and follow east to the railway bridge. If the water is open, cross the railway bridge and begin up the east bank.

Follow the creek, and the banks where necessary, for three kilometres to where the area opens onto broad gravel flats. The flats provide easy open travelling for the next two kilometres where, once again, the trees close in. Travel becomes more difficult at this point and switches back and forth continually between the creek bed and the trees on the east (right) bank. Just over one kilometre from the end of the open flats, the creek forks. Follow the most westerly fork for the next two kilometres until a major cliff and canyon blocks the way.

Return the same way.

Time in: 1½ - 3 hours
Time out: 1 - 2 hours

MOSQUITO CREEK

Intermediate 2
Trail and exploration tour
10 kilometres (6 miles) one way
Elevations: Trail head 6000 feet
Timberline 7300 feet
Map: Hector Lake 82 N/9

Mosquito Creek is a rather uninspiring route into an alpine area of unlimited open slopes which could keep an expert skier happy for days. The intermediate skier is best advised to travel no further than the easy slopes above timberline. Inventory the upper slopes for future exploration.

Begin at the Mosquito Creek bridge, 25 kilometres up the Icefields Parkway. The trail ascends a steep bank above the highway on the north side of the creek to an old clearing through the trees. As is so often the case, the trail continues to climb for another half-kilometre before levelling out into ideal touring terrain.

The trail continues along a bench above the creek and meets the creek again about 2.5 kilometres up. Small meadows provide easy, enjoyable touring along the creek for the next 1.5 kilometres, until the trail goes back into the trees on the south side of the creek. Follow the trail through the heavy timber around the corner of the massive un-named peak towering above to the right.

Around the corner and heading southeast travel becomes more obscure and difficult. Do not hesitate to abort your trip and turn around if you cannot find an obvious route.

Watch carefully for the two drainages which join at 495234. Unless the summer trail has been improved, it is best to explore and bushwhack your way along the ridge between the two drainages. The thick timber does open up and progress can be made easily upwards to timberline. Once out of the trees the entire area opens up to unhindered, easy touring.

Do not attempt to reach Molar Pass to the south unless you are experienced in avalanche evaluation. Rather, enjoy the open, easy slopes around you before turning back down the creek.

Return the same way.

Time in: 2½ - 4 hours
Time out: 1½ - 3 hours

KATHERINE LAKE—HELEN LAKE CIRCUIT

Intermediate 3
Trail and exploration tour
13 kilometres (8 miles) return
Elevations: Trail head 6200 feet
Katherine Lake 7750 feet
Katherine-Helen Col 8150 feet
Helen Lake 7750 feet
Map: Hector Lake 82 N/9

This route is a slight reversal and minor extension of the extremely popular summer trail into an easily accessible area of splendid high alpine terrain. Though many will consider this an easy intermediate route on a nice day, variable weather conditions and the need for accurate map reading warrant the higher classification.

Begin at the summer trail head just north of the Helen Creek bridge, 29 kilometres north on the Icefields Parkway. The first kilometre is rather steep, tightly switchbacking through heavy spruce-fir forest as the trail follows up a ridge above the creek. The ridge soon levels out, and the trail encounters the creek again in about two kilometres (423237).

Follow along the trail or the creek for another two kilometres to 412250. It is possible to continue on up and above the creek to Helen Lake, but a rather awkward gorge must be negotiated. A better ski route continues toward Katherine Lake.

Avoid the gorge by skiing directly north (to the right) and switchback up the hillside to gain the 7700 foot contour at 412253. Contour to the east maintaining a constant height around the corner toward a small series of cliff bands. These may be negotiated through various shelves but are best approached high to 418254.

Once over the cliff bands it is an easy, wide-open, enjoyable ski down to Katherine Lake. The northeast-facing slopes between Katherine and Helen Lakes provide ideal practice terrain for downhill skiing.

Time in: 2 - 4 hours

From Katherine to Helen Lake the area is wide-open and any line can be taken to reach the small col at 407265. Over the col the snow is often very hard wind-packed slab but soon softens below. Ski down bearing slightly northwest (right) to avoid the rock bands above the lake.

From Helen Lake out, the creek may be followed, but the gorge will have to be negotiated. It is easiest to contour southeast to meet your incoming tracks at the 7700 foot contour. (Use extra caution negotiating the tight switchbacks on the final kilometre above the road.)

Total time: 4 - 6 hours

The entire Dolomite area above timberline provides a multitude of exceptional short ski runs. However, much of this is prime avalanche terrain and requires very good judgement of snow conditions.

BOW SUMMIT

Intermediate 3
Practice slope
Maps: Hector Lake 82 N/9
Blaeberry River 82 N/10

Bow Summit is synonymous with Bow Pass, six kilometres north of Num-ti-jah Lodge and Bow Lake on the Icefields Parkway.

Similar to Parker's Ridge, Bow Summit is better known as an off-season practice slope for downhill skiers. Cross-country terrain is limited, but it is a prime area to practice telemark turns and other techniques for downhill skiing with loose heels.

Check with the wardens at Lake Louise for avalanche hazard information. (Skiers have died here, too.)

GLACIER LAKE

Intermediate 2
Exploration tour
24 kilometres (15 miles) return
Elevations: Saskatchewan Crossing 4600 feet
Glacier Lake 4700 feet
Maps: Mistaya Lake 82 N/15

The summer trail to Glacier Lake climbs gradually 800 feet and then drops rapidly 800 feet to the lake. Luckily the hiking route can be avoided in winter, and the total climb can be reduced to 100 feet. However, this route can only be used when the river is sufficiently frozen and should not be attempted early or late in the season.

Begin at the Saskatchewan Crossing Warden Station and ski along the south bank of the North Saskatchewan River, or on the river itself when it helps to short-cut river bends. Past the Saskatchewan River forks travel is generally easiest on the braided river flats of the Howse rather than on the timbered bank. This can be a very uncomfortable trip on a windy day since the valley channels the wind and slows upstream progress. If it has not snowed recently, one will likely encounter wind blown sand on the lower sections.

About 8.5 kilometres upstream (map co-ordinates 134526) watch for an old white trail sign with black lettering on the north shore indicating the trail up to Glacier Lake. The well-contoured horse trail is much easier than attempting to ski up the gorge which drains Glacier Lake. Follow the trail to the lake (it is not the same as the trail marked on the map).

A small, decrepit trapper's cabin can be found at the east end of the lake on the north side of the outlet. There's not much to it, but it does provide some shelter. If you plan to depend on it, check with the wardens before you leave; it could be gone.

Return the same way.

Time in: 2½ - 4 hours
Time out: 1½ - 3 hours

PARKER'S RIDGE

Intermediate 3
Practice slope
Map: Columbia Icefields 83 C/3

Parker's Ridge is better known as an off-season, downhill skiing practice area. But while it is not really a cross-country area, it does receive snow earlier in the fall and later in the spring than most areas. Appropriate cross-country skiing trails are very short, but the open slopes are a great place to practice downhill technique on your skinny skis.

Parker's Ridge is not marked on any map but is easily located as the open slopes above the Hilda Creek Youth Hostel, eight kilometres south of Sunwapta Pass (the north boundary of Banff Park) on the Icefields Parkway.

Check with the warden at Saskatchewan Crossing for avalanche hazard information. (Many have died here in the past.)

SHERBROOKE LAKE

Intermediate 1
Trail tour
3 kilometres (1.8 miles) one way
Elevations: Wapta Lake 5200 feet
Sherbrooke Lake 5900 feet
Map: Lake Louise 82 N/8

Sherbrooke Lake is a very short, interesting trip which provides some good downhill excitement on the return.

Park at Wapta Lodge or at the picnic area just west of the lodge. The trail begins just above the picnic shelter and proceeds upward to the right for 100 metres before switchbacking left in the direction of the lake.

The trail runs consistently uphill for the first two kilometres then levels out over the final stretch to the lake. About 1.7 kilometres up the trail the Paget Lookout Spur turns off to the right—a trail not recommended for skiing due to its extreme steepness and high avalanche hazard.

In a winter of heavy snows the Sherbrooke trail may be difficult to follow in the thinner timber. If you lose the trail, travel along the side-hill through the open timber staying well above the creek.

Travel to the far end of the lake and beyond is not recommended because of extreme avalanche danger. Ski tracks which you may encounter up here are generally those of persons who have come down from Balfour Hut and the Wapta Icefields traverse. All descending skiers travel through this area as rapidly as possible to minimize their exposure to potential avalanches.

Time in: 1 - 2 hours
Time out: 30 minutes - 1 hour

LAKE O'HARA—McARTHUR PASS—OTTERTAIL VALLEY

Intermediate 3 overnight
Trail and road tour
25 kilometres (16 miles)
Elevations: Lake O'Hara 6650 feet
McArthur Pass 7150 feet
Ottertail Junction 4750 feet
Trans-Canada Highway 3850 feet
Maps: Lake Louise 82 N/8
Golden 82 N/7

This trip is best done starting at Lake O'Hara but it can be accomplished in one day from Wapta Lake if conditions are fast and the party is strong. (It is best to wait until late February or March to capitalize on the longer hours of daylight.)

From the Elizabeth Parker Hut ski up the drainage to McArthur Pass or follow the summer trail. The steep climbing eases off within a kilometre, and classic ski terrain leads past Schäffer Lake and up to the pass. (Approach the pass to the north side of center.)

Over the McArthur Pass the summer trail switchbacks sharply, is difficult to follow, and is best avoided until reaching the gentler valley bottom. From the pass ski southwest (left) into the centre of the drainage. A long, steep pitch of open skiing over a boulder field quickly brings you down into the timber and some awkward bushwacking.

Elizabeth Parker Hut

The summer trail can be picked up by skiing northwest (right) in a simple contour through the woods. The trail is fairly accurate as marked on the map. It's more awkward but more fun to proceed down along the creek to the upper forks of McArthur Creek.

Fifty metres up the north fork of McArthur Creek (429860), the summer horse trail bridge is readily visible. Follow this trail down to the Ottertail River. Numerous avalanche slopes off the east side of Mount Owen cross the trail, and a bit of searching on the opposite side of these slides to relocate the trail may be required at times. As always, traverse the avalanche slopes without delay. (When avalanche conditions are extreme a safer route can be followed by simply skiing along the creek.)

At the Ottertail River the McArthur Creek Warden Cabin is easily located on a clear bench above the river.

Time from O'Hara: 2½ - 5 hours

The Ottertail Fire Road begins just behind the cabin and stays on the northeast bank of the river for the next 14 kilometres to the highway, and few good downhill runs mean most of it will have to be skied. (The road does not cross the river briefly as marked on the map.)

Time down the Ottertail: 2 - 5 hours

Total time from O'Hara to the highway via the Ottertail can easily vary from 5 to 10 hours depending on the amount of fresh snow. It is fastest and safest to do this trip when the snow is well-settled and trail-breaking can be kept at a minimum. The area experiences very little winter use except for a few kilometres at both ends.

LITTLE YOHO VALLEY

Intermediate 3 overnight
Road, trail and exploration tour
22 kilometres (14 miles) one way
Elevations: Trail head 4200 feet
Takakkaw Falls viewpoint 4900 feet
Little Yoho Valley 6800 feet
Maps: Lake Louise 82 N/8
Hector Lake 82 N/9
Blaeberry River 82 N/10

The highlight destination of the Little Yoho Valley is the Stanley Mitchell Hut, operated by the Alpine Club of Canada. For details of its use contact the Alpine Club of Canada in Banff at Box 1026 or phone (403) 762-3664. Canadian Mountain Holidays, Banff, arranges guided ski weeks in the area and uses the hut as a base of operations.

The Little Yoho Valley abounds with ideal steep ski terrain for advanced cross-country skiers and ski mountaineers. Intermediate skiers can also enjoy the area but are well advised to hire a guide.

For a description of the first 13 kilometres, see the *Yoho Valley Road* in the novice section.

From Takakkaw Falls continue along the road and follow the regular summer horse trail to Laughing Falls. Travel is simple and direct to Laughing Falls with the exception of Hollingsworth Hill. This is not a hill by itself but rather an incredibly direct, well-graded cut up a long steep hillside. It runs for almost a half-kilometre without change and can be rather hazardous on the downhill return. Take it slowly and remember the hairpin turn.

Watch for a sign near Laughing Falls to indicate the turn up to the Little Yoho Valley. This connecting trail, not marked on the topo map, is often difficult to locate in the wintertime as deep snow hides the trail blazes. If you cannot locate the trail, switchback your way up through the mature spruce forest staying just north (right) of the Little Yoho River. (The climb is rather steep as it is necessary to gain 600 feet in less than one kilometre of map distance.)

As the terrain levels out watch for, or search out, the main summer trail on the north side of the river roughly as marked on the map. Travel is easy and direct along the summer trail to the Stanley Mitchell Hut.

Check with the Yoho wardens concerning emergency shelter in the Takakkaw Falls area, in case you cannot make it in all the way in one day.)

Return the same way.

Time in: 1 - 2 days
Time out: 1 full day

Advanced

ASSINIBOINE VIA BRYANT CREEK

Advanced, camping
Trail tour
19 kilometres (12 miles)
Elevations: Spray Reservoir 5550 feet
Assiniboine Pass 7100 feet
Lake Magog 7050 feet
Maps: Spray Lakes Reservoir 82 J/14
Mount Assiniboine 82 J/13

The 19 kilometres listed above are very deceiving, since that is only the distance from the end of the Spray Reservoir. The Spray Lakes Road to the end of the reservoir is not plowed in the winter, although it may be open halfway if loggers are working in the area. Likewise, the road is sometimes still passable into December, especially with four wheel drive vehicles. (Information may be obtained from the Provincial Forest Ranger in Canmore.) When the road is snowed shut access to the end of the reservoir is possible by oversnow vehicles. The Spray Valley approach through Banff Park is limited to skiers, however (see description under *Spray Valley beyond 8 Mile).*

The trail from the end of the reservoir to the Bryant Creek Warden Cabin is a wide, gentle wagon road, easy to follow and completely obvious. There is one long, steep hill which climbs over a rock band at grid reference 045388.

Immediately over the rock band a small meadow is encountered on the left, at the far end of which stands the Bryant Creek Shelter—a cabin similar to the Egypt Lake shelter. (Arrangements for use can be made with the Warden Service in Banff.)

From the shelter resume the wagon trail to the Bryant Creek Warden Cabin. The trail continues as marked on the map, skirting the northern edge of the meadows. (Do not attempt the Marvel Lake alternate route in winter. Wonder Pass is 700 feet higher than Assiniboine Pass, and the route is exposed to extreme avalanche danger.)

From the end of the Bryant Creek meadows the trail is more difficult to follow as it crosses and recrosses the creek several times. It is generally as marked on the map. A new summer high trail does exist on the north side of the valley, but it is very difficult to locate in the winter. (Check with the Banff wardens in case the situation has improved, as it does provide a better line of travel.)

Both trails converge at the base of a rock band, grid reference 986418, and climb steeply through the band before levelling out into the pass.

From the pass ski directly down through a difficult-to-define gap to the abandoned Magog Lake airfield (marked on the map). Numerous trails exist in this area. Maintain a southwest bearing and keep heading toward Mount Assiniboine. Regardless of which trail you pick, you will ultimately come out at Lake Magog.

For information on cabins in the area, see the trip report for *Assiniboine via Sunshine.*

Return the same way or over Allenby Pass (see report for *Assiniboine-Allenby Return).*

Time in: 6 - 10 hours
Time out via Bryant Creek: 4 - 6 hours

MOUNT ASSINIBOINE VIA SUNSHINE

Advanced, camping
Exploration tour
29 kilometres (18 miles) one way
Elevations: Sunshine 7200 feet
Citadel Pass 7750 feet
Policeman Meadows 5750 feet
Og Lake 6750 feet
Lake Magog 7050 feet
Maps: Banff 82 0/4
Mount Assiniboine 82 J/13

The approach to Mount Assiniboine from Sunshine Village is one of the classic cross-country tours in the Canadian Rockies. But the journey is fraught with hazards for the unwary: the section between Sunshine and Citadel Pass is very susceptible to white-out conditions which can only be overcome with accurate compass travel; the descent from the pass is prone to avalanches; and the journey is deceptively long, often requiring that at least one night be spent on the trail. Departing parties should carry full camping gear and avalanche equipment, and always check with the wardens at Sunshine for weather and snow stability forecasts before setting out.

For the section to Citadel Pass, see the route description for *Sunshine —Citadel Pass.* (Be prepared for white-out conditions above timberline and calculate your bearings before you leave.)

From Citadel Pass follow the route down to the Golden Valley as marked on the map for the summer horse trail. The top of the pass provides an easy run for 1.5 kilometres until it begins to drop away steeply for 600 feet turning sharply to the south-southwest and the headwaters of the Simpson River.

The Valley of the Rocks leading south toward the pyramid of Mount Assiniboine.

Two-thirds of the way from the top of the pass there is an obvious route left across the open slopes into the Golden Valley. The traverse would save considerable distance and altitude. A summer horse trail does cross this slope, but unless avalanche conditions are completely stable, it would be utterly insane to attempt such a shortcut. (The slope under the snow is entirely grass-covered and is excessively prone to avalanching.)

There is also an avalanche threat from the slopes above to the right so move down the centre of the pass quickly. A gully leads directly to the bottom.

As you are coming down the lower half of the pass, Policeman's Meadow is directly ahead and across the valley. Get a good bearing on the meadow if you intend to stay overnight at the old trapper's cabin there. (Don't depend on this cabin, since its future is unknown. Information can be obtained by writing British Columbia Provincial Parks Branch, Box 118, Wasa, B.C. V0B 2K0.)

From the bottom of Citadel Pass ski up the Golden Valley bearing along the centre or left-of-centre. The valley has not been eroded by the usual rivers and streams like other mountain valleys, and there is no normal stream course to follow. Travel is up-and-down-and-around following the best course you can pick through the Golden Valley and the Valley of the Rocks. (When snow conditions are stable you can skirt much of the timber by travelling along the far left side.)

In the upper end of the Valley of the Rocks the timber opens up and, aside from the continuing up-and-down nature of the terrain, skiing is very open and enjoyable. Continue through the notch, past Og Lake, and on toward Assiniboine, following the trail as marked on the map.

As you approach Lake Magog the first buildings you encounter are Strom's lodge and cabins on the bench well back from the lake. These buildings are not open to the public, except through prior arrangement with the operators. The operating dates, on a weekly basis, usually range from late Febraury to the end of April. The lodge is generally booked a year in advance, and information on availability is best obtained through Canadian Mountain Holidays in Banff.

The Naiset Cabins are located south of Strom's, just above Magog Creek on the edge of the trees. These refurbished cabins are open for public use during the winter and serve as an ideal base camp for day trips in the area.

Only under excellent conditions can a strong party make the trip from Sunshine to Assiniboine in one day. Be prepared to camp or assure arrangements for the Policeman's Meadow Cabin.

Time in: 1 - 2 days

ASSINIBOINE, RETURN OVER ALLENBY PASS TO BANFF

Advanced, camping
Trail tour
44 kilometres (27 miles)
Elevations: Lake Magog 7050 feet
Assiniboine Pass 7100 feet
Bryant Creek forks 6200 feet
Allenby Pass 8000 feet
Half-way Hut 6400 feet
Banff 4538 feet
Maps: Mount Assiniboine 82 J/13
Banff 82 0/4

Allenby Pass was the original winter route to and from Assiniboine established by Erling Strom and the Marquis d'Albizzi in 1928. It remained the standard route until bus service to the Sunshine Ski Area provided an alternate route which saved 15 kilometres and 2500 vertical feet of extra climbing. Today the route is rarely skied as an approach to Assiniboine but rather as an alternative return to Banff.

From Lake Magog follow the summer trail to the Magog Lake airfield (now called the O'Brien Meadows) and on up to Assiniboine Pass. Over the pass stay to the south (right) side and attempt to locate the trail. The north side of the pass is blocked by precipitous rock bands. To the south side of the rock bands the trail is quite steep and requires extra caution.

Below the rock bands the upper reaches of Bryant Creek alternate between bogs and thick bush. It is best to stay on the summer horse trail and follow it along the base of Cascade Rock to the Allenby Junction. A broad, open, denuded run-out slope is crossed and indicates the Allenby fork just ahead. Watch for a sign on the north side of the trail.

It is easiest to follow the Allenby trail as marked on the map, but Allenby Creek can also be used if you encounter difficulty locating the trail. An alternative exploration shortcut can be accomplished by cutting across the Bryant Creek flats, through the old burn, and onto the Allenby trail as it climbs the corner of the southeast extension of Og Mountain.

Follow up Allenby Creek, through the trees, and into the open area below the pass. The slopes on the west (left) side often avalanche into the bottom of the drainage; travel should be approximately as the trail is marked on the map, east and slightly above the drainage.

Once into the pass ski along the treeline on the northeast (right) side as marked on the map. Do not attempt the gap on the west side of the middle hump where "Allenby Pass" is printed on the map.

Once over the pass watch for signs and flagging which indicate the ski route down and to the left of the watercourse. Avoid the summer horse trail which leads away to the right in the upper section of the trees. The ski trail stays in heavy protective timber and works down between rock bands and small waterfalls.

Once to the bottom continue out along the trail watching for blazes and openings in the trees. Half-way Hut is located at 995496, on the opposite side of the creek from the spot indicated on the map. (Check with the operators of Strom's lodge as to the cabin's availability if you intend to use it.) It is possible to ski directly out in one day but requires ideal conditions and a strong party. Expect to camp somewhere along Brewster Creek.

The trail away from Half-way and down the creek is as marked on the map, climbing west away from the creek at the start and then coming back down to the creek. It is a long, long, straightforward trail with few distractions. Glide, shuffle, and enjoy the hours passing away under your skis. Move quickly across the avalanche fans which reach to the valley bottom.

The section from Strom's Ten-Mile Cabin back to Banff is often well-packed and provides a faster rate of travel for the afternoon stretch to Banff.

CASTLE MOUNTAIN MAIN PEAK

Advanced cross-country or ski mountaineering
Road, trail and exploration tour
24 kilometres (15 miles) return
Elevations: Trail head 4700+ feet
Tower Lake 6950+ feet
Rockbound Lake 7250 feet
Top of rock band 7700 feet
Top of bulge 8000 feet
Summit 9000+ feet
Map: Castle Mountain 82 0/5

This route to the main summit of Castle Mountain is entirely by ski except for the final ten metres which are easily completed by walking up small, north-facing, snow-filled couloirs and scrambling over easy rock. The ascent can be done either on cross-country skis or with ski-mountaineering equipment. The former provide a faster trip, but the heavier equipment may result in a more enjoyable descent.

Begin as for Tower and Rockbound Lakes. Consider three hours a fair time to reach Rockbound. (WARNING: if it takes longer, forget the rest of the ascent.) Proceed above the southwest shore of the lake to the point where the lake drains. This places you at the base of an obvious avalanche slope which provides the easiest means of cracking the major rock band surrounding the lake. (Do not proceed beyond this point if conditions are at all unstable.)

An obvious left-trending diagonal continues above the immediate slope to the top of a prominent but minor rock bulge. Traversing below this bulge in hopes of cracking the top section of the rock band further left places the skier on extremely hazardous avalanche slopes. To get above the bulge it may be easier to take off your skis to walk up the windblown ridge.

Atop the bulge (747856) plot a contouring course which gradually loses a bit of altitude to cross the major back drainage gully (742859). If you have mountaineering skis and skins, an almost direct line could be followed from here to the peak, though this would involve an excessive amount of up-and-down along the way. Although the back bowl area contains numerous side slopes and gullies not apparent on the map, it is a simple matter to proceed around on a relatively constant gradient.

Work around and upwards, aiming just left of the saddle between the main peaks and the unnamed peak (730852). This brings one just below the ridge at 736847. From here to the base of the final rocks of the main peak is a straightforward diagonal traverse just below the ridge. Again one is exposed to potential avalanche slopes, and great caution must be exercised. At the final rocks pick a usable gully and walk up to the summit.

Time from Rockbound to the summit: 3 - 4 hours
Total time highway to summit: 6 - 7 hours

Rockbound Lake showing the beginning of the Castle Mountain route.

FAY HUT

Advanced or Intermediate 3
Exploration and trail tour
13 kilometres (8 miles) one way
Elevations: Trail head 4850 feet
Fay drainage junction 5500 feet
Fay Hut 6900 feet
Maps: Mount Goodsir 82 N/1
Lake Louise 82 N/8

The Fay Hut is a climber's base cabin which is rarely used in the winter because of the problems of finding it and of negotiating the final rock band beneath it.

Begin as for *Tokumm Creek (Prospector's Valley).* The first ten kilometres are very straightforward, but count the drainages on your right as you ski up the valley. Many skiers become confused and attempt to ascend the third drainage as it looks very open and quite skiable, but the hut is in the fourth drainage and requires extremely good compass work to identify it from a tight valley bottom.

An obscure summer trail takes off to the right on the south side of the Fay drainage (grid reference 555776) but it is very difficult to follow and exceedingly steep and tight to ski. Ski up the creek until it narrows into a tight gorge. Turn back to the right (southeast) and traverse up the open side slopes, always aware of the avalanche threat, into the semi-open timber. Continue upward, climbing steeply along snow chutes and through the trees to one of two noticeable notches in the major rock band overhead. Depending on snow conditions one or both of the notches may be passable, or as is sometimes the case, neither notch will be passable. (You may have to return home or camp out.) The Fay Hut stands about 150 metres back at the apex between the two notches.

Of the skiers who attempt this trip only about fifty percent are successful in finding the hut. Plan accordingly.

Return the same way.

Time in: 4 - 6 hours
Time out: 2½ - 4 hours

STANLEY GLACIER VALLEY

Advanced cross-country
Trail and exploration tour
8 kilometres (5 miles) return
Elevations: Trail head 5200 feet
Start of meadows 6000 feet
Upper slopes 6500-7000 feet
Map: Mount Goodsir 82 N/1

The general characteristics of this trail are written up under *Stanley Glacier Trail (Novice 3)*, but three areas adjacent to the main route can, under the right conditions, offer some phenomenal powder runs for the advanced skier.

Returning down the valley bench, the burn is sufficiently open that an almost direct fall-line descent can be made through an area which is characteristically powder-filled (thanks to the partial wind cover provided by the remaining trees).

In the hanging valley proper, the northeast side is characterized by numerous avalanche slopes whose lower fans provide excellent skiing well below the fracture zones.

The far end of the valley, beyond the abrupt forest line, provides moderate, open ski slopes where one can easily spend a half-day continuously making new tracks.

TAYLOR LAKE AND O'BRIEN LAKE

Advanced 1
Trail tour
9 kilometres (5 miles) Taylor Lake return
Elevations: Trail head 4850 feet
Taylor Lake 6750 feet
O'Brien Lake 6950 feet
Map: Lake Louise 82 N/8

To me this is one of those "I wonder why people bother" type trails. The popularity this trail has experienced is probably due to the parking lot at the bottom (it is usually plowed so people probably assume it is a good place to ski). Not only is it a difficult trail, but heavy timber keeps the trail in chill shadow and views to a minimum. Only after a fresh snowfall does it become an enjoyable run for good skiers.

The parking lot is alongside Taylor Creek, eight kilometres west of Castle Junction. The initial two kilometres of trail are quite acceptable, but from then on it's an almost continual climb to the lake. The trail is very tight, the corners are blind, and the hills are very steep. Collisions are common. On a nice day the view at the lake may be worth it.

From Taylor Lake to O'Brien Lake forget about locating a trail. Bushwack along without losing altitude until you come to the O'Brien Creek drainage. Ski up the drainage to the lake. Return to Taylor Lake on the same track. Add appropriate time and distance.

From Taylor Lake, return cautiously down the same trail.

Time in: 2 - 4 hours
Time out: 1 - 2 hours

DOLOMITE PEAK CIRCUIT

Advanced 1
Trail and exploration tour
19 kilometres (12 miles) return
Elevations: Trail head 6200 feet
Katherine Lake 7750 feet
Dolomite East Col 8700 feet
Mosquito Creek bridge 6000 feet
Map: Hector Lake 82 N/9

The Dolomite Peak circuit should be saved for a fine spring day when the weather is guaranteed to remain clear, since the majority of the route is above timberline and susceptible to white-outs.

Begin as for *Katherine Lake—Helen Lake Circuit* and follow the route to Katherine Lake. Ski to the north end of Katherine Lake and turn east up an easy slope and onto Dolomite Pass. Descend slightly and traverse east and south below Dolomite Peak into the main drainage. On a southeast bearing, ski toward the col on the right side of the col drainage. The climb into the east col at 8300 feet is generally simple.

Once over the col the first 100 feet of descent are steep and wind-packed. It is sometimes best to walk down the top section until the snow improves and the steepness eases. The entire basin ahead is open, fast, enjoyable skiing. (Exercise caution on potential avalanche slopes.)

Follow the drainage into the trees and down to Mosquito Creek. Ski down along Mosquito Creek for one kilometre and watch for the summer trail as it branches to the right away from the creek. Then follow the trail down to the highway. (The creek can be followed all of the way out, but usually there is a better track along the summer trail.)

It is best to arrange this trip with two cars, leaving one at the Mosquito Creek bridge to welcome tired skiers.

Total time: 4 - 8 hours

CROWFOOT PASS

Advanced 1
Exploration tour
14 kilometres (8 miles)
Elevations: Trail head 6300 feet
Crowfoot Pass 7750 feet
Hector Lake 5750 feet
Map: Hector Lake 82 N/9

Crowfoot Pass is a small saddle between Bow Peak and Crowfoot Mountain. The route can be done on cross-country skis by a good skier, but it is more popular as a short test trip on mountaineering skis.

Park along the highway, two kilometres north of the Helen Creek bridge (it is not necessary to start at the summer trail head one kilometre further north). Contour along the east and south side of the hill, between the highway and the river, and head roughly for the forks of Crowfoot Creek and the Bow River.

If you can find the summer trail once across the Bow River, follow it. However, it is usually more trouble to follow than it is worth, and the route is as feasible up the creek bed (best left until February or March so that sufficient snow can drift into the creek pockets). Once up the creek to timberline the area opens out to small, rolling hills and easy, direct travel to the pass. (An exciting return can be made down the same trail if you can't arrange a pick-up vehicle at Hector Lake.)

To complete the traverse continue over the pass and follow down the obvious drainage on the south side. Once back to timberline the usual route goes straight down the creek.

There are some steep sections of ravine which may be more safely walked than skied. The only alternative to the steep, confined, but open creek travel is to negotiate the timber down the hillside east of the creek. (There are definite advantages to having mountaineering skis so you can tie your heels down.)

Whichever route you pick, head directly for the lake. The fastest way out is straight across the middle of the lake.

Simpson's cabins have been destroyed and no longer provide a landmark to locate the trail back to the highway. However, it is possible to bushwhack through almost anywhere up to the highway. (If you can arrange your pick-up vehicle to arrive early and have the driver ski down to the lake to meet you, you will save about an hour of frustration and trail-finding as well as vehicle-finding when you come out.)

Time into the pass: 2 - 3½ hours
Total time: 3 - 6 hours

WAPTA ICEFIELDS TRAVERSE

Advanced, ski mountaineering
Exploration tour and glacier travel
43 kilometres (27 miles)
Elevations: Peyto Lake 6050 feet
Peyto Hut 8100 feet
Peyto-Bow Neve Crest 8750 feet
Bow Lake 6350 feet
Bow Hut 8300 feet
Nicholas-Olive Col 9550 feet
Vulture Col 9750 feet
Balfour Hut 8200 feet
Balfour Pass 8050 feet
Balfour High Col 9800 feet
Niles-Daly Col 8650 feet
Wapta Lake 5200 feet
Maps: Blaeberry River 82 N/10
Hector Lake 82 N/9
Lake Louise 82 N/8

Though this may be a straightforward trip by mountaineering standards, it is nevertheless a major glacier traverse. Experience in glacier travel, crevasse rescue, map-and-compass travel, and avalanche slope evaluation is essential. Mountaineering equipment is recommended.

There are numerous alternate routes onto and off of the Wapta Icefields. Only the most common—access from Peyto and Bow Lakes and exit to Wapta Lake—will be described.

It is imperative that you register out with the Warden Service and that you reserve hut space for the nights required. This can be done in person at the Banff Warden Office, by phoning (403) 762-3324, or by writing Banff National Park, Box 900, Banff, Alberta, T0L 0C0.

The sleeping capacities of the huts vary from a low of ten at the Peter Whyte Hut to a high of twenty at the Bow Hut. It may be necessary to re-schedule your trip or bounce dates around if you do not reserve ahead of time.

The contents of the huts also vary from hut to hut and from year to year. (Check with the Lake Louise wardens on hut conditions and available contents.) It is best to travel independent of the huts for it is possible that you may not reach a hut one night, or you might arrive after a wolverine has just finished destroying it. Use the huts and enjoy them, but do not depend on them.

Peyto Lake to Peter Whyte Hut: Begin either from the highway opposite Peyto Lake or from the Peyto Lake Viewpoint on the Bow Summit. If you intend to return on your same track it is easiest to start from the lake. From the highway bushwhack to the lake, ski across, and proceed up the delta

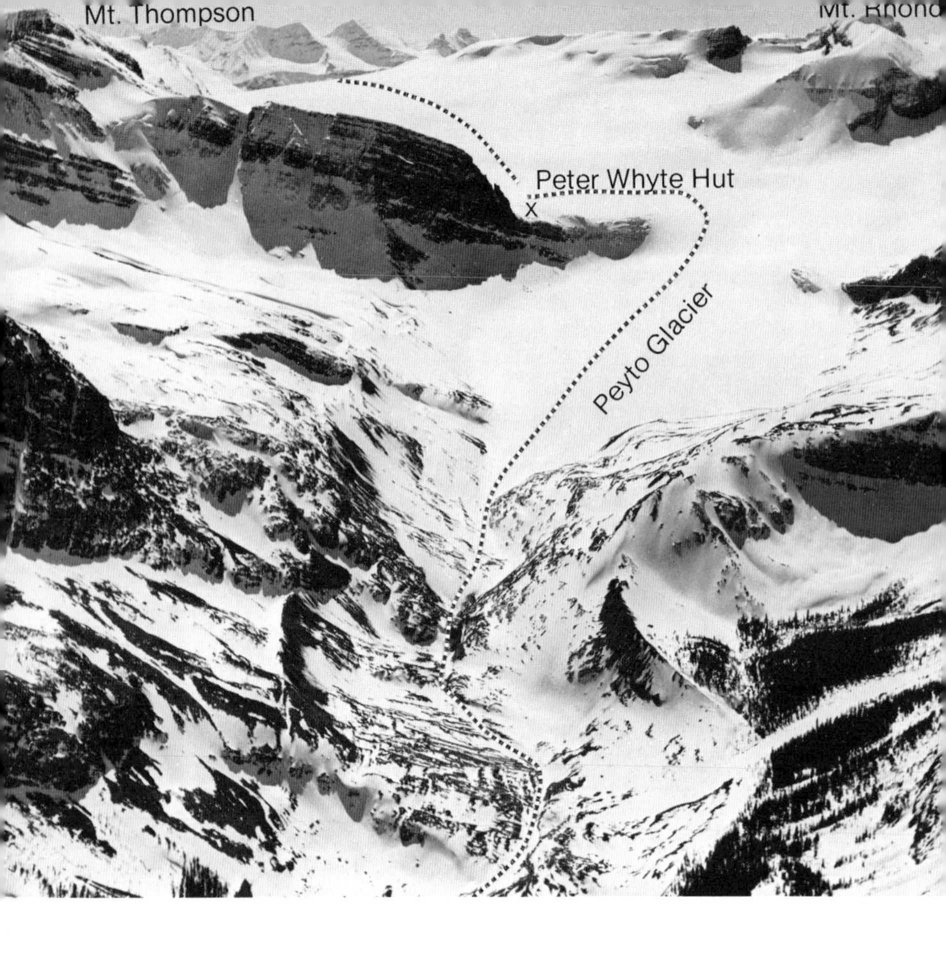

drainage; from the viewpoint contour west and gradually work down the slope to arrive at the valley-bottom near the upper end of the delta. The latter is a steep, heavily-treed slope, but it is the quickest way to the Peyto Glacier.

Follow up the stream bed through several narrowing side passages. As the main gorge tightens climb up and above to the southeast (left) side of the creek. It is usually necessary to take your skis off to climb a fifty foot pitch through the steepest section of the gorge. Once above this, rolling moraines lead to the glacier proper.

Approach the ice at the centre of the toe where the crevasses are minimal and proceed up the glacier along the centreline. As you approach the lower cliff bands of Mount Thompson gradually swing south (left) in a wide arc to get around and behind the rock band.

The Peter Whyte Hut—two fiberglass igloos—sits on a rock shelf just around the corner and off the ice (grid reference 314239).

Time from Peyto Lake Viewpoint to Peter Whyte Hut: 3 - 4 hours

Peter Whyte Hut to Bow Hut: Travel from the Peter Whyte Hut on the Peyto Glacier to the Bow Hut is very straightforward. Simply head south and aim for the centre of the snowfield between Mounts Rhonda and Thompson. Once over the rolling benches the world levels out to an incredibly flat expanse of pure white. Aim for Saint Nicholas Peak (346196) and continue across the flat on this bearing until about one kilometre away. Then turn east (sharp left) and begin the descent to the hut. Bow Hut is located on a rock spur just below Saint Nicholas, above and to the side of the glacier toe (grid reference 348206).

Note: on the topographical maps Saint Nicholas Peak appears in two different locations—346196 and 368192. In the text, and to everyone indigenous to the Rockies, Saint Nicholas refers to the former, more westerly peak only.

Time from Peter Whyte to Bow Hut: 1½ - 2½ hours

Bow Lake to Bow Hut: Park in the plowed parking area beside the entrance of the road into Num-ti-jah Lodge. Start out skiing straight across the lake headed for the centre of the valley which drains below Saint Nicholas. (The summer trail along the shore is longer and quite unnecessary.)

From the end of the lake, ski up the creek and into a large barren basin. This open basin leads on to a tight gorge. If there is enough snow it is possible to continue on straight up the creek.

The summer trail, and the alternate route, crosses to the east (left) side early into the gorge and continues along the side slope above the creek. Finally, the route opens up above treeline into a tight cirque basin. Continue up the main drainage to within a half-kilometre of the cirque headwall and turn to the northwest (sharp right). A steep climb up several rolling steps brings you to the Bow Hut (348206). (The upper sections of this access valley are extremely prone to avalanches; be certain of conditions before following this route.)

Time in: 2½ - 4 hours

Bow Hut to Balfour Hut: Though on the photograph it appears that one can ski directly from Bow Hut onto the Vulture Glacier by following a simple line east of Saint Nicholas Peak, it is safer and easier to take the normal route around Saint Nicholas.

From the hut ski west and south, up and around Saint Nicholas to the Nicholas-Olive Col. This is a very low col which is only about 100 feet higher than the more dangerous direct route onto the Vulture Glacier. Continue over the col and out onto the Vulture, heading south along the east side of the twin peaks of Mount Olive. Stay well out on the glacier, maintaining at least 300 metres away from the mountain to avoid crevasses and rock fall.

A straightforward, enjoyable ski brings you quickly down the Vulture Glacier to Balfour Pass. The hut is located on a rock outcrop just above the pass on the north side (grid reference 368156).

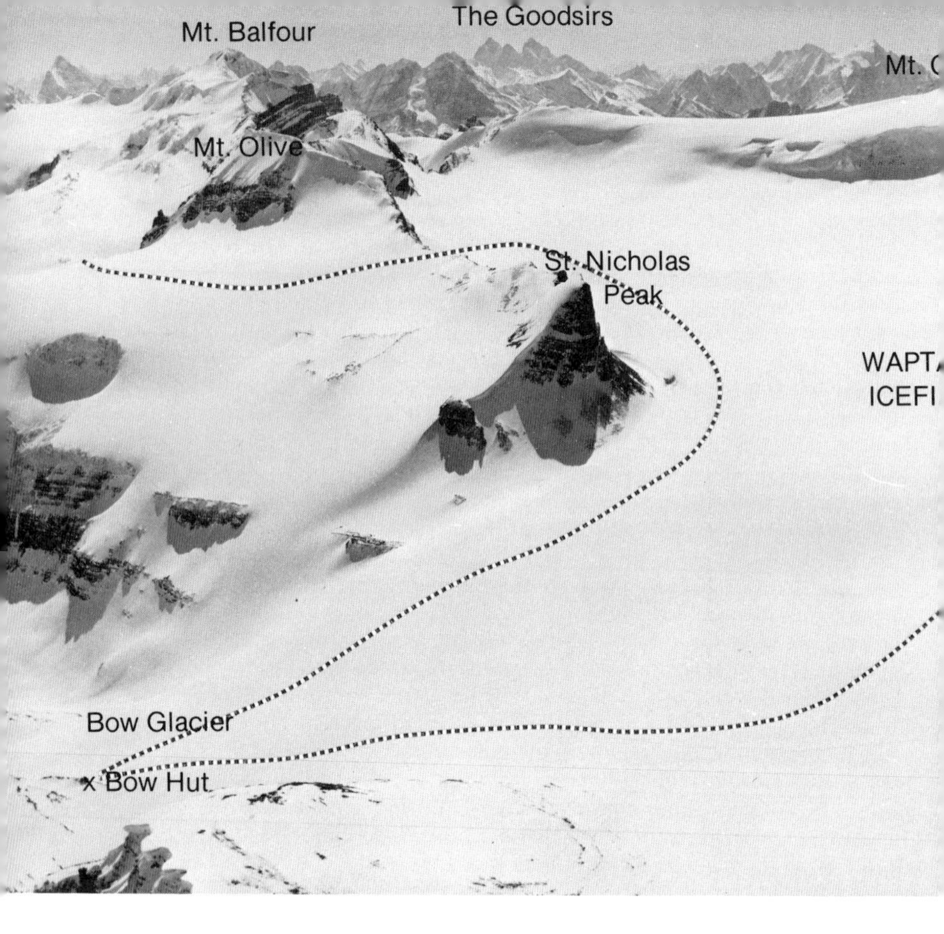

Time from Bow to Balfour Hut: 2½ - 4 hours

A more direct alternate route can be taken through Vulture Col. The south side of the col is very steep, and snow conditions are generally very hard and crusty for the first 200 feet of descent. (Recommended only for good skiers under stable conditions.)

Under ideal conditions the times between the huts are very short, providing ample opportunity to enjoy short ascents of such peaks as Mount Gordon, Mount Olive, and Saint Nicholas Peak. However, the area is very prone to storm and white-out conditions, and it may often require a full day to travel laboriously by map and compass from hut to hut. Keep a sharp eye out for the weather and travel accordingly.

Balfour Hut to Wapta Lake: The last leg of the Wapta Icefields Traverse is the longest. It requires the most time and traverses the most dangerous areas. A pre-dawn start is recommended so that the Sherbrooke avalanche chutes may be descended before mid-day spring instabilities occur.

From the Balfour Hut ski down to the pass, over the moraines and onto

the Waputik Icefield along the east slopes of Mount Balfour. The north spur of Balfour is heavily corniced and is subject to cornice-released avalanches at any time of the day. Travel quickly and efficiently, with an eye on the cornices above, directly up the lower icefield to the midway icefall. This broken, crevassed area is obvious from the hut and is often littered with fresh debris from the glaciers hanging above to the west.

Negotiate the icefall on the east (left) side as efficiently as possible and avoid stopping until you are well above it and onto the smooth unbroken shoulder which leads up to the high col. At 9,750 feet, the Balfour High Col (grid reference 387118) is the high point of the trip; except for a short climb to the Niles-Daly Col, everything is downhill from here on.

Proceed southeasterly down from the Balfour High Col in a large arc across the top of the Daly Glacier. If the snow pack is hard, one can ski for almost four kilometres without having to do anything more than an occasional push with your ski poles.

Though the area is relatively unbroken, there are a couple of major sinkholes which must be watched for carefully if visibility is poor. At the end

of the run continue the arc on a constant contour toward the isolated peak of Mount Niles.

A short climb into the Niles-Daly Col generally leads to a brief lunch break and a chance to ponder the seriousness of the confined run to Sherbrooke Lake immediately below.

Ski down from the col bearing slightly west (right) along the upper sections toward the Niles Creek drainage, stopping for route selection only in avalanche protected areas. This necessitates quick thinking and rapid travel between protected vantage points as the route works down the series of benches.

Niles Creek runs into Sherbrooke Creek, and the route continues along Sherbrooke Creek onto the lake. Ski directly across the middle of Sherbrooke Lake and follow the summer trail, as on the map, out to the highway.

Time from Balfour Hut to Wapta Lake: 6 - 8 hours

CASTLEGUARD MEADOWS

Advanced, camping (ski mountaineering)
Exploration tour and glacier travel
15 kilometres (9 miles) one way
Elevations: Trail head 5400 feet
Glacier toe 5850 feet
Castleguard Meadows 7350 feet
Map: Columbia Icefields 83 C/3

On a sunny day in the spring the Castleguard Meadows rank as one of the most beautiful trips in the Rockies. Under ideal conditions with a strong group the journey can be accomplished in a long day, but the ski potential of the area warrants a one or two night camp.

Begin at the Big Bend on the Icefields Parkway, 12 kilometres south of Sunwapta Pass (the north boundary of Banff Park). The highway is not quite as marked on the map. Either watch for a bridge and an old road below the highway at 958797 or drive through to the parking area on the bend before the long hill.

The old army road is roughly as marked (on the south side of the open gravel wash) and can be approached via the old bridge, or by merely skiing across the gravel flat and up the south bank. Once onto the old road simply follow it up the valley and over a forested ridge. (The river passes through the ridge via a very tight gorge. It is not skiable.)

Once onto the gravel flats beyond the ridge travel becomes very open and straightforward. Pick a line, any line, straight up the valley to the Saskatchewan Glacier. This glacier is probably the flattest, easiest, and safest glacier to travel in the entire Rocky Mountains. However, this is no reason not to take the usual precautions for travelling over glaciers.

The center of the ice tongue provides the safest route of travel at present and will probably remain so. As you pass through the gap between Mount Athabaska and Mount Saskatchewan slowly veer south, aiming to leave the ice at 870756.

Off the ice, a short climb up the natural draw leads onto the height of land and over to the beginning of the Castleguard Meadows. The meadows provide easy open travelling with a multitude of interesting short runs along both flanks.

Good snow drifts abound along the side of the meadow for snow caves. A very interesting alternate campsite is the entrance to the Castleguard Cave. A steel gate 40 metres into the cave blocks access to the cave itself, but the entrance-way is large enough to accommodate 20 skiers and still have plenty of room. It is a large, dry, unique place to camp.

Since present park policy is to discourage cave exploration, I'll simply say the entrance is at approximately 851690. Do not depend on finding it. It is easy to miss if you don't know where to look. Permission to enter the cave (and the key) must be obtained from the Superintendent of Banff National Park if you are intent on doing some caving.

Return the same way.

Time in to the middle meadows: 4 - 6 hours
Time out: 2 - 4 hours

An easy overnight loop trip can be made by skiing down the Castleguard River and out along the Alexandra River Fire Road. However, it is long, mundane, boring, and in the woods. (Avoid the canyon in the upper sections of the Castleguard River, otherwise it's straightforward.)

LAKE O'HARA—OPABIN PASS—WENKCHEMNA PASS—MORAINE LAKE

Advanced cross-country and ski mountaineering
Exploration, trail and road tour
18 kilometres (11 miles) plus the Moraine Lake Road
Elevations: Lake O'Hara 6650 feet
Opabin Pass 8550 feet
Eagle's Eyrie 7400 feet
Wenkchemna Pass 8550 feet
Moraine Lake 6190 feet
Maps: Lake Louise 82 N/8

The Lake O'Hara to Moraine Lake traverse is one of the most spectacular day trips available to advanced skiers. While the trip can be completed in less time on cross-country equipment, heavier mountaineering skis are usually preferable.

Since the trip is long and rigorous, it is best to spend the night at Lake O'Hara and jump off to an early start in the morning. From Lake O'Hara Lodge ski along the south side of the lake to the Opabin drainage. Follow up the creek and onto the Opabin moors—an area which is wide and open with scattered trees providing easy idyllic skiing past Opabin and Hungabee Lakes.

As the terrain becomes steeper cross to the right side of the drainage and onto the rolling hills in a direct line for the pass. The area is so open that almost any line of travel can be assumed, but the right side of the plateau is more convenient. Travelling on the right puts one in the proximity of the Schäffer-Biddle slides, however, so caution should be taken to remain well below the run-out areas.

The approach onto the Opabin Glacier has always been easiest from the centre of the valley, although this may change in time. Once onto the ice continue right of centre or along the northeast (far left) side. One large

Opabin Pass

sinkhole must be avoided and small crevasses should be cautiously crossed with standard precautions. (In a normal winter the Opabin glaciers on both sides of the pass present very few open crevasses or problem areas, still they should be respected as glaciers and the requisite additional equipment should be carried.)

The final approach to Opabin Pass is easiest from the left side even though the centre of the bowl is more direct.

Time to Opabin Pass: 2½ - 4½ hours

The Prospector's Valley side of Opabin and Wenkchemna Passes presents very steep and potentially dangerous avalanche slopes which cannot be avoided. Additional avalanche equipment is essential.

From Opabin Pass an exciting, open, and fast downhill run to the Eagle's Eyrie can be made in 10 to 15 minutes. The Eyrie provides a great lunch stop, but the visit entails losing an additional one hundred feet from the more direct contour to the base of Wenkchemna Pass.

The bowl leading up to Wenkchemna Pass is entirely treeless and has a scree base, thus it is extremely prone to avalanches especially after a fresh snowfall or on a warm, spring afternoon. Assess the situation carefully before proceeding up to the pass.

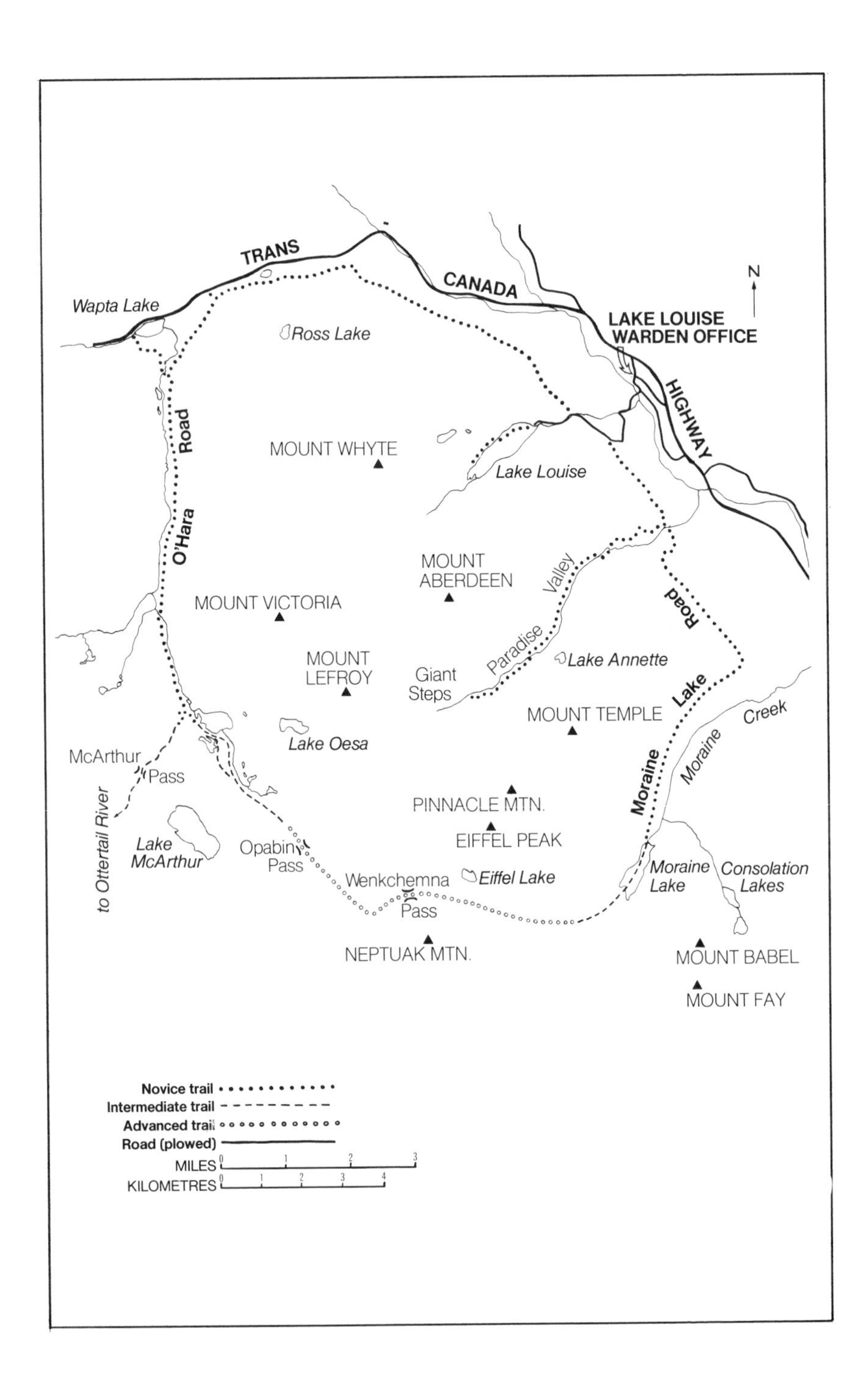
TRANS
CANADA
HIGHWAY
N
LAKE LOUISE
WARDEN OFFICE
Wapta Lake
Ross Lake
O'Hara
Road
MOUNT WHYTE
Lake Louise
MOUNT ABERDEEN
Paradise
Valley
Giant Steps
Road
MOUNT VICTORIA
MOUNT LEFROY
Lake Annette
Moraine
Lake
MOUNT TEMPLE
Lake Oesa
McArthur
Pass
to Ottertail River
Lake McArthur
Opabin Pass
Wenkchemna
Pass
PINNACLE MTN.
EIFFEL PEAK
Eiffel Lake
Moraine
Creek
Moraine Lake
Consolation Lakes
NEPTUAK MTN.
MOUNT BABEL
MOUNT FAY
Novice trail
Intermediate trail
Advanced trail
Road (plowed)
MILES
0
1
2
3
KILOMETRES
0
1
2
3
4

The last 100 metres to the pass are usually windblown and void of snow necessitating a short scramble carrying your skis.

Time from Eagle's Eyrie to Wenkchemna Pass: 1½ - 2½ hours

From the top of Wenkchemna Pass an almost direct line can be taken to Moraine Lake. (Forget about the summer trail; it is difficult to follow in the upper reaches and only adds time.) Proceed downward on a rough bearing toward the hanging glacier between Mounts Babel and Fay. Maintain an easy rate of descent keeping well to the south of Eiffel Lake.

Continue along the moraine keeping the major longitudinal moraine ridge just above to the right of you. Near the base of the Wenkchemna Glacier there are two or three major sink holes which should be passed on the north (left) side.

At the end of the glacier drop down into the drainage and follow the creek to Moraine Lake. Ski across the lake rather than bothering to locate the summer trail.

Time from Wenkchemna Pass to Moraine Lodge: 1 - 3 hours
Total time O'Hara to Moraine: 6 - 10 hours

The Moraine Lake Lodge is closed in the winter, and there are no camping facilities. Luckily the Moraine Lake Road is heavily skied and usually provides a fast track for the final two or three hours to the Lake Louise Road.

ICE RIVER VALLEY

Advanced winter camping
Road and trail tour
48 kilometres (30 miles) return
Elevations: Leanchoil Bridge 3650 feet
Lower Ice River Warden Cabin 4200 feet
Ice River Meadows 4900 feet
Maps: McMurdo 82 N/2
Mount Goodsir 82 N/1

The Ice River Valley is very spectacular, very remote, and very rarely travelled. The Ice River is best known for its summer access to the west side of the Goodsirs.

See report under novice section for the Ice River Fire Road and ski to the end of the road. (Time: 3 - 6 hours.) On the north side of the river is the Lower Ice River Warden Cabin, and across the river is a B.C. Forest Service cabin. Neither cabin is open for public use so use your tent or dig a snow cave.

From the Lower Ice River Cabin cross the bridge, ski left behind the provincial cabin, and locate the blazes marking the horse trail up the Ice River above the east bank. The trail originally stayed inside the park skirting the west bank for the first 1.5 kilometres then crossing to the east bank where the boundary diverges from the river. In the early seventies a major avalanche wiped out a section of trail piling debris too deep to clear. Damming and flooding at this point washed out other sections. The old bridge is still there but don't be confused by it on your return.

Follow the summer horse trail up the east bank and move quickly across the several avalanche slopes which cross the trail. About six kilometres up from the bridge one passes the Upper Ice River Warden Cabin, and in another kilometre the Ice River meadows begin to open up.

Travel through the meadows is best done along the river bank, traversing back and forth on the snow bridges whenever necessary and avoiding piles of avalanche debris. (The Upper Ice River Valley should definitely be avoided when the avalanche hazard is high.)

Return the same way.

Time in: 1½ - 2 days
Time out: 1 day

Jasper Trails

"In the Crisp of the Morning." Taken in the Tonquin Valley by pioneer skier Joe Weiss during the 1930's.

JASPER NATIONAL PARK

Jasper National Park occupies a vast area covering approximately 11,000 square kilometres of the northern Rockies. Moreover, it is surrounded by equally wild terrain on all sides. The landscape is characterized by wide river valleys, three distinct sub-regions of the Rocky Mountains, major icefields and glaciers and a great diversity of wildlife. Only 800 square kilometres of the park are sheltered valley bottom land, with at least sixty percent being characterized as alpine.

Two major highways bisect the park. The Yellowhead Highway, Highway 16, runs east-west, and the Icefields Parkway, Highway 93, runs south to Lake Louise. Jasper townsite is located at the intersection of Highways 93 and 16 and has winter population of 4,000. A quieter relative of Banff, Jasper offers complete visitor services. Beyond the highways and townsite, secondary roads to Maligne Lake and Marmot Basin Ski Area provide access to prime ski terrain. All these roads are open in winter, except during snow and avalanche closure periods.

The winter weather is similar to the rest of the mountain parks, but snowfall (a function of elevation) is generally less than Banff which is 335 metres higher in elevation than Jasper. Because the Rockies are subjected to two distinct weather patterns, great variations are possible throughout the winter, although Jasper is seldom affected by strong chinook conditions. Extreme cold spells lasting two weeks or more are common and cold periods can appear suddenly.

The snowpack is deeper at higher elevations and closer to the Continental Divide. The eastern valleys may experience very low snowpacks. During the early winter, depth hoar or sugar snow is usually present at the bottom of the snowpack making for frustrating trailbreaking and extreme avalanche hazard.

The summer trail system in Jasper is well established and provides a basic framework for winter skiing. Many of the trails are well adapted to skiing with opportunities for all levels of skiers; they range from regularly maintained (track-set) to simple routes requiring trail breaking and considerable route finding.

Ski information is available at the Parks Information Centre in Jasper townsite (open from 9 a.m. to 5 p.m. daily). Snow and avalanche conditions are available from the Warden Service office. The park naturalists offer guided ski trips emphasizing the natural history of the park.

Detailed topographic maps are for sale at the Park Information Centre. Many of the 1:50,000 scale topographic maps for Jasper have recently been revised and updated. The newest ones give contour elevations in metres. These intervals vary on each map: some use an interval of 20 metres below the 2000 metre elevation line and 40 metres above the 2000 metre line. This confusing method should be noted when using these particular maps. Throughout this ski guide, the grid reference system, designated by six numbers in brackets, is used to denote specific points (the system is explained on the margin of the 1:50,000 topographic maps).

Maintained cross-country trails in Jasper are located at two centralized locations. The trails on the benchlands above Jasper are track-set through the winter on a semi-regular basis; the Whistlers Campground is included in this program. The Maligne Lake area, because of consistent snow and a pristine winter setting, has become a very popular centre for cross-country skiing in Jasper. The main trails are track-set on a regular basis. The Maligne Lake Chalet is open daily during the ski season except Tuesdays and Wednesdays.

Voluntary registration for ski touring is available at the Park Information Centre or at the Warden Office; this service requires the return of the registration (signing-in) when the trip is completed. Overnight trips (including winter camping and use of huts and cabins) require a park use permit, also available at the Information Centre. Backcountry Warden patrol cabins and other government facilities are locked and not available to the public.

Professional guide services and ski touring/avalanche schools are available locally. Week-long guided ski tours to many areas of the park are also available. Information can be obtained through the Parks Canada Visitor Services office or the Park Information Centre.

Snowmobiles are permitted on designated trails in Jasper National Park. A permit is required. Since some ski trails are used by snowmobiles, conflicts and incompatibilities exist.

Novice

PYRAMID BENCH TRAIL

Novice 3
Cross-country trail tour
4 kilometres (2.5 miles)
Map: Jasper 83 D/16, or
Jasper Park Ski Trail Sheet

An enjoyable but short loop trail starts at the Pyramid Riding Stables parking area, 4 kilometres from Jasper on the Pyramid Lake Road.

Start at the far end of the parking area, following the trail through a mixed forest of aspen, spruce, fir and pine. Some of the large Douglas fir trees in this area have survived numerous forest fires, standing now as sentinels above the rest of the forest on the benchlands.

The trail reaches the edge of a steep stream embankment above the Athabasca Valley after .8 kilometres. The view south and east to the surrounding peaks is superb from this vantage point. Here the trail continues along the edge of the embankment and loops back to the parking lot.

Time around loop: 45 minutes

PATRICIA LAKE CIRCLE

Novice 3
Cross-country trail tour
5 kilometres (3 miles)
Map: Jasper 83 D/16, or
Jasper Park Ski Trail Sheet

This loop trail is an excellent opportunity for a longer outing, nature observations or training. There is a variety of steep sections and tight corners, with plenty of level forested terrain between.

Start by parking at the Pyramid Lake Riding Stables and ski back along the access road, crossing Pyramid Lake Road. Beginning the trail here, it is suggested to ski clockwise following the left fork to Cottonwood Slough and down to the shore of Patricia Lake. The trail climbs very steeply for 100 metres and then levels out. Elk can often be seen in the forest along this loop.

Time around loop: 1 - 2 hours

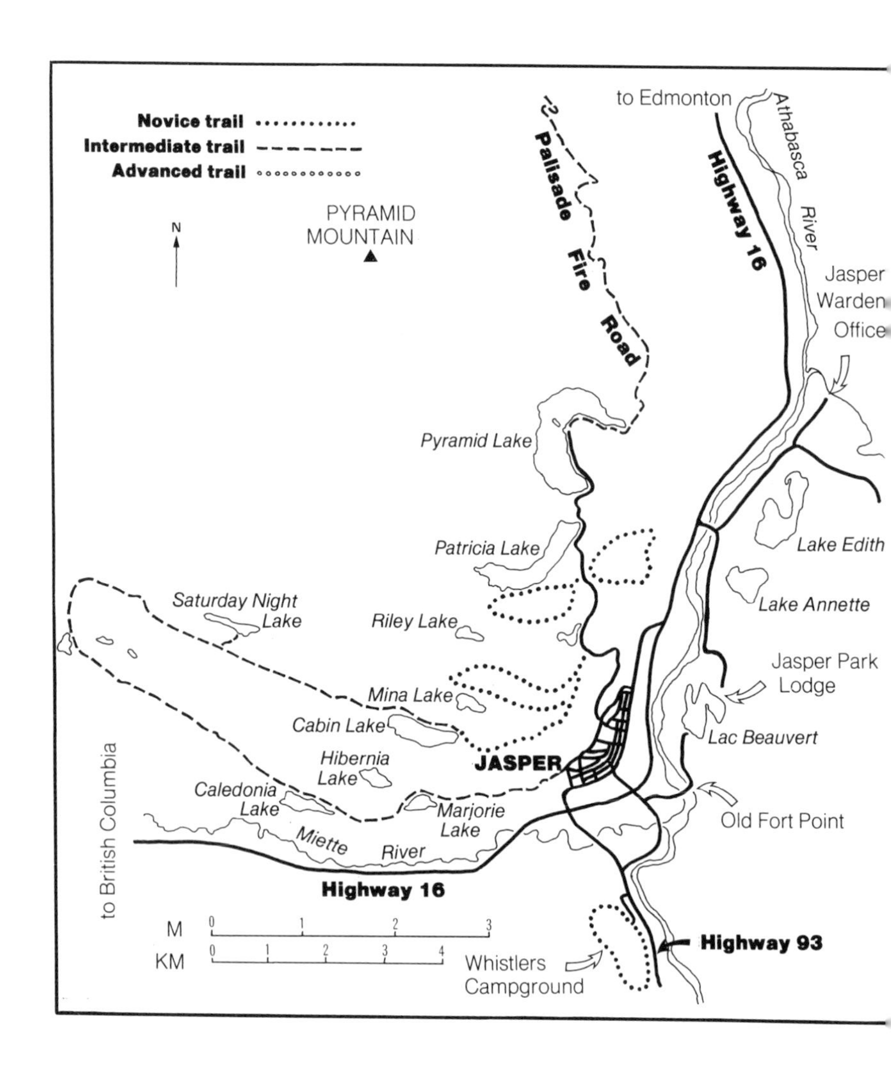

Novice trail
Intermediate trail
Advanced trail
N
PYRAMID
MOUNTAIN
to Edmonton
Palisade Fire Road
Highway 16
Athabasca River
Jasper
Warden
Office
Pyramid Lake
Patricia Lake
Lake Edith
Lake Annette
Saturday Night
Lake
Riley Lake
Jasper Park
Lodge
Mina Lake
Cabin Lake
Lac Beauvert
Hibernia
Lake
JASPER
to British Columbia
Caledonia
Lake
Marjorie
Lake
Old Fort Point
Miette River
Highway 16
M
KM
Highway 93
Whistlers
Campground

MINA LAKE LOOP

Novice 3
Road and trail tour
6.5 kilometres (4 miles)
Map: Jasper 83 D/16, or
Jasper Park Ski Trail Sheet

This very enjoyable loop trail offers a variety of rolling terrain through moderately dense forest cover and slightly more solitude and length than the other bench trails.

The trailhead is located 2.2 kilometres from Jasper on the Pyramid Lake Road at the Cottonwood Slough parking area. The first section follows the Cabin Creek fire road for 1.6 kilometres then turns right and heads along the Mina Lake trail. The skiing is through rolling terrain with two short, steeper sections to add variety. At the far end of the loop, the trail swings back east and a spur trail at 3.5 kilometres to Riley Lake is encountered where a short side trip may be made. The remainder of the trail is through similar terrain until the fire road is reached and followed back to the parking area.

Time around loop: 2 - 3 hours

PYRAMID AND PATRICIA LAKESHORES

Novice 1
Trail tour
6 kilometres (3.5 miles) Pyramid Lake
5 kilometres (3 miles) Patricia Lake
Map: Jasper 83 D/16

Both Pyramid and Patricia Lakes offer limited skiing opportunities along their lakeshores. There are no established trails and inconsistent freezing and possible springs cause holes and thin ice to appear from time to time on both lakes. Blowing snow may cover and obscure these hazards, adding to the problem.

If the skier stays close to the shoreline, an enjoyable outing is possible, further enhanced by wide views to many of the peaks up and down the valley. The skiing is level and even when the snowpack is limited these lakeshores offer enough cover for excellent practice and conditioning. Access from Jasper townsite is by the Pyramid Lake Road and plowed pullouts along the lakes are available.

Time: 1 - 4 hours for both lakes

WHISTLERS CAMPGROUND LOOP

Novice 1
Cross-country trail tour
5 kilometres (3 miles) total loop
Map: Jasper 83 D/16

Whistlers Campground, closed during the winter months, offers novice skiers, experts in training, and the family a handy track-set loop within minutes of Jasper townsite.

Travel 3.2 kilometres south on Highway 93, turn right onto the Whistlers Campground/Skytram road and follow the short campground access road to the dead end parking area. The track, maintained by Jasper National Park, follows the loop periphery road around the entire campground and ends back at the parking area. In the past, the road lights have been turned on at night during the ski season, allowing evening skiing opportunities.

Time around loop: 30 - 60 minutes

VALLEY OF THE FIVE LAKES

Novice 3 to Intermediate 2
Trail tour
11 kilometres (7 miles) to Old Fort Point
8 kilometres (5 miles) to Wabasso Lake
Maps: Medicine Lake 83 C/13
Jasper 83 D/16

The Valley of the Five Lakes is actually a series of minor forested depressions at the base of the Maligne Range, some 5 to 15 kilometres south of Jasper. This entire area occupies the Athabasca Valley bottom proper with only a few high points and landmarks and numerous side trails to contend with. Hence travel can be disorienting, even though it is comforting to know that Highway 93 lies only 3 to 4 kilometres to the west. At the north end lies Old Fort Point near Jasper, while Wabasso Lake marks the south terminus. Because of three entry-exit points, many options are possible.

Access to the midpoint trail is located at the marked parking area 10 kilometres south of Jasper on Highway 93. A short ski of 800 metres through the pine forest, across a bridge and up a low, open ridge presents a good view west and a choice of continuing north or south on the main trail from this midpoint intersection. Northward, or left, the trail continues over the hogback, meeting the junction of the access trail to the actual five lakes. By bearing left at this junction, the skier will be on the main trail (Parks designation #9) which alternately descends and climbs a series of small terrain features, follows a drainage and crosses Tekarra Creek. After some 6.2 kilometres the trail to Old Fort Point (Parks designation #1A) is met. Turn right and ski two kilometres to the parking area where a second car can be left.

Time in to Five Lakes junction: 30 minutes to 1 hour
Time from Highway 93 to Old Fort Point: 3 - 5 hours

By turning south or right at the midpoint intersection, a rather straightforward trail travels along a creek and marshlands through prime winter elk range. After 5.5 kilometres a bridge should be crossed back over the creek where a short 200 metre trail bearing to the right leads to Wabasso Lake. (See Wabasso Lake entry to continue out to Highway 93.)

Time from Highway 93 to Wabasso Lake: 2 - 4 hours
Time from Old Fort Point to Wabasso Lake: 5 - 7 hours

WABASSO LAKE

Novice 3
Trail tour
3 kilometres (2 miles)
Map: Medicine Lake 83 C/13

The trail to Wabasso Lake starts from the marked parking area 15 kilometres south of Jasper on Highway 93. After a short, steep initial climb and descent over a worn rock outcrop, the trail follows level terrain through the montane forest, crossing a creek after 1.5 kilometres. Passing a summer marsh, the trail crosses another stream twice on narrow log bridges and quickly climbs a short incline. From here it is 500 metres to the Lake where the trail can be followed around the left shore. A connection can be made to the Valley of the Five Lakes trail at the far right corner of the lake.

Time in: 30 minutes to 1 hour
Time out: 30 minutes to 1 hour

MOAB LAKE

Novice 1
Road tour
19 kilometres (12 miles) return
Map: Athabasca Falls 83 C/12

The Whirlpool Valley Fire Road to Moab Lake is a flat valley bottom approach to the famous and historic Athabasca Pass. A few views do redeem this otherwise thickly forested setting. The fire road is open to snowmobile use to Moab Lake, as is alternate Highway 93A from the picnic site at the confluence of the Whirlpool and Athabasca Rivers to Athabasca Falls on the Icefields Parkway. The fire road does provide an opportunity for flat road skiing, and if the prospect of machines along the way does not disturb one, this area is good for novices searching for a few hours of straightforward level skiing.

Drive to the Meeting of the Waters picnic site on Highway 93A. Ski south along the unplowed road for 2.3 kilometres and turn right up the fire road. The Moab Lake gate is reached after 6.5 kilometres. The Lake is 500 metres further along. Return is the same.

Time in: 3 hours
Time out: 3 hours

GERALDINE LOOKOUT

Novice 3
Road tour
18 kilometres (11.5 miles) return
Elevations: Athabasca Falls 1173 metres
Geraldine Lookout 1700 metres
First Geraldine Lake 1620 metres
Map: Athabasca Falls 83 C/12

The fire road to Geraldine Lookout provides an opportunity for skiers to climb out of the valley on a wide, moderately steep trail. This road, one of four fire road possibilities for skiers in Jasper, is generally not too popular, perhaps because of often variable snow conditions on the lower sections and seemingly monotonous forest travel. However, for a quiet day-trip through the winter woods with a good view thrown in at the top, this trail is worthy of more use.

Start out from the Athabasca Falls parking lot, 31.0 kilometres south of Jasper on the Icefields Parkway. Ski along alternate route 93A from the parking lot, which is not plowed in winter, and across the bridge over the Athabasca River. Here a view of the frozen and subdued Athabasca Falls is worth a stop. The full force of the Athabasca is directed over the

Cambrian rock strata to form the falls. Ski down the road, which is open to snowmobiles during certain times of the winter, for 1.1 kilometres to the actual Geraldine Fire Road intersection.

Turn left up the fire road, which is gated and not open to snowmobiles at any time, and follow the obvious level track through the montane forest. The first 2.0 kilometres to the Fryatt Valley trail head provide a quiet winter setting, and the observant skier may see downy woodpeckers, mountain chickadees and other winter birds or the tracks of the wary lynx. The road climbs steadily and if snow conditions have been a bit crusted or glazed lower down, they should improve with the gain in elevation.

After 5.5 kilometres the spur trail to the Geraldine Lakes is passed on the left and a second gate appears as the road swings to the northwest. The views from then on improve steadily. Across the Athabasca Valley is Mount Kerkeslin, 2956 metres high, with white snow outlining its red quartzite ledges. The last 2.5 kilometres to the fire tower climb two or three more steep sections before the view from the top is revealed.

Below the tower viewpoint stretches the broad Whirlpool Valley, snaking out of sight to the west to the legendary Athabasca Pass. Directly across the valley is Mount Edith Cavell with a different profile from the south. (The tower should not be climbed and its outbuildings are not open to the public).

The return journey down the wide road is a simple venture. However, the two or three steeper sections and corners will provide fast skiing, especially if conditions are icy. As always, downhill skiers have the right-of-way.

Time in: 3 to 4 hours
Time out: 1 to 2 hours

The 1.8 kilometre long spur trail to the first Geraldine Lake, although steep and narrow in spots, is skiable. It intersects the fire road just before the second gate, 5.5 kilometres from its start. Climbing 120 metres to the lake through heavy forest, the trail follows approximately the outlet stream to the north shore. The summer trail continues along the west shore to the steep rockfall at the end. This should be considered the end of the line for all but the most advanced skiers. The return ski can be quite wild as the numerous steep sections and narrow trail will require extreme care and ability beyond that necessary for the fire road tour.

Time in: 1 - 2 hours from the fire road
Time out: 30 minutes - 1 hour

WHISTLERS CREEK

Novice 3 to Intermediate 1
Trail and exploration tour
5 kilometres (3 miles) to upper creek one way
Elevations: Trail head 1800 metres
Upper Whistlers Creek 2100 metres
Indian Pass 2440 metres
Marmot Pass 2240 metres
Map: Jasper 83 D/16

The undesignated trail up Whistlers Creek is the only opportunity for cross-country touring in the immediate vicinity of the Marmot Basin Ski Area. It is a fine ski trip in itself or provides an option for downhillers who have a few skinny-ski types in the group.

Drive to Marmot Basin, 20 kilometres south of Jasper. Park in the next to last parking lot (#3). The trail head is not marked, but is located directly opposite the parking lot entrance, across the road and up the steep ditchside. Ski immediately through an opening in the trees and across an open bog area along the left edge. At the far end (left corner) locate an obscure trail heading into the forest. This rough, narrow cut follows along the sidehill above Whistlers Creek, contouring left for 1.5 kilometres and merging into the creek bottom. Once out on the creek, simply follow it to the upper open glades where views to Terminal Mountain improve steadily. Most novices will find this a good stopping point.

The upper end of the valley is marked by a split in the drainnage and two possible alternatives for further skiing, both requiring higher levels of skill. By bearing right, Indian and Whistlers Pass are 3.5 kilometres to the northwest through the treeless, exposed upper basin. Snow conditions are often very windpacked here. A line along the north side of the basin will avoid possible avalanche hazard off Terminal and Manx Peak.

Up the other, lefthand drainage, Marmot Pass is located. Ski in a southeast direction, toward the obvious low point at the base of the red-brown ridge of Terminal Mountain. Stay in the trees as long as possible, avoiding the steeper slopes on the approach to the pass. The trees run out where the slope lessens and the pass lies directly ahead in a small notch. There are a number of small avalanche-prone gullies and slopes all the way to the pass. Portal Creek lies on the other side of Marmot Pass, making a loop connection possible (see Portal Creek description). However, avalanche hazard on this side of the pass is very real and must be thoroughly considered. A car pickup would also be required.

The return down Whistlers Creek is fast and tight; keep speed down, watch for ascending skiers and do not miss the turn-off back into the forest.

Time into Upper Whistlers Creek: 3 hours
Time out: 1 - 2 hours

SUMMIT LAKES - JACQUES LAKE

Novice 3 or Intermediate 1
Trail tour
23 kilometres (14.5 miles) Jacques Lake return
Elevations: Trail head 1463 metres
Summit Lakes 1494 metres
Jacques Lake 1500 metres
Map: Medicine Lake 83 C/13

The trail head for the Summit-Jacques Lakes trail is located at the south end of Medicine Lake 29 kilometres up the Maligne Road. Park in the plowed lot just past the inlet creek where the road makes a big curve away from the lake. Start skiing north from the parking area, across the frozen creek and onto the wide fire road emerging from the trees.

The massive limestone slabs of the Queen Elizabeth and Colin Ranges form a natural corridor for this trail. In fact the spectacular thrust faulting of the front ranges can readily be observed while skiing through this ideal terrain. A few gentle ups and downs, a wide trail and vistas framed by the lower subalpine forest make this a most enjoyable trip, no matter how far one chooses to travel. The first half is excellent novice touring, past Beaver Lake to the first Summit Lake at 5.0 kilometres. It is easiest to continue directly along the right or east shorelines of both lakes and pick up the trail to Jacques Lake at the far end of the second lake. The trail skirts the bottom edges of three impressive avalanche tracks on the short section in the trees between the lakes and the usual cautions should be exercised here.

Return the same way, watchful for skiers on the one or two short downhill runs.

Time in: 1 - 2 hours
Time out: 1 hour

The Trail on to Jacques Lake is rated as intermediate due to some narrow, tight skiing and the additional distance. The forest is more dense and the trail crosses a low divide at the corresponding gap in the northwest-southeast trending limestone ridges. At the fork it is possible to ski either trail as each parallels the other, offering their own interesting variations. By following the basic drainage course, the southwest end of Jacques Lake is soon reached. To push on the one kilometre to the other end of the lake and the campsite it is best to keep to the left or north shore as holes are not uncommon in the ice.

Return is by the same route.

Time in: 4 - 5 hours
Time out: 3 - 4 hours

LAKE TRAIL LOOP - MALIGNE

Novice 2
Cross-country trail tour and exploration
3 kilometres (2 miles)
28 kilometres (17.5 miles) to Narrows return
Map: Athabasca Falls 83 C/12, or
Jasper Park Ski Trail Sheet

The maintained cross-country trails in the Maligne Lake area have earned tremendous popularity in the past few years. Excellent snow conditions when lower areas are marginal, superb scenery and the winter services of the Maligne Lake Chalet have contributed to establishing this area as a nordic centre in Jasper.

Historically, Maligne has a ski touring heritage that dates back five decades. Joe Weiss, the legendary Jasper guide, made a lone trip down Maligne Lake in 1929. His journey took him into the Brazeau country, returning by the Athabasca Valley to Jasper. His enthusiasm for skiing potential in the Rockies was responsible for many major winter expeditions. On January 15, 1930, Weiss and four other Jasper Ski Club members started out for Banff and reached their destination fifteen days later after experiencing very harsh conditions. This and other trips in the Maligne area served to convince succeeding generations of the winter possibilities on skis.

To reach Maligne Lake from Jasper, follow Highway 16 east for 3.0 kilometres, cross the bridge over the Athabasca River and follow the Maligne Road for 45 kilometres. Food, rentals, ski equipment and information can be obtained from the Chalet (usually closed Tuesdays and Wednesdays) adjacent to the parking area.

The Lake Trail is short and level, following along the northeast shore. Start at the Chalet, follow the track past the boathouse and continue along to the viewpoint at the bay. The trail leaves the shoreline here and loops back through the spruce-fir forest and meadows, ending at the parking area. This trail is a good starting place for beginners, and once confidence is gained the skier can move up to the next level. The Maligne trails do, in fact, provide a graduated system of difficulty and length, allowing for a learn-by-experience approach, and opportunities exist for skiers of all ages and abilities.

Time: 30 minutes to 1 hour

From the view point at the bay it is very tempting to ski further down the lake, even though there is no trail as such. A word of warning is required, however: the thickness of ice on the lake varies considerably from place to place. Wet spots and snow-covered holes of open water are possible any place and are especially frequent where side streams enter the lake. It is possible to ski for many kilometres down either shoreline, but it is essential to stay on the meandering shore and avoid the temptation to cut corners across the numerous small bays. Skiing along the shores is flat but the snow is often very windpacked and drifted due to the predominant blowing conditions across the lake.

Time to the Narrow and return: 6 - 8 hours

MOOSE LAKE LOOP - MALIGNE

Novice 2
Cross-country trail tour
4.5 kilometres (3 miles)
Map: Athabasca Falls 83 C/12, or
Jasper Park Ski Trail Sheet

The majority of trails in the Maligne area are found west of the plowed parking lot (no cars allowed beyond the Chalet in winter) by skiing past the Chalet, along the lakeshore and over the Maligne River on the road bridge.

The Moose Lake Loop is reached by skiing 500 metres past the Chalet to the Bald Hills Fire Road gate. Travel up the fire road, turn left at the Maligne Pass trail head sign and continue through the spruce-pine forest over moderate terrain for 600 metres to the Moose Lake turnoff to the left. Here the trail steepens downhill with a fast short run to Moose Lake. (Watch for others coming up this section).

From here the trail loops back to Maligne Lake all too quickly, travelling along the level shoreline for a few hundred metres and rejoining the Maligne River bridge.

This is ideal cross-country terrain, enhanced by the maintained, set tracks. The Moose Lake trail is an excellent warm-up or conditioning loop when skied in this counter-clockwise fashion. It is a step above the Lake Trail.

Time: 30 minutes to 1 hour

LORRAINE LAKE LOOP - MALIGNE

Novice 3
Cross-country trail tour
7.5 kilometres (4.5 miles)
Map: Athabasca Falls 83 C/12, or
Jasper Park Ski Trail Sheet

The Lorraine Lake trail is a grade above the Moose Lake Loop and the two may be skied in succession (or even as a figure eight) because of their proximity.

Start from the Chalet and follow the track over the Maligne River bridge to the Bald Hills Fire Road. Ski up the road to the intersection trail heading right to Lorraine Lake through rolling terrain and mixed forest. Lorraine Lake and the other depression landforms in this area are typical of small glacial kettle formations. As large valley glaciers receded, chunks of ice broke free and were abandoned. Gravel fill washed in around the ice and as it slowly melted away a depression or well was left. Some filled with water producing these isolated lakes.

The trail continues along the lake and joins the Evelyn Creek trail. Turn right and go down this trail to loop back to the trail head near the fire road gate. This downhill section is moderately fast with numerous corners. As this loop is just as often skied in reverse and is very popular in its own right, it is prudent to watch for others coming up.

Time: 2 - 3 hours

KINNEY LAKE - MOUNT ROBSON PARK

Novice 3
Trail tour and exploration
8 kilometres (5 miles) return
Maps: Mt. Robson 83 E/3E
Mt. Robson Provincial Park Map

Mount Robson, the highest peak in the Canadian Rockies, rises to 3954 metres above sea level. Towering over the Fraser River, this massive uplift of peaks, glaciers and steep valleys, renowned for superb scenery, offers little in the way of established skiing opportunities.

Kinney Lake is one exception and provides a short and scenic trip for the day skier. The trail head is located down a short access road at the Mount Robson viewpoint, 88 kilometres west of Jasper on Highway 16. The trail is wide, level and travels through a remarkable forest of cedar, hemlock and fir reminiscent of coastal settings. This lush vegetation is a function of high precipitation values on the west slope of the mountains and due to the weather-making abilities of Mount Robson itself.

The trail follows the edge of a Robson River subdued greatly from its summer torrent. About halfway along, an avalanche track empties onto the trail, providing a clear view to the steep starting zones above. Kinney Lake is reached after crossing a bridge over the river. The valley is relatively wide here but ends abruptly on all sides. The incredible bulk of Mount Robson rises to the northeast while the elegant form of Whitehorn Mountain lies dead ahead beyond the end of the lake.

It is possible to ski to the far end of the lake, but it is imperative to stay on the northeast (right) shore as thin ice and slush are almost continually present. The trail does continue on up above the river, climbing steeply to the Valley of a Thousand Falls and ultimately to Berg Lake. This, however, is not an ideal ski route crossing hazardous avalanche terrain, extremely steep and exposed rock cuts and involving considerable route-finding.

Return the same way, being considerate of others ascending the trail.

Time in: 2 hours
Time out: 2 hours

Note: in the past, cross-country ski trails have been marked and maintained in other areas of Mount Robson Provincial Park. The trails up Swiftcurrent Creek and in the Lucerne Lake area are two examples. Recent staff shortages, however, have limited trail services. Current information on trails, snow and avalanche conditions can be obtained from park headquarters at Red Pass, B.C., 75 kilometres west of Jasper on Highway 16 or from the Park Supervisor, Box 579, Valemount, B.C. VOE 2Z0 (Tel: 604 566-4325).

Intermediate

SATURDAY NIGHT LAKE CIRCLE

Intermediate 3
Trail tour
22 kilometres (14 miles)
Map: Jasper 83 D/16

Penetrating the benchlands west of Jasper, the trail to Saturday Night Lake is an opportunity for an extended trip into rolling hill and valley country. Though it is possible to ski the entire 22 kilometre loop in one very long day, the length possibly dictates overnight considerations. Of course, either end of the trail can be skied for a short distance with a return the same way.

Start at either the Cottonwood Slough parking area, 2.2 kilometres from Jasper on the Pyramid Lake Road, or at the trail head at the far end of the mobile home subdivision at the west end of Jasper townsite. If starting from Cottonwood the trail first follows the fire road to Cabin Lake and then heads west along the north side of the lake, reaching the looping back point after 11 kilometres. Here the trail heads east, back toward Jasper, through more hills and valleys, almost always in the forest. The return portions are on a gentle downhill grade ending at the west end of the townsite.

Time around entire loop: 8 - 10 hours

PALISADE LOOKOUT

Intermediate 1
Road tour
22 kilometres (14 miles) return
Elevations: Trail head 1180 metres
Lookout 2075 metres
Map: Jasper 83 D/16

The fire road to the Palisade Lookout is a view-redeeming trip. The long, steep and densely wooded ascent over 11 kilometres of wide road is rewarded by an outstanding view for those who persevere. The lookout sits atop the sheer limestone cliffs of the Palisade at an elevation of 2075 metres. The view unfolds eastward down the wide Athabasca Valley and all the way south back up the valley to the higher peaks. It is an excellent location to observe the three sub-provinces within the Canadian Rockies: the foothills, the front ranges and the main range. Pick a clear day to take full advantage of this vista.

Start at the fire road gate at the end of the Pyramid Lake Road, 6.5 kilometres from Jasper townsite. The first sections follow the road through montane forests typical of the benchlands above the town. The mixed stands of lodgepole pine, spruce and aspen poplar make up the all-important valley bottom habitats for the majority of wildlife in the mountain parks. The winter snows provide an invaluable record of wildlife activities; watch for elk, deer, wolf and lynx tracks along the road.

The grade is moderate and views improve as the road climbs. At the 7.5 kilometre point the road forks. Follow the right, narrower spur on over steeper terrain for 3.2 kilometres to the fire lookout. There is not much room to wander around the lookout for those with remaining energy, besides the descent down the road will require some effort over the steeper sections.

A snowcat is occasionally used on the lower road to the spur during the winter to service the telecommunications station on Pyramid Mountain. This favourably packs the wide road, allowing skiers to practise controlled turns, but be alert for this vehicle on the road.

Time in: 4 - 5 hours
Time out: 2 - 3 hours

SIGNAL MOUNTAIN FIRE ROAD

Intermediate 1
Road tour
18 kilometres (11 miles) return
Elevations: Fire Road gate 1160 metres
Signal Mountain Lookout 2120 metres
Maps: Jasper 83 D/16
Medicine Lake 83 C/13

The wide road up to Signal Mountain Lookout represents one of six possible unplowed road tours in Jasper. All of these fire roads are generally quite acceptable for skiing, with the possible exception of Signal Mountain, the Whirlpool Valley Road to Moab Lake and the Cavell Road, which are open to public snowmobile use. The use of snowmobiles in National Parks is a subject of continuing debate. The skier must decide for himself if this use detracts from the winter experience or is simply a nuisance.

Drive up the Maligne Road from the junction on Highway 16 for five kilometres to the gated entry of the fire road. The skiing is straightforward through dense pine and spruce forest. The road does climb steeply in a few places and reaches lower tree limit at 2080 metres. Here the summer campground lies at the bottom of a final sidehill road section that heads up to the white lookout buildings on the exposed ridge. The campground is the turnaround point for snowmobiles.

It is possible to ski up to the lookout site, but the road cut drifts in making for a very tricky traverse on the steeply sloped, windpacked snow. The alpine meadows on the north flank of Signal Mountain offer further opportunity for exploration touring and a chance to practise downhill techniques on the rolling terrain. Mount Tekarra and Excelsior Mountain rise above the windblown ridges to the south and the lower Athabasca spreads out below.

Return down the road exactly as the trip up. Be alert for snowmobile traffic up and down the road.

Time in: 4 - 5 hours
Time out: 2 - 4 hours

WATCHTOWER BASIN

Intermediate 3
Trail and exploration tour
22 kilometres (14 miles) return
Elevations: Trail head 1400 metres
Lower Basin 1900 metres
Upper Basin 2200 metres
Map: Medicine Lake 83 C/13

The Watchtower is a prominent peak of the Maligne Range and the small valley it stands guard over has been favoured ski terrain for many years. The rustic and historic Watchtower Cabin burned down in 1977, taking with it the memories of many cozy winter nights.

The trail head is located 18.5 kilometres up the Maligne Road at the far end of the parking lot marked by the Watchtower sign. The trail travels through dense forest with numerous steep sections until turning south and entering the basin proper.

From the parking area ski down a short steep section to the Maligne River and cross either the narrow footbridge or, a few metres upstream, directly over the ice. Turn right following the trail along the river for a short distance and then almost immediately turn left and start a very steep but relatively short climb over a rough section. Many skiers find it necessary to walk up (and down) this 100-200 metre stretch; it is definitely not ideal for skiing but fortunately it is short.

From here on the trail climbs steadily, passing through some open summer bog areas where occasional glimpses through the spruce-fir forest reveal the grey limestone slopes of the Colin Range to the north. After 3.0 kilometres the trail begins to climb in earnest. It passes through three steep sections and then turns directly south leaving the sidehill slopes to head up into the initial narrow sections of the Watchtower Valley.

The forest is left behind and generally open, level terrain is

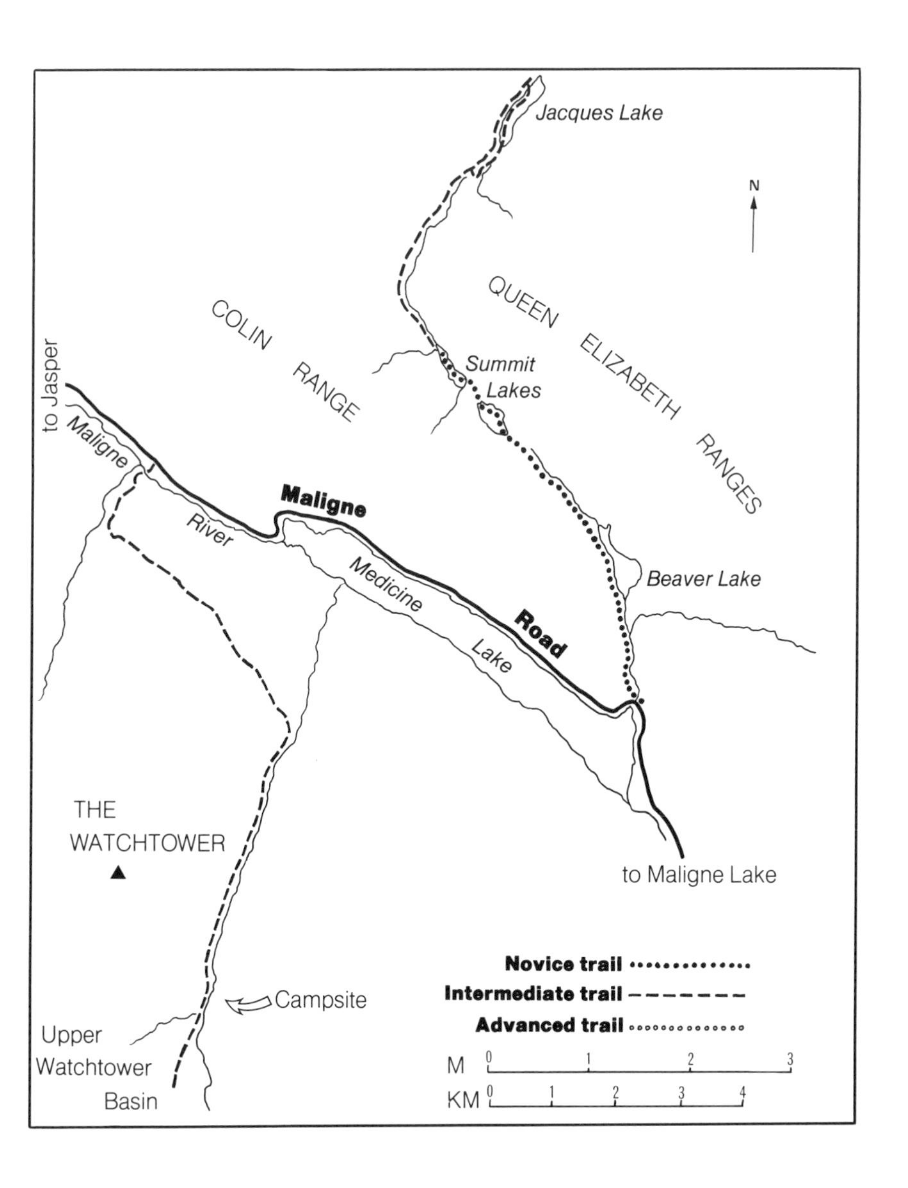
Jacques Lake
N
QUEEN ELIZABETH RANGES
COLIN RANGE
to Jasper
Summit Lakes
Maligne
Maligne
River
Medicine
Lake
Road
Beaver Lake
THE WATCHTOWER
to Maligne Lake
Novice trail
Intermediate trail
Advanced trail
Campsite
Upper Watchtower Basin
M 0 1 2 3
KM 0 1 2 3 4

encountered where the trail strikes the creek. It is now a matter of following the frozen creek into the upper basin. Watchtower peak, looming high above to the north, comes into full view for the first time. The lower slopes at the far end of the valley are especially well suited for further skiing, but it should be kept in mind it is another five kilometres to the far end. In addition, these open slopes accumulate large amounts of wind-transported snow which lie on steep scree; this obvious avalanche terrain should be treated with respect.

Overnight camping in the valley should be restricted to the summer campground located about four kilometres into the valley from where the trail first levels out, on the true righthand bank. It is recognised by the privy. Water can generally be found by breaking the ice at the side of the creek about 50 metres upstream from the campsite.

The return ski down the steeper sections of trail can be very exciting and quite demanding if the lower slopes are crusted or there is a lack of snow cover. By keeping speed down, the four or five tight, fast corners can be negotiated with a minimum of incidents. If it becomes necessary to walk, do so off the side of the trail.

Time in: 3 - 5 hours
Time out: 2 - 4 hours

EVELYN CREEK LOOP - MALIGNE

Intermediate 2
Cross-country trail tour
12 kilometres (7.5 miles)
Elevations: Trail head 1680 metres
Fire Road turn-off 1960 metres
Map: Athabasca Falls 83 C/12

Combining sections of wide fire road, steep trail and twisting corners, the Evelyn Creek loop at Maligne Lake offers variety and views and requires a definite level of proficiency above the Lorraine Lake trail (see *Novice* trails section).

Start from the Chalet and ski west over the bridge to the Bald Hills Fire Road. Ski up the road for 3.5 kilometres, ascending about 260 metres through the lodgepole pine forest, to the intersection with the trail down to Evelyn Creek. Turn right onto the trail and begin the steep descent, paying attention to two sections in particular. It is essential to keep speed down here as the forest is quite thick, and a crash and burn technique is not advised. After two kilometres the trail joins the Evelyn Creek trail at a footbridge. Moose are often evident along this creek as they forage for winter browse among the willow.

The return is straightforward down the Evelyn Creek trail, however numerous fast sections, blind corners and narrow passages make for an exciting, knee-shaking run. It is wise to take this one section at a time, stopping at blind points to assess the unknown. Be particularly watchful for others churning their way up this popular trail. The run ends at the trail head next to the fire road gate. As with the other loops in the vicinity, this trail can be, and just as often is, run in reverse.

Time: 3 - 4 hours

EVELYN CREEK TRAIL TO LITTLE SHOVEL PASS

Intermediate 3 to Advanced
Cross-country trail tour and exploration
10 kilometres (6 miles) to bridge return
21 kilometres (13 miles) to Little Shovel Pass return
Elevations: Trail head 1680 metres
Evelyn Creek Bridge 1810 metres
Little Shovel Pass 2225 metres
Map: Athabasca Falls 83 C/12

By skiing half the Evelyn Creek loop to the footbridge, Little Shovel Pass can be gained on the famed Skyline Trail. Start at the parking area, cross the Maligne River bridge and head up the marked trail at the sign just before the fire road. The first section to the footbridge is the same as the Evelyn Creek loop description and the same warnings apply, namely watch for descending skiers coming around the tight, blind corners. The bridge is reached in 4.8 kilometres after passing by Lorraine and Mona Lakes and through a delightful forest setting. On a bright winter day a pair of well-waxed skis seem to fly along this up and down trail. The trip to the footbridge can be a main destination, and a lunch-stop or break may be made there.

Time in: 1 - 3 hours
Time out: 1 - 2 hours

From the footbridge it is 5.5 kilometres further to Little Shovel Pass and a climb of 415 metres. Only experienced skiers with ample time and avalanche equipment should consider going to the pass. Once across the bridge, ski left following the side of the creek. The summer trail cuts right here, back up the sidehill, but it is best to continue along the creek. After 100 metres, gradually swing into the righthand (west) fork of the creek, which might appear a bit vague. The track is usually packed up this creek, however, making the way easier to detect. The higher summer trail traverses the steep, south-facing slopes above, crossing at least three possible avalanche gullies. Once on the snow-covered righthand fork of the creek, the skiing is quite enjoyable. If there is not enough snow cover, minor route finding on and off the creek bed may be required. It is three kilometres to the flat, narrow valley head.

As the open slopes begin to rise, turn right (northwest) up a side drainage - (503419), ascending to rolling terrain through increasingly open tree cover. Little Shovel Pass lies ahead to the northwest, partially hidden by the steep snowy avalanche slopes on the left and windblown rocky slopes to the right. The high summer trail should be joined in the lowest line heading into the narrow passage to the pass, though it will probably be indistinct or invisible. Beyond the pass the Skyline Trail continues into the Snowbowl. Return is by the same route.

Time in: 4 - 6 hours
Time out: 3 - 5 hours

BALD HILLS LOOKOUT

Intermediate 2
Cross-country trail tour and exploration
11.5 kilometres (7 miles) return
Elevations: Trail head 1680 metres
Bald Hills Lookout 2120 metres
Map: Athabasca Falls 83 C/12

The Bald Hills and surrounding area have been used for many winters by the Maligne Lake Ski Club and other groups, attesting to the exceptional snow conditions and renowned scenery.

The trail to the Bald Hills lookout site follows the fire road entirely. Starting at the parking lot, ski past the Chalet and cross the Maligne River. Join the fire road and climb 480 metres over a distance of 5.7 kilometres through a forest that changes from lodgepole pine near the bottom to windblown sub-alpine fir at the top. There are some steep sections, but it is wise to stick with the track on the road as the adjacent steep terrain can be avalanche-prone. (On these steep uphills, stay single file and give downhill traffic the right of way. Be prepared to move out of the way to avoid collisions).

The high elevation places the end of the road near tree-line where winds and blowing snow can be quite common. On a nice day the view is ample reward for the climb. Leah and Samson peaks to the east, Charlton and Unwin and the Brazeau Group to the south, stand sentinel over snow-covered Maligne Lake, the largest glacier-fed lake in the Canadian Rockies. Mary Schäffer in 1908 was one of the first to visit the lake, and since then thousands have journeyed to witness its scenery, many of those now in the winter months.

Beyond the lookout site, the rolling alpine tundra provides ample opportunity for further exploration. By skiing directly south along the crest of the hills for three kilometres, a rocky high point can be reached by experienced skiers. (The open steep slopes behind the lookout area are avalanche-prone and should be avoided). Caribou tracks are sometimes seen at this end of the Bald Hills and by carefully scanning the adjacent slopes this elusive animal might be seen.

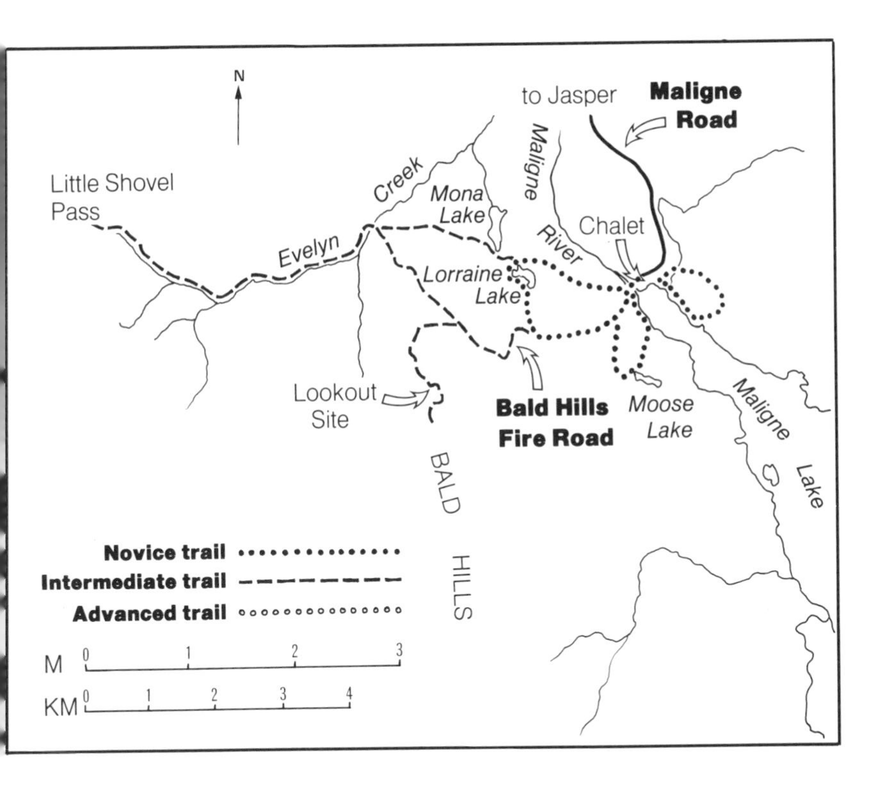

It is advisable to return by the fire road, but even with the steep sections and sharp corners, there is generally lots of room to snowplow or stop.

Time in: 2 - 4 hours
Time out: 1 - 2 hours

MOUNT EDITH CAVELL ROAD

Intermediate 1 or Advanced
Road and trail tour
28 kilometres (17.5 miles) return
Elevations: Road start 1222 metres
Road end 1756 metres
Cavell Meadows 2271 metres
Maps: Jasper 83 D/16
Amethyst Lakes 83 D/9

The road to the base of Mount Edith Cavell is not plowed in winter, providing good ski access to a very scenic area close to Jasper townsite. The road is paved and there is little chance of hitting rocks early in the winter. However, since the road is open to snowmobiles, skiers will have to share it with a motorized contingent which is usually heavier on weekends than midweek.

Start at the gated Cavell Road turnoff located eleven kilometres south of Jasper on the 93A Highway. Simply follow the road as it climbs rapidly for the first three kilometres above the Astoria River. Three viewpoints along the road provide impressive vistas west up the Astoria to the Tonquin Valley and Mount Fraser. Another short climb and the Cavell Youth Hostel is reached at Kilometre 11.5. (Arrangements for overnight use should be made in advance through the Canadian Youth Hostel office in Edmonton - Phone (403) 439-3089.)

At this point the massive north face of Mount Edith Cavell becomes the dominate feature. This superb quartzite peak was formerly known as La Montagne de la Grand Traverse by the fur brigades heading up the Athabasca River. The former name is a mouthful but is perhaps more appealing, romantic and descriptive. By following the road to its end at the parking area, the full sweep of the face looms above. Powder avalanches and spindrift seem to continually billow down across the wall. Most skiers will find it necessary to head back down from this point because of time considerations. The return down the road is obvious.

Time in: 4 - 5 hours
Time out: 2 - 3 hours

The summer footpath on the outwash flats beyond the parking lot can be followed by skiing left from the parking area. This area is menaced by avalanche runouts and occasional ice breakage from the exquisite Angel Glacier hanging at the lip of the cirque above. Alternately, the footpath up the steep lateral moraine can be followed on skis but takes some careful manoeuvering and minor route finding. Follow the path from the parking area above the stairs and left across the bridge, ascending the right side of the moraine until the trail cuts sharply back left and traverses steeply up to the top of the moraine. From here the trail lies between the backside of the moraine and the forested slope. The trail continues steeply up to tree limit and the meadows beyond.

On both these extension tours past the parking area quickly changing weather, avalanche slopes and steep narrow trails warrant special care and experience. Travel beyond the end of the road should be considered *Advanced.*

PORTAL CREEK TO CIRCUS CREEK - MACCARIB PASS

Intermediate 2
Trail tour
8 kilometres (5 miles) return
25 kilometres (15.5 miles) to Maccarib Pass return
Elevations: Portal Creek Trail head 1469 metres
Circus Creek bridge 1760 metres
Maccarib Pass 2210 metres
Map: Jasper 83 D/16

The Portal Creek trail represents the first leg of the beautiful and popular Maccarib Pass access route into the Tonquin Valley. This first section to the footbridge over Circus Creek is an enjoyable day trip offering some excellent views of Peveril Peak and the Trident Range as the trail is ascended.

The trail head is located six kilometres up the Marmot Basin Ski Area access road. Park in the plowed lot at the Portal Creek road bridge. The summer trail starts at the far end of the parking area, but early in the winter the horse trail starting on the other side of the road bridge allows for easier initial skiing.

A direct route following the bottom of Portal Creek from the footbridge is the easiest and most common route once the water is frozen and winter snows have filled in the boulders. Elevation is gained quickly and views of Peveril Peak appear and disappear through the subalpine forest cover. One avalanche run-out zone is crossed. The summer trail along the north side of the creek is an alternative choice and must be used early in the season before skiing on the creek is possible.

The junction of Portal and Circus Creeks, or the bridge over Circus Creek if using the trail, provides a convenient stop and turnaround point for a short day tour. The ski down on either trail or creek is steep and in sections fast with tight turns. Be on the lookout for skiers heading up.

Time in: 1 - 2 hours
Time out: 30 minutes - 1 hour

The flanks of Peveril and Lectern Peaks form The Portal, which entices one to ski further to the expansive meadows and Maccarib Pass beyond. It is essential to stay on the confines of Portal Creek if pushing on. The summer trail traverses high on the open southeast slopes of Peveril Peak and crosses extremely hazardous avalanche gullies. Besides, skiing here is pointless since the trail climbs up steeply and then drops back down again. If continuing on from the Circus Creek footbridge, simply ski 50 metres down the creek to its junction proper with Portal Creek and continue on at that point.

From the creek junction it is 8.4 kilometres further to Maccarib Pass. Skiing along the creek in this section is flatter and through a wider valley bottom. The route climbs about 427 metres through the upper subalpine zone into the wide expanses of meadow land and the summit of the pass.

Locating Maccarib Pass at 2210 metres can be somewhat deceiving, especially on a stormy day. Once leaving the trees and the obvious drainage, it is prudent to bear right as the route makes a ninety degree dog-leg to the northwest over the last two kilometres (grid reference 214416). The idea is to avoid getting on the steeper slopes immediately to the right while also resisting the temptation to ski too far south or left into the endless alpine meadows. If it is essential to get to the pass and the weather is poor, travel by map and compass. If the pass is not a primary objective, there is ample skiing opportunity on the gladed slopes lower down. Many of these slopes in and on both sides of Maccarib Pass are potential avalanche terrain due to the considerable snowfall and wind conditions.

A trip to Maccarib Pass is enticing and possible in one day for strong parties, but attention should be paid to the time available, especially during the early winter.

Time in: 4 - 6 hours
Time out: 3 - 4 hours

TONQUIN VALLEY VIA ASTORIA RIVER

Intermediate 3, overnight
Road, trail and exploration tour
11.5 kilometres (7 miles) to Cavell Hostel one way
28 kilometres (17.5 miles) to Amethyst Lakes one way
Elevations: Cavell Road (bottom) 1222 metres
Cavell Hostel 1707 metres
Amethyst Lakes 1981 metres
Maps: Amethyst Lakes 83 D/9
Jasper 83 D/16

An alternate access to the Tonquin Valley, the Astoria River approach enters the valley at its south end. The Eremite Valley and Wates-Gibson Hut are special attractions in the Tonquin region and perhaps are more easily accessible by this route. In addition, the Astoria River combined with the Maccarib Pass route provides the opportunity for a multi-day loop trip. Skiing the loop in either direction is equally feasible, however the two starting points are nine kilometres apart, requiring two vehicles or a winter hitch-hike.

The first section of this trip involves skiing up the unplowed Cavell Road, described in the Mount Edith Cavell Road entry. Most prefer (or are forced due to distance) to split the in-trip into two days, staying overnight at the Cavell Youth Hostel (overnight aggrangements are necessary). From the parking area at the bottom of the Cavel Road it is 11.5 kilometres to the hostel and 28.0 kilometres to Amethyst Lakes; bear these distances in mind when planning trips.

Join the main summer trail to the Tonquin Valley slightly past the hostel, cross the Cavell Lake outlet stream and head out through dense forest descending to the Astoria River. A footbridge crosses the river and the trail is followed to the Old Horn Warden Cabin. Here the best route is to follow the frozen Astoria River upstream. The summer trail climbs steeply, switchbacking up the exposed slopes of Old Horn Mountain and is best avoided. Following the river will require some route-finding and minor bushwacking to avoid occasional open water, side channels and marsh areas. By staying with the drainage, the confluence with the outlet creek from Chrome Lake (grid reference 170358) is reached after thirteen kilometres of skiing from the hostel.

If interest lies in Chrome Lake, the Eremite Valley area or the Wates-Gibson Hut, ski up the left-hand drainage for 500 metres to Chrome Lake; the Eremite Valley is directly south of the lake at the far end.

The Wates-Gibson Hut, operated by the Alpine Club of Canada, is another 2.5 confusing kilometres beyond Chrome Lake. It is located on the north shore of Outpost Lake (153353). From the outlet of Chrome Lake ski along the north shore for 100 metres in a westerly direction, ascend a short creek bed and continue westerly until an open glade is reached. Ski up and through the open meadows and Penstock Creek to the base of a large, exposed boulder slide on the north side of the creek. A side trail on the

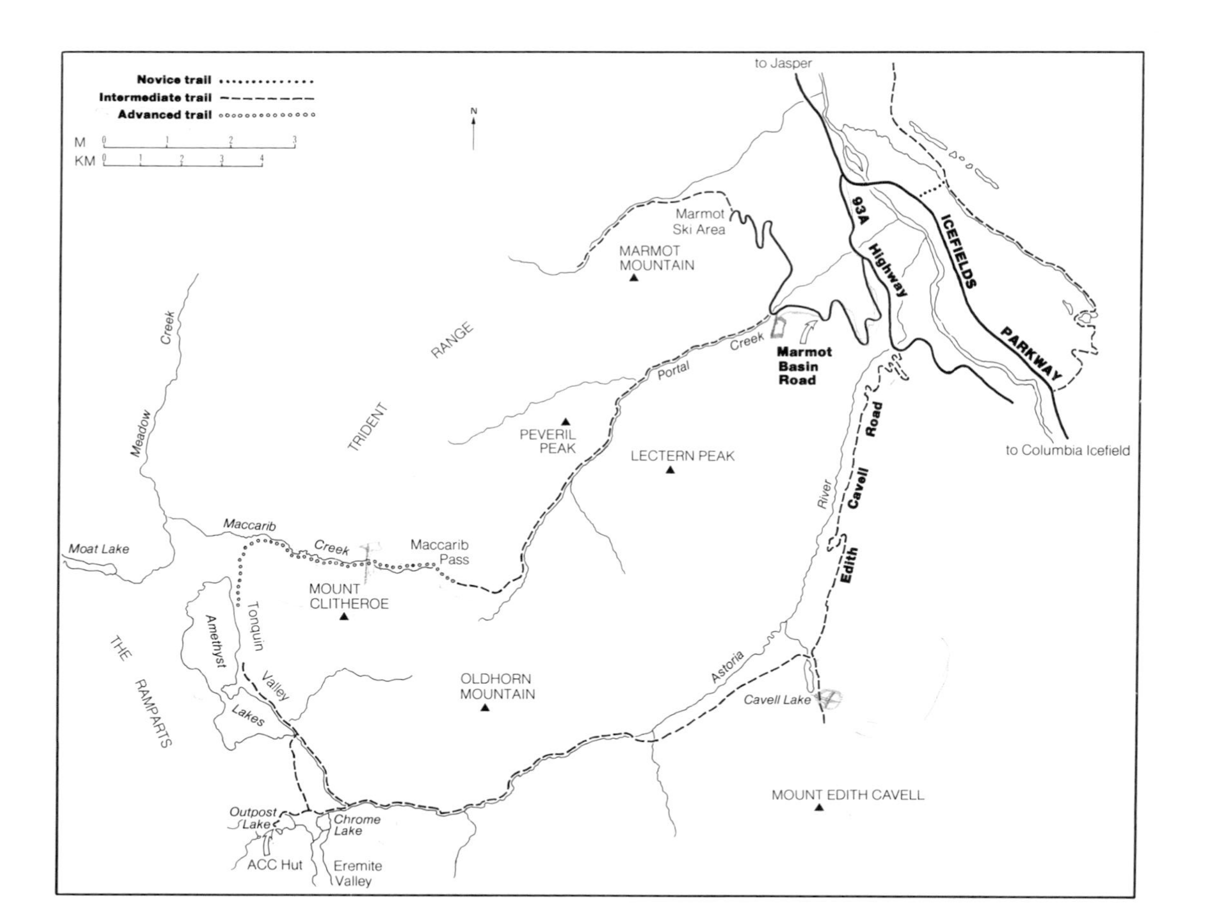

Novice trail
Intermediate trail
Advanced trail
M 0 1 2 3
KM 0 1 2 3 4
N
to Jasper
to Columbia Icefield
ICEFIELDS PARKWAY
93A Highway
Marmot Basin Road
Marmot Ski Area
MARMOT MOUNTAIN
Portal Creek
PEVERIL PEAK
LECTERN PEAK
TRIDENT RANGE
Meadow Creek
Maccarib Creek
Maccarib Pass
Moat Lake
MOUNT CLITHEROE
Tonquin Valley
Amethyst Lakes
THE RAMPARTS
OLDHORN MOUNTAIN
Astoria River
Edith Cavell Road
Cavell Lake
MOUNT EDITH CAVELL
Outpost Lake
Chrome Lake
ACC Hut
Eremite Valley

south side of Penstock Creek climbs steadily through thick timber to Outpost Lake and the locked hut. (Information on the Alpine Club of Canada and arrangements for the use of huts can be obtained through the club office, Box 1026, Banff, Alberta TOL OCO - phone (403) 762-3664). It is advisable to travel independent of the hut, since it is difficult to locate or may not be reached by night. Both the Alphine Club and Canadian Mountain Holidays in Banff offer ski touring excursions to the area each winter that utilize the hut as a base of operations.

If the Tonquin Valley and Amethyst Lakes proper are the main destination, follow the Astoria River right at the confluence with the creek from Chrome Lake. The south end of the Amethyst Lakes is 2.8 kilometres up the Astoria. To connect through the Tonquin Valley and complete the loop, see the Maccarib Pass entry.

Two points should be kept in mind concerning this route to the Tonquin: (1) The area around Chrome and Outpost Lakes can be very confusing, and map knowledge and a good sense of direction are definite assets (unfortunately no trails are shown on the current map edition); (2) snowmobiles are allowed by special permit, when conditions are judged favourable, up the Astoria River the the Amethyst Lakes.

Time in from Cavell Hostel to Amethyst Lakes: 6 - 8 hours
Time out: 5 - 8 hours

SUNWAPTA FALLS TO ATHABASCA RIVER

Intermediate 2
Trail tour
26 kilometres (16 miles) return
Elevations: Sunwapta Falls 1392 metres
Athabasca River Crossing 1362 metres
Maps: Athabasca Falls 83 C/12
Fortress Lake 83 C/5

This trail does not receive a great deal of winter use, although the skiing is generally quite enjoyable. The forest is typical valley bottom growth, tending to be quite dense, but fortunately the trail follows an open river bank here and there, providing some excellent views to the wilder regions of the Upper Athabasca Valley. This is one of the few trails that descends going in and climbs coming back. The overall elevation change is moderate, the trail itself generally wide and snow conditions are better than lower down in the Athabasca Valley. Quite often the trail to at least Long Lake may be packed by Warden Service snowmobile patrols. This can be a blessing or a frustrating experience depending on snow conditions.

Start at the Sunwapta Falls access road entrance 55 kilometres south of Jasper on the Icefields Parkway. Cars should be parked off the highway in the small cleared space at the access road. Ski down the road 500 metres to the footbridge over the falls and head south down the marked trail.

Stands of lodgepole pine and a few short, fast descents mark the first five kilometres to where the trail passes the first summer campsite and joins the open flats of the Athabasca River. The views south to Mount Confederation, Mount Quincy and the vast expanses of the seldom visited Athabasca headwaters country are a distant contrast to the surrounding forest.

At this point route-finding may require close attention to tree blazes as it is sometimes best to take to the frozen side channels. The riverside proper is followed for only 1.4 kilometres when the trail heads back into the trees until the short side trail to Long Lake is met. From here it is two kilometres to a point near the confluence of the Athabasca and Chaba Rivers where the summer ford across the Athabasca is located.

The total distance of 26.0 kilometres return from the starting point usually means a long day. It is all uphill back out although not steep.

Time in: 3 - 5 hours
Time out: 4 - 6 hours

POBOKTAN CREEK

Intermediate 1
Trail tour
13 kilometres (8 miles) to Poligne Creek return
Elevations: Trail head 1541 metres
Poligne Creek bridge 1760 metres
Map: Sunwapta Peak 83 C/6

Poboktan Creek provides access for two major backcountry exploration trips to either Maligne Pass or Poboktan Pass (see *Advanced* trips). However, the first section of trail is a suitable day trip, climbing into a beautiful side valley at middle elevations. The forest is open enough for glimpses of the many surrounding peaks including Poboktan Mountain to the south.

Start at the trail head located 72 kilometres south of Jasper on the Icefields Parkway. Park in the large lot immediately south of the bridge over Poboktan Creek. (If the lot is not plowed, park at the Sunwapta Warden Station, well out of the way). Find the trail on the north side of the creek.

Within just enough time to allow ski wax to start working effectively, the trail climbs a steep section gaining elevation above the creek. The upper rolling section through the open lodgepole pine forest is interesting ski terrain, accentuated by fleeting views into the Poboktan Valley beyond. The junction with Poligne Creek and a footbridge are met after 6.5 kilometres, an ideal spot for lunch and as a turnaround. It is possible to continue south all the way to Poboktan Pass, a further eighteen kilometres, but an overnight must be considered.

Return the same way which is considerably faster on the steep descents (pay particular attention to the one hairpin corner near the bottom).

Time to Poligne Creek: 2 - 3 hours
Time out: 1 - 2 hours

NIGEL PASS

Intermediate 2
Trail tour
16 kilometres (10 miles) return
Elevations: Highway 1890 metres
Nigel Pass 2195 metres
Map: Columbia Icefield 83 C/3

Situated at the boundaries of Jasper and Banff Parks, Nigel Pass is a sometimes forgotten frontier area, possibly due to the driving distance from the more popular townsites. It does offer an interesting day trip into an area which boasts heavy snowfall and excellent scenery.

Start at the Nigel Pass trail head on the Icefields Parkway (117 kilometres south of Jasper, 115 kilometres north of Lake Louise). Park well off the highway in the small cleared area. Ski directly down the unplowed, old Banff-Jasper road for 1.5 kilometres to the Camp Parker Warden shelter and corral; go through the station and down the trail to Nigel Creek. Follow directly up the creek through one or two narrow passages to a wide, open meadow area. Avalanche slopes descend from the east (right) slopes and should be skirted.

Nigel Pass is the low ridge-like line directly up the drainage. Pick a route through the sporadic forest and meadow until the edge of the escarpment is reached. (Exercise extreme caution along the rocky cliff top as corniced snow may conceal the void below). The Brazeau River stretches beyond to the northeast, cutting through the front ranges and foothills.

The return trip features gentle slopes and equally good views to Mounts Athabasca and Saskatchewan.

Time in: 3 - 4 hours
Time out: 2 - 3 hours

Advanced

TONQUIN VALLEY VIA MACCARIB PASS

Advanced, camping
Trail tour
21 kilometres (13 miles) to Amethyst Lakes
Elevations: Portal Creek trail head 1469 metres
Maccarib Pass 2210 metres
Tonquin Valley 1981 metres
Maps: Jasper 83 D/16
Amethyst Lakes 83 D/9

The Tonquin Valley in winter is a backcountry ski paradise. Generally flat, open terrain, a backdrop of the magnificent Ramparts and excellent snow cover set the area apart as special. The route via Maccarib Pass is highly scenic, although long, and travels through the upper subalpine life zone. Treeline is reached just below Maccarib Pass. (The route to the pass is described in the Portal Creek section.

The pass and creek flowing down into the Tonquin Valley take their name from an Indian word meaning caribou. Woodland or mountain caribou make their home in the high open meadows characteristic of the area. Taking advantage of windblown and snow free areas, the small herds of caribou feed mainly on lichens and dried sedges.

From the crest of Maccarib Pass, the route down is straightforward and gradual, following the drainage west into the flat, open creek bottomlands. Here, an already scenic trip is further enhanced with the first spectacular views of The Ramparts. This uplift of quartzite peaks forming the Great Divide and boundary between Alberta and British Columbia is one of the great vistas in the mountain national parks. The first peaks visible above Moat Pass are Barbican, Geikie, Turret and Bastion; as one nears the lower end of the creek and Tonquin Valley proper, the remaining summits of Drawbridge, Redoubt, Dungeon and Parapet come into full view. With snow outlining the sedimentary layers of rock and small avalanches billowing down the 1000 metre faces, the scene is an eyeful.

Because of the length of the trip into Tonquin Valley, overnight arrangements are usually essential and the choices are many. Winter camping is available at the Portal Campsite before Maccarib Pass (eight kilometres from the trail head), at Maccarib Campsite (seven kilometres beyond Maccarib Pass), at the campsite on the east shore of Amethyst Lakes, and at the Surprise Point campsite across the outlet stream at the south end of the lake. This last camping spot is twenty-six kilometres from the trail head and makes for a long day.

There are two opportunities for indoor accommodation in the

Tonquin. The first is available at the outfitter's camp at the north end of the lake. Arrangements must be made in advance through Gordon Dixon, P.O. Box 550, Jasper, Alberta T0E 1E0 (phone 403 852-3909). The other choice is the Wates-Gibson Hut of the Alpine Club of Canada located at Outpost Lake. Again arrangements must be made in advance through the club office at P.O. Box 1026, Banff, Alberta T0L 0C0. (For directions to Outpost Lake, see the Astoria River entry).

Opportunities for side and day trip explorations in the Tonquin are plentiful. Moat Pass and Vista Pass occupy the northwest corner of the area, providing vast, open and level ski terrain. At the far south end beyond Amethyst Lakes, Chrome Lake and the Eremite Valley have been popular ski destinations for years. Access from Tonquin Valley proper to these southern reaches of the area is by way of a rough summer trail through the thick forest. This trail can usually be found with a bit of searching from the Surprise Point campsite. A map is desirable when exploring the periphery environs of the Tonquin due to the openness, obscure summer trails and size of the area.

Time in: *6 - 8 hours*
Time out: *6 - 8 hours*

FRYATT VALLEY

Advanced, overnight
Trail tour and exploration
26 kilometres (16 miles) return (using river crossing)
Elevations: Athabasca River 1220 metres
Bottom of headwall 1780 metres
Hut 2000 metres
Map: Athabasca Falls 83 C/12

The Fryatt Valley is a good example of an area that has gained perhaps an excess of popularity due to the existence of free overnight accommodation. The Sydney Vallance memorial cabin, located at an elevation of 2000 metres on upper Fryatt Creek, was originally built by the Alpine Club of Canada as a mountaineer hut. This wooden shelter is now administered by Parks Canada and accommodates only twelve persons at a time as per parks regulations. It is on a strict reservation system and persons planning on using the cabin must obtain a permit from the Park Information Centre in Jasper (phone 403 852-4401). There is a wood-burning stove, and since the cabin is located in a fragile area with little natural growth, the firewood is flown in by helicopter. Anyone expecting to use this facility and others like it has a special responsibility to conserve the limited wood so it will last an entire winter. The continued existence of huts and shelters in the mountain parks is very tenuous and depends directly on an attitude of care and respect. Keep the cabin and site clean, close up tightly when leaving, do not cut any natural vegetation in the area,

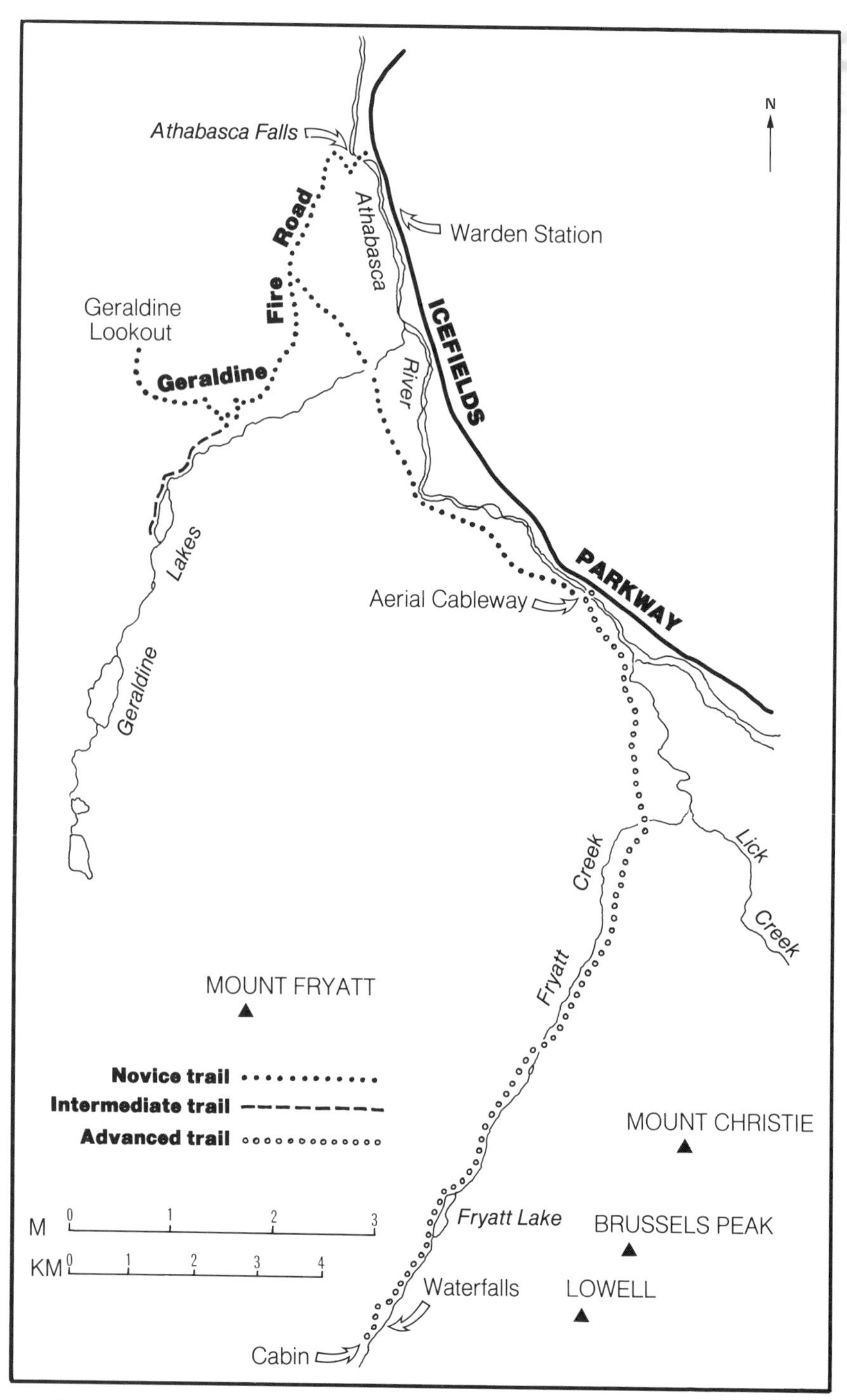
N
Athabasca Falls
Warden Station
Athabasca
River
ICEFIELDS
PARKWAY
Fire Road
Geraldine Lookout
Geraldine
Lakes
Geraldine
Aerial Cableway
Lick
Creek
Creek
Fryatt
MOUNT FRYATT
Novice trail
Intermediate trail
Advanced trail
MOUNT CHRISTIE
M 0 1 2 3
KM 0 1 2 3 4
Fryatt Lake
BRUSSELS PEAK
Waterfalls
LOWELL
Cabin

leave kindling for the next user, and pack out everything brought in. Report conditions and misuse to parks staff when returning.

The Fryatt Valley is a confined stream and glacier-eroded side drainage of the main Athabasca Valley. Its upper reaches are surrounded by high peaks, alpine glaciers and rolling open terrain. Mount Fryatt, 3308 metres, lies out of sight to the north, while the austere rock shaft of Mount Brussels dominates the horizon to the east of the valley.

The normal trail head is located 2.4 kilometres up the Geraldine Fire Road as described in the Geraldine Lookout entry. Starting at the sign, ski along the summer trail through dense forest, paying attention to blazes; a footbridge across Fryatt Creek is reached after thirteen kilometres of monotonous skiing with few views.

Most skiers, however, prefer to cross the Athabasca River, shortening the overall distance. The usual crossing is located at the aerial cableway (incorrectly marked on Athabasca Falls map 83 C/12) 6.7 kilometres south of the Athabasca Falls Warden Station on the Icefields Parkway. Park well off the side of the highway and ski down to the river; the cablecar is locked and not available for public use. Check the snow covered Athabasca River carefully upstream a bit from the cable for solid ice; cautiously ski one at a time across the river at a safe location. Open water and thin ice are possible anytime.

A short trail heads up the river bank below the cable tower and joins the main trail. Follow this section for 3.4 kilometres to the bridge over Fryatt Creek where the trail enters the forest and starts to climb, sometimes very steeply, over the next 4.0 kilometres. During winters of heavy snow cover, it is feasible to ski directly up the creek. It is impossible to know if the creek is passable above the bridge, however, unless a positive report is available.

Upper Fryatt Creek is recrossed on a second bridge and a series of impressive avalanche runout zones is immediately encountered. Move through quickly, staying in the trees along the creek. Head straight up the drainage picking the best line to a large glacial moraine dam. Beyond lies Fryatt Lake which is passed on the west side. Continue to ski up the drainage through large timber toward the infamous Fryatt headwall straight ahead. Head for a point some 100 to 200 metres right of the falls, staying clear of the large avalanche track further to the right.

The cabin (incorrectly marked on Athabasca Falls map 83 C/12 as being at the lake) now lies about 600 metres distant (220 vertical metres) above the headwall. There is no trail, and most find it necessary to carry skis up this section, route-finding a way to the top. Traverse gradually to the left over towards the top of the falls on a diagonally ascending line, using extreme caution on the exposed rocks. Once over the lip, follow near the west side of the creek and begin searching for the cabin (402174) above and to the right (northwest) of the creek in a clearning of small stunted trees. Water can be found in frozen pools in the creek below the cabin. A word of warning: many misjudge the distance to and up the headwall or miss the cabin entirely and are forced to spend the night out unprepared.

Once in the upper Fryatt Valley, the scenery, terrain and snow cover provide ample incentive for exploration beyond the cabin. Avalanche hazard is present on all the slopes and small glaciers occupy some of the saddles between the peaks at the valley head.

The return trip down the headwall requires extreme care; most find it safer to carry skis, retracing steps. The trail made on the way up should wisely anticipate the return down. Similarily, if skiing down the creek, be certain it is possible all the way to the bridge and be cautious of open water and holes between the boulders.

Time in: 6 - 10 hours
Time out: 6 - 8 hours

SUNWAPTA FALLS TO FORTRESS LAKE

Advanced, camping
Exploration and trail tour
47 kilometres (29 miles) return
Elevations: Sunwapta Falls 1392 metres
Fortress Pass 1332 metres
Fortress Lake 1327 metres
Maps: Athabasca Falls 83 C/12
Fortress Lake 83 C/5

Beyond the Athabasca River crossing point described in the *Sunwapta Falls to Athabasca River* entry lies the wild, remote Chaba Valley and Fortress Lake. This area is not often visited, and because of summer river crossing problems, winter may be the most appropriate time.

Follow the trail from Sunwapta Falls to the crossing at the Athabasca River. Consider this crossing carefully as deep snow may hide open water. Trails now become indistinct and the very expansive flats of the Chaba River are gained by heading south and west upstream from the confluence.

It is ten kilometres from the Athabasca crossing to Fortress Pass, one of the lowest breaks along the Continental Divide. Crossing to the west side of the Chaba is possible at a number of points depending on snow conditions and extent of open water which can be quite common even during very cold periods. Two possible crossings are at the river braidings, three and seven kilometres upstream from the confluence.

Once on the west side, route-finding to the rather indistinct, forested pass is generally straightforward. The break in the high peaks guarding the pass is rather obvious. Old trails may appear from time to time heading in that direction. The shore of Fortress Lake is 600 metres west of the Chaba. If the divide here was a few metres lower in elevation, the lake would probably drain east to the Arctic watershed instead of west to the Pacific.

Time in: 7 - 9 hours
Time out: 7 - 9 hours

COLUMBIA ICEFIELD

Advanced, winter camping, ski mountaineering
Glacier travel, exploration
8 kilometres (5 miles) to top of Athabasca Glacier one way
Elevations: Highway 93 1981 metres
Top of Glacier 2865 metres
Maps: Columbia Icefield 83 C/3
Parks Canada Columbia Icefield relief map (1:50,000)

The Columbia Icefield, one of the most publicized features of the Canadian Rockies, is rarely seen by the majority of visitors. Ski mountaineering is the traditional means of access, and travel on the Icefield during the winter requires a high degree of skill and experience. The following notes are offered not as a guide but rather as current information.

Until recently, heavy ski mountaineering equipment was utilized by all parties on the Icefield, but lighter cross-country touring gear is now seeing more use. Spring is the recommended time for travel, with March, April and May being perhaps the best months. The major objective of Icefield travel is usually a combination of skiing and climbing since many of the summits represent classic ski mountaineering objectives.

The Columbia Icefield occupies a high plateau surrounded by some of the major peaks in the Rockies. It is a sanctuary of alpine glaciation, sending out arms of ice that spill over its 3000 metre edge to the valleys below. The Icefield is guarded by difficult access on all sides and incredibly poor weather conditions. Whiteouts are possible anytime and are quite common.

The Saskatchewan Glacier offers perhaps the least difficult access route, but still represents a major glacier traverse (see *Saskatchewan Glacier* description).

The Athabasca Glacier, one of the most visited in North America, offers little in the way of easy travel over its five kilometre length. The Athabasca ascends 920 vertical metres from its toe to the rim of the Icefield proper. The lower section is liberally covered with millwells, some very wide and deep. The upper one-third is compressed into three major icefalls. Travel directly through the icefalls has become extremely difficult over the past few years, requiring a circuitous effort. Low winter snowfalls and down wasting have changed this area considerably. Many accidents have occurred on the icefalls adding to their reputation. Some mountaineers prefer a route that hugs the right (northwest) edge of the glacier which lessens some of the crevasse problems, but severely exposes one to the snow and ice avalanches pouring off the cliffs of Snow Dome. This route should be studied and considered carefully before it is attempted. Once above the second icefall, a narrow, steep ramp must be ascended through the third and last icefall to gain the Icefield proper. This ramp is cut by many deep crevasses, not altogether obvious. Needless to say, travel on and up the glacier requires complete glacier travel equipment and techniques.

Once on the Icefield, many travel options are available depending on objectives. It should be emphasised that the Columbia Icefield, although relatively level in appearance, contains many regions of huge crevasses. In the spring, these snow-covered crevasse fields can be very difficult to perceive. Roped travel with complete glacier travel and winter camping equipment and a strong self-reliant party is essential. This is advanced ski mountaineering.

The Icefield Information Centre, one kilometre from the Athabasca Glacier, opens the beginning of May. Current informtion and travel permits are available from either the Jasper (403 852-4401) or Banff (403 762-3324) Warden Services, or from Parks Canada Information Centres.

EXTENDED TRIPS

Jasper National Park offers some of the finest possibilities for extended ski trips in the Canadian Rockies. The long, wide valleys and sheer size of the park combined with an excellent summer trail system as a framework provide imaginative skiers with many options.

Snow depths in the main valleys can be less than experienced further south in Banff, since the elevation is generally lower. Winter temperatures can be very cold with extended -30° periods quite common. Late winter/early spring is generally the recommended time for extended skiing when the snowpack has had a chance to consolidate, days are longer and temperatures warmer. Few backcountry cabins are available, other than those noted in the Tonquin and Fryatt Valley descriptions. Warden patrol cabins are locked and not open to the public.

Jasper is well known for its abundance of wildlife which depends heavily on the same sheltered valleys for winter survival. Stable wolf populations, elk herds and scattered bands of mountain caribou are further rewards for the backcountry skier, but isolated wildlife must be respected during the winter when animal energy reserves are low and stress from human contact is high.

Anyone planning extended ski trips in Jasper and the other mountain parks must consider the vital questions of weather, avalanche hazard, equipment and personal ability very carefully. A ski trip involving variable snow conditions, winter camping, heavy awkward packs and endless hours of breaking trail should only be attempted after experience is gained on shorter jaunts. A competent leader or guide is recommended, or at least a strong party of four. Prior skiing experience in the Rockies is a definite asset.

Extended trips require winter camping, and simply because a disguising blanket of snow is present, a zero-impact ethic should not be forsaken. Winter campers are expected to use the established backcountry campsites wherever possible. A park use permit is available free at the Park Information Centre as is the voluntary registration.

The following extended ski trips represent possibilities to whet the appetite and are not meant as route descriptions. Enthusiasm is no excuse for experience and experienced backcountry skiers will no doubt discover many more intriguing winter journeys.

WHIRLPOOL RIVER TO ATHABASCA PASS

The route of the fur brigades across the mountains still captures the imagination of backcountry travellers. Winter may well be the best time for travel up the Whirlpool Valley, especially when the river is continuously frozen and snow covered to allow ski travel. It is approximately 60 kilometres from Highway 93A near Jasper to the summit of Athabasca Pass (see *Moab Lake* description). The elevation gain is not severe, but route finding may be troublesome in some areas.

A further section may be added to this backcountry tour to make a loop of truly classic proportions. From Athabasca Pass it is possible to ski down the western slope following either Pacific and/or Jeffrey Creeks to the Wood River. Following the Wood upstream through a heavy snowpack, probable open water, narrow canyons and heavy bush, Fortress Lake can be reached. From the lake the Continental Divide is recrossed back into Jasper over forested Fortress Pass and the Chaba River is followed downstream to the confluence with the Athabasca. The trail is followed to Sunwapta Falls on the Icefield Parkway, a total distance of some 130 kilometres from the starting point.

POBOKTAN — BRAZEAU — NIGEL

Starting from the Sunwapta Warden Station (see *Poboktan* description) or from Nigel Pass in Banff (see *Nigel Pass* description), a ski trip of approximately 60 kilometres over Poboktan Pass and through the upper Brazeau Valley is possible. The summer hiking route can be followed nearly throughout, but variable snow conditions may be met, especially along the Brazeau River. Poboktan Pass is a vast, open, rolling alpine area and can experience blowing snow and low visibility at any time.

POBOKTAN CREEK — MALIGNE PASS

Starting from the Sunwapta Warden Station on the Icefield Parkway or from Maligne Lake, a 40 kilometre route along the Maligne River and over Maligne Pass provides a medium length backcountry tour. Much of the way is through forest, but the rolling upper reaches of the pass provide excellent terrain complete with views in all directions.

THE SKYLINE TRAIL

The high ridge of the Maligne Range is very popular hiking terrain in Jasper. It is less suited to backcountry skiing due to windblown ridges and avalanche hazard. However, a two or three day ski tour is possible. Much of the route follows the summer trail with two or three variations required due to impassible cornices at the Notch and avalanche slopes, particularly on the northeast slopes of Amber Mountain. Starting or ending at either the northern trail head at the Signal Mountain Road or at the south end at Evelyn Creek near Maligne Lake (see separate descriptions), the route covers approximately 45 kilometres, most of it above tree limit.

NORTH BOUNDARY TRAIL

The North Boundary is a legendary name in long distance travel in the Canadian Rockies. Because of predominant forest travel, it is perhaps overrated, but the trail does provide the basic criteria for an extended backcountry ski trip. It is long, isolated, presents extremes in snow conditions and offers no exit or easy way out once a trip is started.

The start and finish may in fact pose the greatest difficulties. At the east access, a long walk or ski, depending on snow amounts, along 27 kilometres of the unplowed Celestine Road is required just to reach the trail head at Celestine Lake. It is seldom possible to cross the Athabasca River at Jasper House to short-cut this initial section.

At the west end, in Mount Robson Provincial Park, the descent from Berg Lake through the rock bands and cliffs to Kinney Lake represents the other obstacle. In between is unbroken snow through some of the wildest regions in the mountain parks. A good place to think about life and the pursuit of happiness. The entire length, including initial road skiing in Jasper, would be about 205 kilometres.

SOUTH BOUNDARY TRAIL

The South Boundary follows secondary river valleys through the Front Ranges of the Rockies. The Rocky, Medicine Tent, Cairn and Brazeau Rivers provide the corridors for this 180 kilometre trip which closely parallels the east and south boundary of Jasper National Park. Starting points are located at either the Jacques Lake trail head in the north or the Nigel Pass trail head in Banff National Park (see separate descriptions). This area is usually characterized by lower precipitation, and conditions can vary considerably from consolidated snow to mud and running water. The South Boundary is wild, seldom travelled country with no easy exits.

Appendix

"Sincerely yours, Lottie Hollingsworth" (undated photograph from the Archives of the Canadian Rockies).

KANANASKIS PROVINCIAL PARK

At the time of this writing, Kananaskis Provincial Park is still in the development phase. Highway #40 has been paved into the park for 52 kilometres (35 miles) south from the junction with the Trans-Canada Highway and driving time from Calgary to the Kananaskis Lakes is only slightly more than that required to reach Banff townsite.

Many cross-country ski trails have already been opened for use. These trails are not merely summer trails covered with snow, but rather loops prepared with the skier in mind. Some of the routes are over summer-use trail, but have been expanded and marked to take advantage of additional terrain which comes available in winter. In time the cross-country trails will be expanded to about 200 kilometres.

The park already has a number of major trail heads with parking areas from which numerous loops lead out and return. Some of the novice trails are machine-groomed when conditions warrant. The majority of these trails are designed for the novice and intermediate family skier and, as might be expected, the trails are very popular and crowded on weekends and holidays.

Overnight camping is available in winter and hotel accommodation and food services are provided at Fortress Mountain Ski Area, 13 kilometres (8 miles) north of the Kananaskis Lakes.

Oversnow vehicles are not permitted in the park.

Snow conditions will be similar to those at the Fortress Mountain Ski Area, and skiers can receive last minute updates by listening to radio ski reports or by calling Fortress Mountain information in Calgary.

An information centre at Kananaskis Lakes is open year-round to provide maps and brochures. In addition to ski trail maps provided by the parks department, trails in the Kananaskis Park and surrounding recreation area are comprehensively treated in the *Kananaskis Country Trail Guide* by Tony and Gillean Daffern (available from Rocky Mountain Books, 106 Wimbledon Crescent, Calgary, Alberta).

Further information can be obtained by writing or calling:

Kananaskis Provincial Park
Box 59
Canmore, Alberta T0L 0M0
Phone: (403) 678-5508

Check list day pack

spare tip
spare basket
repair kit
first-aid kit
lunch
stopping jacket
camera
extra mitts
light sweater
maps and compass
waxing kit
wind pants and jacket
sun glasses
waterproof matches
toilet paper

Check list advanced trips

avalanche beacon
avalanche probe
shovel
bivouac sac
spare cable
survival food
down jacket
overboots or old socks
rope
ice screws
crevasse pulleys
snow knife
climbing skins
ice axe
prussick slings
climbing harness

Check list overnight trips

sleeping bag
ensolite
space blanket
pots
stove and gas
bowl, cup and spoon
candles
tent

shovel
snow saw
extra socks
extra underwear
extra wool shirt
warm-up pants
overboots or old socks
towel and toothbrush
food
water bottle
extra food
extra sugar

Basic First Aid Kit

*bandaids
*adhesive tape 1″ wide
triangular bandages, compress
safety pins, assorted sizes
"kling" bandage, or panty hose
moleskin and/or molefoam
*sun cream and lipsaver
tensor (Ace) bandage
sanitary napkin (kotex)
alcohol towelettes
folding scissors
tweezers
*matches
*short candle
*sewing kit
condoms
emergency space blanket
*tylenol, tempra, or campain—Acetaminophen
Chlor-tripolon 4 mg.—Chlorpheniramine
Gravol, Dramamine—Diphenhydrinate
*salt tablets
your own favorite or required medications
luggage label and soft lead pencil

(*Items to be kept at the top of the pack or in an accessible pocket.)

First Aid Reading

Steele, Peter. *Medical Care for Mountain Climbers.*

William Heinemann Medical Books Ltd. London. 1976. 220 pp. approximate cost $12.00.

By far the most pertinent, comprehensive, and enjoyable book available. If you intend to carry a manual in your pack, this is it.

Wilkerson, James A. *Medicine For Mountaineering.*

The Mountaineers. Seattle. 1976. 309 pp. approximate cost $9.00

Overly comprehensive for most readers. Great for advanced home reading.

Darvill, Fred T. *Mountaineering Medicine.*

Skagit Mountain Rescue Unit. 1973. 44 pp. $1.00

Look for it in sports stores or equipment catalogs. Inexpensive, brief and very compact. Carry it if you can't get Peter Steele.

Washburn, Bradford. *Frostbite.* Museum of Science.

Boston. 1963. 25 pp. approximate cost $2.50

An excellent short overview on frostbite by one of the world's leading researchers.

Lathrop, Theodore G. *Hypothermia: Killer of the Unprepared.*

Mazamas. 1973. 23 pp. $1.00

An excellent short overview on a subject that too many people take for granted.

Houston, Charles S. and S.L. Cummings. *Proceedings Yosemite Institute Mountain Medicine Symposium.*

Yosemite Institute. 1976. 104 pp. $9.00

Superb reference material containing contemporary knowledge and opinions covering a wide range of mountaineering medical problems. Watch for a new, updated, more comprehensive edition coming soon.

Clarke, Charles, Michael Ward and Edward Williams. *Mountain Medicine and Physiology.* Alpine Club.

London. 1975. 140 pp. $7.00

A British symposium similar to the Yosemite Institute, but more concerned with high altitude and exercise physiology.

Ward, Michael. *Mountain Medicine.*

London. Granada Publishing Limited. 1975. 365 pp. approximate cost $30.00.

An intensive study into problems of cold and high altitude.

Index

"Dolomite" John Porter resting near Deegan's Rock in the Ptarmigan Valley during the winter of 1952.

INDEX

These are the words he told me
at fifty degrees below
as the wolves sang out in a funeral choir
and hunkered down in the snow:

"Now do this act before you freeze;
let it be the final thing—
cross your arms and legs so you'll skid out
behind a saddle horse in the spring."

"Game Warden Lament" from *Timberline Tales*
by Jim Deegan

Garry *Gibson ascending Mount Resplendent on skis during the winter of 1932.*